"All of us possess opinions (wise and foolish). All have influence (positive and negative). And all of us should communicate with greater Christlikeness. Based on his teaching experience, lifelong learning, and acquired wisdom, Dr. Thiessen's book teaches intellectual piety. This is an accessible text blending insights from philosophy, biblical teaching, and cultural critique that are essential in our tribalistic church and society. The final prayer is worth the price of the book."

—**Richard L. Smith**, director, Kuyper Center for Christian Studies, Buenos Aires

"Wow! This book is not to be missed. Elmer Thiessen's life's work has been dedicated to developing a Christian mind. In *Healthy Christian Minds* he focuses on how Christians should relate to those with whom they profoundly disagree. His answer: by cultivating biblical intellectual virtues. Both readable and rigorous, this book offers Christians who care about Truth an alternative to the rabbit hole of culture wars."

—**Trevor Cooling**, professor emeritus of Christian education, Canterbury Christ Church University

"In a time when relationships too often break down due to seemingly insurmountable differences, Elmer Thiessen offers a kind of therapy, grounded in the Bible, and taking the best from philosophy, to provide a middle path that aims to help the reader develop the intellectual virtues. This book is an excellent tool for those wanting to explore ways of becoming what God intended us to be."

—**Phil Enns**, dean of academic affairs, Parami University

"*Healthy Christian Minds* provides an important and timely study of Christian intellectual virtues, e.g., the love of knowledge and truth, commitment and openness, and humility. It is clearly written, informative and original in its discussion of the virtues in relation to Christian belief and commitment. It is relevant to a range of audiences: professors and instructors, students, reflective Christians who want to think about the form Christian commitment should take, and finally, honest enquirers, religious or otherwise. Essential reading!"

—L. PHILIP BARNES, emeritus reader in religious and theological education, King's College London

"Elmer Thiessen boldly yet graciously sets forth a vision for redeeming unhealthy minds corrupted by sin. To this end, he provides a biblical framework for understanding the intellectual virtues and corresponding vices that promote or impede the communal pursuit of truth in our post-truth era. Full of tested wisdom and concrete examples, Thiessen's giftedness as a thinker, writer, and educator rewards the reader with powerful insights and practical guidance."

—PERRY L. GLANZER, professor of educational foundations, Baylor University

Healthy Christian Minds

Healthy Christian Minds

A Biblical, Practical, and Sometimes Philosophical
Exploration of Intellectual Virtues and Vices

———▶◀———

ELMER JOHN THIESSEN

CASCADE *Books* • Eugene, Oregon

HEALTHY CHRISTIAN MINDS
A Biblical, Practical, and Sometimes Philosophical Exploration of Intellectual Virtues and Vices

Copyright © 2024 Elmer John Thiessen. All rights reserved. Except for brief quotations in critical publications or reviews, no part of this book may be reproduced in any manner without prior written permission from the publisher. Write: Permissions, Wipf and Stock Publishers, 199 W. 8th Ave., Suite 3, Eugene, OR 97401.

Cascade Books
An Imprint of Wipf and Stock Publishers
199 W. 8th Ave., Suite 3
Eugene, OR 97401

www.wipfandstock.com

PAPERBACK ISBN: 979-8-3852-1112-8
HARDCOVER ISBN: 979-8-3852-1113-5
EBOOK ISBN: 979-8-3852-1114-2

Cataloguing-in-Publication data:

Names: Thiessen, Elmer John, 1942– [author].

Title: Healthy Christian minds : a biblical, practical, and sometimes philosophical exploration of intellectual virtues and vices / by Elmer John Thiessen.

Description: Eugene, OR: Cascade Books, 2024 | Includes bibliographical references and index.

Identifiers: ISBN 979-8-3852-1112-8 (paperback) | ISBN 979-8-3852-1113-5 (hardcover) | ISBN 979-8-3852-1114-2 (ebook)

Subjects: LCSH: Virtue epistemology. | Virtues. | Vices. | Knowledge, theory of. | Philosophical theology. | Intellect. | Bible—Criticism, interpretation, etc.

Classification: BD176 T44 2024 (paperback) | BD176 (ebook)

VERSION NUMBER 09/16/24

Unless otherwise stated Scripture quotations are from The Holy Bible, New International Version ® NIV®. Copyright © 1973, 1978, 1984, 2011 by Biblica, Inc. Used with permission. All rights reserved worldwide.

Scripture quotations marked NRSV are from the New Revised Standard Version Bible, copyright © 1989, National Council of the Churches of Christ in the United States of America. Used by permission. All rights reserved worldwide.

Scripture quotations marked RSV are from the Revised Standard Version Bible, copyright 1952 [2nd. edition, 1971] by the Division of Christian Education of the National Council of the Churches of Christ in the United States of America. Used by permission. All rights reserved.

Scripture quotations marked NEB are from the New English Bible, copyright © Cambridge University Press and Oxford University Press, 1961, 1970. All rights reserved.

Contents

List of Illustrations | vii
Preface | ix

1 The Nature and Study of Intellectual Virtues | 1
2 Love of Knowledge and Truth | 29
3 Intellectual Humility | 55
4 Commitment and Openness | 83
5 Intellectual Forbearance, Fairmindedness, and Intellectual Courage | 109
6 Conclusion | 139

Endnotes | 163
Bibliography | 185
Subject Index | 193
Scripture Index | 199

List of Illustrations

Figure 1—Overlapping Ellipses | 11

Figure 2—Ladder of Truth | 39

Figure 3—Belief Systems | 101

Preface

It was supposed to be my final book.[1] I even made a point of announcing the same at a church gathering where I reported on my "last book." But writing seems to be in my bones. So, I broke that promise and wrote my autobiography in anticipation of the celebration of my eightieth birthday.[2] But even as I was writing my autobiography, another topic was percolating in my mind, and I was experiencing a growing urge to write a book on this topic. The Psalmist puts it so well: "My heart grew hot within me, and as I meditated, the fire burned; then I spoke with my tongue" (Ps 39:3).

What was it that was prompting my inner spirit to pick up my pen once more? (Thankfully the pen has been replaced with a keyboard, though I do remember starting my first book with a pen.) The topic that was catching my attention and my passion is so well captured in the title of Alan Jacobs's delightful book *How to Think: A Survival Guide for a World at Odds*. We are going through some turbulent times regarding how we think. Indeed, we are in a world at odds in our thinking. Not only do we disagree with each other, but we are becoming increasingly polarized, locked into information silos, filter bubbles, and echo chambers which create alternate realities constructed out of alternative facts. We think the worst of those who disagree with us—"demonizing the other," it is called. And any attempt to express disagreement or argue with the other is conveniently silenced by labeling this as "weaponizing." I cringe every time I hear the word. But what is at the root of all this?

As a college and university professor (now retired), I had of course experienced the usual reluctance of students to change their minds. My ethics courses were among the most popular courses I taught, and over the years I had to spend more and more time trying to disabuse my students of the silly notion that right and wrong depended on their personal beliefs. "It's true for me," and that was the end of the discussion, as far as they were concerned. And how dare I challenge their ideas on sexual liberation or their pro-choice stance with regard to abortion. Trying to cultivate the virtue of open-mindedness in my students was a major challenge in my teaching career.

Since my retirement, things have gotten much worse at our colleges and universities. Of all places, it is at universities where all ideas should be critically discussed and evaluated. The cultivation of the love of knowledge and truth should be paramount. And yet colleges and universities have become toxic environments where cancel campaigns abound.[3] Controversial guest speakers are hounded by students, if they are even allowed to speak on campuses. Assistant teachers get into trouble for giving expression to ideas that are not deemed politically correct.[4] And some professors are even being fired for the same. The atmosphere on campuses is so toxic that self-censorship is widespread among professors. Instead of dialogue and critical inquiry, we have the silencing of alternate voices at our universities. Surely there is something very wrong here.

We are living in a post-truth era. This word was first used in 2008. The editors of the *Oxford English Dictionary* inform us that use of the term "post-truth" increased by around 2,000 percent in 2016 compared to the previous year. Interestingly, this spike in usage occurred in the context of the EU referendum in the United Kingdom and the presidential election in the United States. Oh yes, those early Donald Trump years! Who can forget them. We learned about alternative facts, as though reality itself could be changed. Then there were lies, and more lies. And charges of fake news and stolen elections. And yet, despite all this, the Trump base never wavers in its support for its leader.

I have tried hard to understand this phenomenon. Sadly, I couldn't help but note that the critics of Trump seemed to be equally stuck in their own intellectual silos. Democrats and liberals were most often completely unable to see what might be prompting Trump's popularity. Then there was Hillary Clinton's infamous speech which blithely placed half of Trump supporters into a "basket of deplorables." This is surely the height of intellectual arrogance and probably contributed significantly to

Clinton's loss in her run for the presidency. As it should have! I would suggest that the rise of populism is a reaction to the arrogance of liberal progressives, the intellectual elite, and the chattering classes. What I find equally hard to understand is the blindness of liberal Democrats to their own intellectual arrogance. Please don't get me wrong. I don't think this vice is limited to the political left and the chattering classes. Both sides are guilty of intellectual arrogance and closed-mindedness. And sadly, these intellectual vices are becoming more widespread.

The Trump phenomenon is of course only one example of growing polarizations about nearly any issue in our societies. There are deep differences about climate change. Conspiracy theories abound and are held with passionate intensity. In Canada we witnessed loud and large demonstrations in the nation's capital protesting a COVID-19 vaccine mandate for cross-border truckers in January of 2022. Then there were the vaccine deniers, who continued to proclaim their convictions despite abundant evidence that the vaccines were protecting millions of people. Slogans for "Black lives matter" evoked counter-slogans for "White lives matter." And the list goes on.

In the church, too, we are encountering growing polarizations. There are the deep divisions between theological liberals and conservatives. There is the divide between those who are committed to social activism and those who see evangelism as the first priority for the church. Critical race theory has been hugely divisive in the church. Sharp divisions also occur with regard to LGBTQ+ demands and gay marriage, with many church discussions being one-sided and agenda-driven, and some denominations holding votes on this issue year after year until they finally achieve the required 51 percent majority. Truth is once again simply determined by raw political power. And this is happening in the church, of all places!

All polarizations have the effect of shutting ourselves off from dialogue with the other side. Our differences are so deep we cannot even understand each other, let alone talk to each other. But what is at the root of these growing polarizations and their devastating consequences?

As I pondered this question, I began to see with greater clarity that both sides of such polarizations suffer from closed-mindedness and intellectual arrogance. Both sides are shutting themselves off from a genuine and communal search for the truth which is often understood as the supreme intellectual virtue. Both sides are failing to practice intellectual hospitality. We are dealing here with a problem of unhealthy minds which are diseased and corrupted by intellectual vices and ultimately by sin. All this was prompting me to think about writing another book.

But there is more. I have also encountered bewilderment about what to do about the problem of growing disagreements and polarizations. How do you cure unhealthy minds? The standard cure, and one that we have inherited from Plato and the Enlightenment, is to look to reason to solve these problems. What people need is better arguments and a little more information and then the disagreements will disappear. Education is the answer. Training in detecting misinformation should help. Maybe even a bit of therapy. But there are problems with these proposed solutions. More education doesn't seem to help. After all, even educated people disagree strongly with each other, often to the point of calling each other names or yelling at each other. And more information just doesn't seem to clear away our disagreements. Vaccine deniers, for example, are not swayed by providing the latest statistics on the efficacy of COVID vaccines. We are simply not as rational as we think we are. We need to look elsewhere for solutions. But where to find them?

I return again to Alan Jacobs's insightful and entertaining book, *How to Think*. His introduction begins with this statement: "Why we're worse at thinking than we think."[5] After telling us about the many books he had read about thinking in preparation for writing his own book, Jacobs concludes that despite their varying models of thinking, the books he read had one trait in common: they were depressing to read.[6] He goes on to provide a list of ways in which thinking can go wrong. But the central problem for Jacobs is that "we suffer from a settled determination to avoid thinking."[7] And so he devotes much of his book "to exploring the power of the forces that inhibit thinking," assuming that an accurate diagnosis of our condition is a first step to treating the problem.[8]

I'm not so sure. Indeed, in his concluding chapter Jacobs admits that his book will only help if you are "a certain *kind of person*"—"the kind of person who, at least some of the time, cares more about *working towards the truth* than about one's current social position."[9] Here Jacobs finally gets to the heart of the problem and a possible solution. Diagnosing the forces that inhibit thinking is not enough. We need to address the issue of character, the kind of persons we are. The central problem is not *how* we think but *who* is doing the thinking. We need to look at the intellectual vices that make us bad thinkers. Now to be sure, Jacobs's analysis does touch on intellectual virtues and vices, at least implicitly, but I think a more explicit focus on them is needed. Hence my work on the book you are currently reading.

First, I had to immerse myself in the literature on intellectual virtues and vices, as this was a relatively new topic for me. Thankfully, some excellent philosophical treatments of intellectual virtues and vices have been published in recent years. (A brief literature review will be provided in chapter 1.) I then decided to offer a course on intellectual virtues and vices in the life-long learning program (LALL) at Wilfrid Laurier University in Waterloo. When I finally offered the course in 2018, I had a full class of thirty students, with another twenty on a waiting list. The course seemed to be addressing some concerns regarding contemporary culture, and it prompted a lot of enthusiastic participation in class discussions. One student wrote the following in an evaluation of the course: "Since some of my beliefs did not necessarily reflect those of the instructor, the course itself provided a wonderful learning opportunity to be more open-minded and to allow other perspectives to unfold. I feel this course has helped me to be more aware of my own intellectual vices and I really appreciate that. Thank you for a thought provoking and informative course."

Since I was aiming for a Christian readership in writing this book, I also offered to do a series of Sunday school classes on intellectual virtues and vices in the church my wife and I are currently attending. I was given a slot of two sessions in the fall of 2019, so I dealt with open-mindedness in the first class and the love of truth in the second. Again, attendance was high, participation was animated, and I received a number of appreciative comments about the lectures. I offered another two sessions via Zoom in the following year of the pandemic, this time dealing with intellectual humility and a few intellectual virtues that relate more to interpersonal disagreement. So, the contents of this book have been tested in the classroom and in a church context.

This is a book about intellectual virtues and vices. Why the need for another book, given that there is already a considerable body of literature on the topic? Fortunately, or unfortunately, depending on one's point of view, much of what has been written on intellectual virtues and vices has been written by philosophers and for philosophers. Philosophers tend to get carried away with technical detail, and their books are often not easy to read. My aim is to write a short, introductory-level book for the layreader. As already mentioned, this book is written with a Christian readership in mind. The subtitle of the book is important. I want to provide a biblical framework for understanding intellectual virtues and vices, and each of the central chapters includes a review of what the Bible says about a specific intellectual virtue and its corresponding vices.[10] This book also tries to help ordinary Christians understand the practical importance of the central intellectual virtues and vices, particularly for our troubled and polarized times. Each chapter gives concrete examples of intellectual virtues and vices. And while the book reflects the best of philosophical scholarship, it tries to make any philosophical considerations understandable for the lay reader. Academic references have for the most part been relegated to endnotes.

Chapter 1 is more theoretical in nature, describing the general nature of intellectual virtues and providing some ethical and epistemological background for the study of intellectual virtues and vices. I also provide a biblical grounding for intellectual virtues as well as a biblical analysis of the origin of intellectual vices. The next three chapters provide an in-depth study of what I consider to be the most important intellectual virtues—the love of knowledge and truth, intellectual humility, and committed openness. Chapter 5 treats intellectual virtues that are more relational in nature—intellectual forbearance, fairmindedness, and intellectual courage. I am not covering all the intellectual virtues and vices but only those that are especially important for our troubled and divided age. The central aim throughout, but especially in the final chapter, is to help the reader understand and appreciate the practical importance of each of these intellectual virtues as a way of overcoming the deep divides that plague churches and societies in the Western world. The final chapter also includes a brief treatment of how to nurture the development of intellectual virtues.

I want to thank my students at Wilfrid Laurier University and the participants of the adult Sunday school classes at Waterloo North Mennonite Church for their feedback on my first attempts to articulate some of the ideas of these chapters. Thanks also to Bruce Barron for his careful editing of an exploratory essay I wrote on intellectual virtues for the *Evangelical Review of Theology*.[11] Sincere thanks to my wife, Maggie, for her enduring love, her ongoing support of my writing endeavors, and for checking the readability of an earlier draft of this manuscript. I am also grateful for the many helpful comments given by three early readers of the manuscript—Richard L. Smith, Phil Enns, and Darrin W. Snyder Belousek. This book would no doubt have been better if I would have paid even more attention to their suggestions. Finally, thanks to my editors,

Dr. Robin Parry and Elisabeth Rickard, and the team at Wipf and Stock for helping to bring this writing project to completion.

Elmer J. Thiessen
February 12, 2024
ejthiessen@sympatico.ca
elmerjohnthiessen.wordpress.com

1

The Nature and Study of Intellectual Virtues

> Make every effort to supplement your faith with virtue, and virtue with knowledge, and knowledge with self-control, and self-control with steadfastness, and steadfastness with godliness, and godliness with brotherly affection, and brotherly affection with love.
>
> (2 Peter 1:5–7 RSV)

> Let us then strive to think well; that is the basic principle of morality.
>
> (Blaise Pascal, Pensées §200)

This chapter will be a bit more theoretical in nature as it answers some preliminary questions about intellectual virtues and vices. What are some intellectual virtues and vices? Indeed, what is the nature of virtues and vices generally? Why are they important? What are some recent developments in philosophy and theology that have contributed to a growing interest in intellectual virtues and vices? Is the Bible at all concerned about intellectual virtues and vices? How do the grand biblical themes of creation, fall, and redemption relate to intellectual virtues and vices? And is the Great Commandment at all relevant to a discussion of intellectual virtues and vices? To help bring this chapter down to earth, I begin with some reflections on some of my own teaching and church experiences that illustrate the importance of intellectual virtues and vices.

I am a philosopher and have had a long and satisfying career teaching philosophy. I started my teaching career at Waterloo Lutheran University in Ontario, then settled at Medicine Hat College in Alberta for most of my career and, since my retirement, have taught at colleges and seminaries in various parts of the world. Teaching philosophy is a challenge. Philosophy deals with big questions. What is the meaning of life? Is there a God? Is there such a thing as truth? How can we know? Are there objective moral standards? I have enjoyed helping students think about these big questions. But I found there was also resistance to the hard thinking required in trying to answer these questions. Some students were unconcerned about searching for the truth or were simply intellectually lazy. Some students found it difficult to approach these questions with an open mind. And some students arrogantly assumed that they already had all the answers. I must confess that on one or two occasions I got so exasperated at student arrogance, closed-mindedness, and lack of concern about searching for truth, that I got angry while teaching and would later have to apologize for my angry outburst. Maybe I, too, was lacking in some intellectual virtues!

Upon my retirement, my wife and I moved to Waterloo, Ontario, where I began teaching a yearly seminar on worldviews at Emmanuel Bible College. After years of teaching within a secular context, I had to adjust to teaching at a Bible college where many of the students came from conservative Christian backgrounds. It was a challenge to open their minds to considering beliefs they were not familiar with. For me to suggest that the story of creation in Genesis might not rule out some elements of evolutionary theory was a stretch for some of my students. Combatting closed-mindedness was not easy, I discovered, and I had to practice forbearance and patience in teaching.

I also had the privilege of teaching in a life-long learning program (LALL) at Wilfrid Laurier University for a number years after my retirement. I enjoyed offering these six-week courses to retired adults, many of whom were well educated. One year I offered a course on contemporary moral problems and gave them an opportunity to vote on topics they would like to cover. I had to choose the first few topics on my own to get the course started, so I selected the problem of abortion for the first lecture. As the lecture proceeded, I sensed some resistance to my attempt to be fair to both sides of this contentious issue. Indeed, in the survey of topic choices that students handed in at the beginning of the second class, several indicated they did not want the topic of abortion to be covered in the course. Too late! My students were of course reflecting a widespread attitude to the problem of abortion.[12] People just don't want to discuss the topic anymore. Their minds are already made up. "Please don't confuse me with a careful treatment of arguments for and against abortion." Again, I was encountering resistance to treating a moral question with an open mind and a genuine desire to search for truth.

My family and church experiences have also prompted my interest in the topic of intellectual virtues and vices. My upbringing was rather conservative, with my parents attending various Mennonite Brethren churches in the Bible belt of the Canadian prairies. My grandfather, who was a pastor, was very worried about my attending university after high school. My family was even more worried when I switched from physics to philosophy at university, prompted in part by my wanting to test my faith. Indeed, at one point, I was ready to throw my Christian faith overboard when I couldn't find answers to the questions that I was facing. But God was gracious in sending some life-lines that helped to sustain and even strengthen my faith. For much of my adult life I was very active in a conservative Mennonite Brethren church. But as a leader and teacher in the church, I found myself constantly needing to push boundaries as I tried to help the congregation search for biblical truth with minds that were open to the guidance of the Holy Spirit.

Sabbaticals and retirement have enabled me to have some other church experiences, including attendance at some liberal churches. These have been learning experiences! One of these churches spent considerable time processing the LGBTQ+ issue, and while I mostly listened, I did voice my conservative stance on questions surrounding this issue before a final vote was taken. In the end the church adopted an affirmative stance on the issue, but I couldn't help but reflect on how one-sided and agenda-driven our discussions had been. Indeed, when I pointed this out to some leaders towards the end of our deliberations, I was asked to suggest some books that defended a conservative viewpoint and that might be shared with the class the following Sunday. Amazing! They needed help in identifying resources that went counter to the prevailing opinion in the church. And when I later suggested an excellent book that had just been published on the topic, and even offered to donate the book to the church library, the library committee couldn't make up its mind about adding the book to the church library. So they forwarded my suggestion to the leadership of the church, who rejected the offer.[13] Sadly, these are not isolated incidents. So, one conclusion I have reached after many years of attending both conservative and liberal churches is that the intellectual vice of closed-mindedness exists in both.

It is experiences like these that have confirmed for me how important intellectual virtues are, not only for us as individuals but also for churches and for society as a whole. And hence this book.

THE NATURE OF INTELLECTUAL VIRTUES AND VICES

Perhaps the easiest way to zero in on the focus of this book is to simply draw up a list of intellectual virtues and vices. I have already identified some intellectual virtues and vices in the preface and in my personal reflections above. Here are two lists of commonly identified intellectual virtues and vices.

Intellectual virtues: love of knowledge and truth; inquisitiveness or curiosity; intellectual perseverance; intellectual courage; intellectual humility; intellectual generosity; and open-mindedness.

Intellectual vices: intellectual apathy or laziness; intellectual carelessness; intellectual bias; intellectual cowardice; intellectual arrogance; dogmatism; and closed-mindedness.

We need not be too bothered by the fact that not everyone will come up with the same intellectual virtues and vices when they are asked to list them. There is a rough consensus on a core of important intellectual virtues and vices, and that is good enough for my purposes. My intent in this book is to limit myself to those intellectual virtues and vices that I consider to be most important and that are more relevant to the turbulent times in which we live.

These lists prompt a further question as to the general characteristics of intellectual virtues and vices. Why are the above items included in these lists in the first place? What is it that makes us classify certain items as intellectual virtues or vices? I will limit myself to virtues for the time being. What do these virtues have in common? To answer these questions we need to look more carefully at the two words that make up this concept—"intellectual" and "virtues." The notion of virtue is a moral category. Virtues have to do with good character. Aristotle defined virtues as dispositions to do the right thing at the right time and in the right way.[14] Virtues describe what it means to be an excellent human being.

Virtues express themselves as deeply ingrained habits of good behavior. Aristotle included honesty, bravery, integrity, fidelity, generosity, courage, and truthfulness as moral virtues. He also liked to describe virtues as a golden mean between extremes. For example, courage is a mean between cowardice and foolhardiness. I'm not sure this applies to all virtues.[15] But where useful I will be drawing on Aristotle's notion of a golden mean to help us understand some of the intellectual virtues.

I am treating intellectual virtues as a subset of the more general notion of moral virtues.[16] Intellectual virtues have to do with the mind, with our ability to think and our desire to know and find truth. As human beings, we have certain natural or God-given faculties that help us to gain knowledge and discover truth. We have our five senses, which play a critical role in our gaining knowledge. While most of us can see and hear, a question can still be raised as to whether we are careful in our seeing and hearing. Have we cultivated good habits in seeing and hearing? Are we able to catch the details of what we are seeing? Do we really listen when someone is talking to us? Do we pay close attention to what we are reading? These questions have to do with the presence or absence of intellectual virtues.

We also have minds or brains. Some of us are not quite as clever as others, and we should not be blamed for this. In other words, the degree of intelligence that we possess is not in itself an intellectual virtue. But whatever our innate level of intelligence, do we use the brains that we have been given and do we use them well? Now we are raising a question that relates to intellectual virtues. Memory also plays an important part in our gaining knowledge and truth. Again, we can't fault someone for not having a photographic memory. Very few of us have this. But have we cultivated our memory to the best of our ability? Are we able to distinguish between items that are very clear in our memory and those about which we should say that we are not entirely sure? Here again these questions relate to our possession of intellectual virtues.

Philosophers use the term "epistemology" to describe the theory of knowing. Epistemology is the branch of philosophy concerned with the methods, validity, and scope of knowledge. Intellectual virtues have to do with our epistemic or cognitive faculties, our natural or innate powers to gain knowledge and truth. I have already identified some of our epistemic faculties. Here is a more complete list: senses, memory, introspection (the ability to know directly that one exists and who one is), argument and inference, induction (the ability to generalize from particular cases), trust in the testimony of other people, the ability to learn and understand languages, the ability to make comparisons, the ability to demand consistency in our beliefs, the desire for understanding, and the disposition to seek and to be aware of God.[17]

These intellectual faculties can be described in various ways, as abilities, powers, talents, temperaments, or skills. They are natural or innate to us as normal human beings. Of course, Christians like to describe them as God-given. These natural or God-given faculties are hard-wired to develop towards a state of maturity or excellence. Of course, an individual's upbringing and social environment might stifle the development of these faculties or powers. Indeed, Christians maintain that sin can also contribute to a failure to achieve intellectual excellence. Proper nurture is important for us to become mature human beings.

We can't give ourselves credit for having these faculties and powers. Nor do we blame someone for being blind or deaf. We also can't give ourselves full credit for receiving proper nurture that contributed to the development of these faculties and powers. Nonetheless, we are partially responsible for their development. So, we do praise people for taking some responsibility for developing these natural or God-given faculties or powers. We can and should praise someone for being open-minded, for example. And we can and should criticize someone for being intellectually lazy. We do so because here we are entering the moral realm. Now we are dealing with intellectual virtues and vices.

We are now in a position to give a definition of intellectual virtues and vices.[18]

Intellectual virtues are acquired and enduring personal dispositions to use one's cognitive faculties well in the pursuit of knowledge and truth.

Intellectual vices are acquired and enduring personal dispositions to use one's cognitive faculties poorly in the pursuit of knowledge and truth.

Both definitions focus on personal dispositions or character traits.[19] Both have to do with personal intellectual excellences or the lack thereof. Both definitions don't just focus on human faculties or abilities, like having a high IQ or a photographic memory, because you aren't responsible for them. You could still be a bad person even if you had a high IQ. Morality only enters the picture once we consider what a person has done with his or her high IQ. Of course, being a good person involves many other things, like being generous, kind, and courageous. In this book I am focusing on being a good person in terms of what one does with one's epistemic faculties, or the faculties we have that help us in the pursuit of knowledge and truth. I am also assuming that our epistemic or knowledge-acquiring faculties are God-given and therefore an important dimension of our being created in the image of God. We are, therefore, obligated to develop these epistemic faculties well by acquiring intellectual virtues.

PHILOSOPHY, ETHICS, AND EPISTEMOLOGY

In order to help us to better understand intellectual virtues and vices and their importance, I now want to review some more recent developments in philosophy that relate to our topic. I have already mentioned some philosophers and introduced some philosophical terms. The subtitle of this book suggests that my treatment will sometimes include philosophical explorations. So perhaps some reflection on the nature of philosophy and its connection to intellectual virtues and vices might be in order. (Some readers might want to skip the next few sections and move right on to the biblical basis for intellectual virtues.)

All of us are philosophers, whether we accept this label or not. Children keep asking the question "Why?" and they are not content with superficial answers. We continue to ask "Why?" as adults, though perhaps sadly not with the same persistence as children. We argue with others and ourselves. Sometimes we are forced to clarify the language that we use. We all ask deeper questions about life and its meaning. We try to find a unifying explanation of reality. Here is my definition of philosophy: Philosophy involves a critical examination of the basic assumptions underlying all that human beings think and do, the clarification of the language used to express our beliefs, as well as the attempt to formulate a rational, coherent, interpretive picture of reality on the basis of which we can think and live.

There are two important divisions of philosophy that relate in a special way to the study of intellectual virtues and vices. The first is ethics or moral philosophy. Ethics concerns itself with judgments as to the rightness or wrongness, goodness or badness, desirability or undesirability of human actions, dispositions (virtues or vices), and goals. Various theories have been proposed to provide a foundation for making ethical judgments. Of course, there are many today who deny the very possibility of objective, justifiable, and universal ethical principles. Indeed, ethical relativism characterizes the thinking of many people today. But some of us believe there are some ethical principles that can be justified and applied to all persons and cultures and that exist for all time. This is surely what is entailed by the Psalmist when he describes the laws that God built into creation. "Your word, O LORD, is eternal; it stands firm in the heavens.... Your laws endure to this day, for all things serve you" (Ps 119:89, 91). Of course, the application of these universal ethical principles to specific contexts might involve some variation. But this in no way undermines the notion that there are some objective, justifiable, and universal ethical principles.

Whereas much of modern moral philosophy has focused on rules and duties, ancient ethical traditions emphasized character and virtue. Plato talked about excellence in human beings. For Aristotle, the fundament ethical question was not "What shall I do?" but "What shall I be?" Plato saw justice as a quality of character. For Aristotle, not truth but being a truthful person was the key to ethics. Thankfully, there has been a recovery of this ancient approach to ethics in modern philosophy in the Western world in the last fifty years or so. Defining ethics in terms of rules and duties is seen by many philosophers today as too negative, too black and white, too complicated, and too divorced from real life. What we need is a focus on virtue ethics and good character. And what we also need to help us live morally are exemplary models, saints and heroes, who display good character.[20]

This more recent shift to virtue ethics in philosophy runs parallel to the contemporary emphasis on intellectual virtues and vices. Moral character applies not only to how we behave but also to how we think, how we process information, how we reason, and how we argue. Here, too, there are virtues that define what a good person is intellectually. Here, too, there are exemplary dispositions, like being conscientious in the search for truth, being fair in our responses to what we hear, being humble about our own convictions, and being courageous in expressing viewpoints that run counter to established opinion.

A second division of philosophy that has influenced current discussions of intellectual virtues and vices is the study of epistemology. Fundamental epistemological questions include the following: Can we know? How can we know? What are the limits of knowledge? What is knowledge? What is truth? Is there Truth with a capital *T*? Epistemology was for a long time dominated by debates between empiricists and rationalists. More recently, analytic philosophy was preoccupied with defining knowledge, with the following being a favorite definition: knowledge is justified true belief. But there are problems with determining exactly when a belief is justified. How much evidence do you need for a belief to be treated as justified and therefore as known? And of course there is Pilate's famous question: "What is truth?" (John 18:38). When can we be sure that we have arrived at the truth? There seems to be an inescapable subjectivity that surrounds the key ingredients of knowledge. Indeed, one writer has suggested that a veritable "cottage industry" sprang up among epistemologists trying to overcome the problems surrounding the above definition of knowledge.[21] More recently still there has been the postmodern challenge to epistemological questions. There is a growing recognition that observation is theory-laden and that our reasoning depends on unprovable assumptions. All this has led some philosophers to despair about the field of epistemology with some even writing obituaries of epistemology.[22]

But not all has been lost. As in ethics, there has been a rather dramatic recent shift in the approach to doing epistemology, in part due to the difficulties surrounding traditional approaches to epistemological questions. I was first introduced to this shift when reading a book with the title *Epistemic Responsibility*, written by Lorraine Code (1987). Code complains that epistemologists, in their analysis of the meaning and justification of knowledge claims, rarely ask about the *person* making the claims.[23] She goes on to develop an alternate way to approach epistemological questions by focusing on cognitive activity and process rather than products or end-states of cognition.[24] Code treats epistemic responsibility as the chief intellectual virtue "from which other virtues radiate."[25] Her work prepared the way for a subsequent focus on intellectual virtues and vices.[26]

With this shift in thinking about intellectual virtues and vices, the focus is not so much on how much evidence someone has for a claim but rather on whether a person has been careful in gathering evidence and is open to looking at any counter-evidence that might exist.[27] A focus on intellectual virtues and vices looks at the cognitive life or the mind of a person, making sure that he or she is maximizing its potential for finding truth and avoiding error.

So here we have two significant and fairly recent developments in philosophy which have contributed to current discussions of intellectual virtues and vices. In their 2007 study of intellectual virtues, Robert Roberts and Jay Wood describe philosophical reflection about intellectual virtues and vices as "still in its infancy" but holding "enormous promise for the recovery of epistemology as a philosophical discipline with broad human importance."[28] Philosophers have indeed given much attention to the subject in the last few decades.[29] However, most of this literature is written for philosophers and is therefore rather abstract and technical.

In the mid-2000s, virtue epistemologists began analyzing individual intellectual virtues and vices, and this has indeed become a "growth industry" in virtue epistemology.[30] However, most of these works are again written for philosophers, and the illustrations of intellectual virtues and vices are most often taken from the academic realm. There have been a couple of recent attempts to write about intellectual virtues and vices for non-philosophers, but whether they succeed in relating these virtues to "everyday life" is debatable.[31] It is my hope and prayer that my contribution to this literature will be more accessible to non-academics and also highlight the importance of this subject for the Christian church. I also want to provide an explicitly biblical foundation for intellectual virtues which to this point is largely missing in the literature.[32]

FAITH AND REASON

As should be apparent from the title of my book and from what I have already said in this chapter, I am writing specifically for Christians. The subtitle of my book suggests that my treatment of intellectual virtues is meant to be "biblical" in nature. It also suggests that my treatment of intellectual virtues will be "sometimes philosophical." Indeed, this chapter has so far been mainly philosophical in nature. This raises the interesting question memorably raised by the early church father Tertullian: "What has Athens to do with Jerusalem?" Tertullian maintained that the Christian faith, which had its home in Jerusalem, was incompatible with Greek philosophy, which had its home in Athens. Philosophy prides itself in being based on reason. And Christianity is often understood to be based on faith. Hence, their alleged incompatibility.

But there are problems with this supposed dichotomy. There are after all Christian philosophers who somehow combine faith and reason. Perhaps philosophy is not quite as rational as is often assumed. Indeed, I follow Anselm and other Reformed philosophers who maintain that reason is always faith seeking understanding.[33] In other words, all philosophers start with presuppositions accepted on faith and then reason from these presuppositions. All knowledge begins and ends in faith.

But the question still remains: Can thinkers who start with different presuppositional frameworks come to any agreement? Thomas Aquinas has given us a classic answer to this question with respect to faith and reason. Aquinas argues that there is an overlap between the truths of reason (philosophy) and the truths of faith (revelation).[34] More recently and more generally, John Rawls has introduced the idea of an overlapping consensus to describe the common ground we find between competing belief systems.[35] Here a picture might be useful (see figure 1).[36] Imagine a series of ellipses, each representing a different worldview or belief system, but all overlapping to some degree. Each ellipse is unique, and yet there is some common ground. The common ground represented by the overlap will be interpreted and justified in different ways in each particular belief system. The faith-based assumptions underlying each belief system might be different, but there is still some common ground despite the differences.

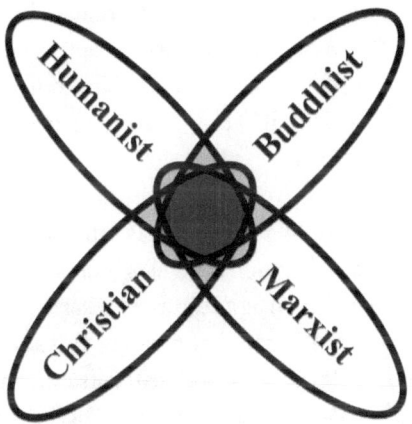

Figure 1: Overlapping Ellipses

Why is there such an overlap? Because we live in the same world. Regardless of our worldviews, we have a common source of data, which imposes constraints on our interpretations of reality. Human nature is also roughly the same. As we have already seen, we share knowledge-gaining faculties. So, we are all trying to understand a common reality. And there is also the very practical issue of people needing to get along despite their differences. All this is what makes an overlapping consensus necessary and possible. Of course, Christians will add that an overlapping consensus is made possible because God created and ordered all that exists. More on this later.

For my purposes, an overlapping consensus is important in that it helps us to understand why a philosophical and a Christian understanding of intellectual virtues might share some common ground. Such an admission however, does not preclude some areas of incompatibility. For example, we might find that the biblical ideal of intellectual humility is not shared by some philosophers. So we need to be on the look-out for both commonalities and differences in a philosophical and a biblical treatment of intellectual virtues. I now turn to an explicitly theological and biblical treatment of intellectual virtues.

THE BIBLE ON PHILOSOPHY AND ETHICS

The title of this section will no doubt raise questions for some readers. Does the Bible have anything to say about philosophical issues like epistemology? And if the Bible does touch on epistemological questions, wouldn't such biblical references apply only to knowing in the religious realm? More generally, isn't it wrongheaded to try to derive a general epistemology from the Bible?

These objections stem from an unbiblical dualism. While the Bible is not a science or philosophy textbook, it is much more than a treatment of religious truth. Indeed, it touches on all spheres of life, from politics to economics to marriage.[37] Even agriculture is described as subject to God's laws, and the farmer is reminded that plowing and sowing and threshing are all dictated by God's laws. "His God instructs him and teaches him the right way. . . . All this also comes from the LORD Almighty, wonderful in counsel and magnificent in wisdom" (Isa 28:23–29). All truth is God's truth, and therefore we should not be surprised to find the Bible touching on all areas of knowledge and truth.[38] Indeed, Dru Johnson argues that there is a "fortuitous overlap" between the biblical and the scientific approaches to knowing.[39] This would reaffirm a point made in the previous section regarding an overlapping consensus between the truths of faith and reason.

Yes, we must be careful not to move too quickly in drawing conclusions about epistemology from the Bible. And there are certainly some hermeneutical hurdles that must be overcome in doing so, given the many authors of biblical texts who are speaking to different contexts and situations. But the Bible clearly touches on epistemological questions frequently, as I will show later in this chapter and in the chapters that follow. And a careful study of the many biblical authors reveals a relatively uniform approach to epistemology, as Dru Johnson and Richard Smith have shown.[40] So I concur with these authors, among others, that there is a biblical approach to knowing which, I would add, includes a biblical approach to intellectual virtues and vices.

Yes, I agree that the Bible nowhere explicitly refers to the notion of "intellectual virtues." And I am very much aware of the pitfalls associated with imposing modern categories onto the Bible. But I hope to show that the Bible has a lot to say about intellectual virtues and vices even though these exact words are not found in Scripture. In order to help us see how the Bible speaks to intellectual virtues, it will be helpful to examine two recent trends in biblical theology. These trends parallel the two trends in ethics and epistemology that I have already considered in providing the philosophical background to intellectual virtues and vices.

First some developments in Christian ethics. Sadly, too many Christians have a rather simplistic view of ethics. Christian ethics has all too often followed the lead of moral philosophy in defining ethics primarily in terms of rules and duties. Certainly, rules and duties form an important part of biblical ethics. We need only think of the Ten Commandments. But there is more to Christian ethics than rules and commandments. Richard Hays helps us to grapple with a broader approach to Christian ethics in his groundbreaking work, *The Moral Vision of the New Testament* (1996). Although Hays focuses primarily on the New Testament, his approach can easily be extended to include the Old Testament. Indeed, Hays reminds us, "It is impossible to read the New Testament rightly without hearing the voice of Israel's Scriptures within these early Christian documents."[41]

Drawing on Hays,[42] I suggest there are five different ways in which Old and New Testament texts can help us in making ethical judgments: (a) Specific rules or commandments that either require or prohibit certain actions and types of behavior or character; (b) Broader principles or frameworks that govern particular decisions about actions; (c) Stories of persons who model exemplary conduct and character. There can of course also be stories of persons who model bad behavior and character. The story of Jesus holds primacy in our understanding of ethics; (d) The narrative of the Bible as a whole, within which we locate our individual stories and the story of the church. The narrative of the Bible gives us a broad and storied framework within which to understand ethics; (e) A biblical worldview which is grounded in the narrative of the Bible. A biblical worldview shapes how we interpret the world and gives us a parallel broad framework from which we grapple with ethical questions.

It should be evident that the above five modes of ethical discourse move from the specific to the more general. I would further suggest that this gradation also moves from the less important to the more important.[43] All five approaches to appealing to biblical texts in order to make ethical judgments are important, but some are more important than others. Hays also reminds us that texts must be granted authority in the mode in which they speak.[44] It would be a mistake to turn a narrative into a rule, for example. We must also be very careful not to let one mode of appeal to Scripture override another. If there are tensions between differing modes of appeal, these should be acknowledged and any attempts at synthesis must do justice to the whole canon of Scripture. And, as already mentioned, we must guard against the danger of reading Old and New Testament ethical texts in one mode only.

There is another important hermeneutical problem that needs to be addressed here. The books of the Bible are written within particular historical, cultural, and social contexts. The worlds of the Old Testament and New Testament are very distant and different from our own. So how do we overcome this distance as we seek to apply the five modes of ethical discourse to our own world? Here we must avoid two extremes. On the one hand, we must not make the distance between the biblical text and the world today so great that the Bible is unable to speak to our contemporary situation.[45] On the other hand, we must be careful not to ignore the gap between these two worlds and therefore adopt a simplistic equivalency approach in moving from the Bible to our contemporary situation.[46] What is needed to bridge this gap is some imaginative creativity, or even "improvisation."[47]

One caution is in order. Acknowledging that all biblical texts are embedded in a particular culture does not rule out the possibility that there might be some ethical norms that are transcultural. Indeed, there are some ethical norms that are reaffirmed throughout the books of the Old Testament and the New Testament. I consider the Ten Commandments to be one example of transcultural ethical norms which are affirmed throughout Scripture. Further, as I will argue in the next section, understanding God as creator entails that there are some universal norms that apply to all cultures and peoples.

The above multi-mode approach to biblical ethics should help us to see how the Bible addresses intellectual virtues and vices. If we think of biblical ethics only in terms of specific rules, then we will probably discover that the Bible has little to say about intellectual virtues and vices. In what follows in this chapter and the remaining chapters of this book, I will be drawing on all five modes of ethical discourse found in the Bible in order to articulate normative intellectual virtues. I believe there are some ethical principles (mode b above) that relate to specific intellectual virtues. For example, I believe the Great Commandment has some implications for how we relate to others intellectually. More on this later. We will also be looking at biblical examples of intellectual virtues (mode c above). Moses is described as the most humble person on earth (Num 12:3). Why? And did he also exemplify intellectual humility? Later in this chapter I will also show how the biblical narrative and worldview of the Bible (modes d and e) speak directly and indirectly to the intellectual virtues discussed in this book.

There is one further development in Christian ethics that needs to be addressed. I have already pointed out that all too often Christian ethics has followed the lead of moral philosophy in defining ethics primarily in terms of rules and duties. While this is certainly part of Christian ethics (modes a and b above), there is more to Christian ethics. The Bible also has a lot to say about virtue and good character. The Leviticus account of the Ten Commandments is prefaced by a call to be holy. "Be holy because I, the LORD your God, am holy" (Lev 19:1). Paul informs us that God chose us "before the creation of the world to be holy and blameless in his sight" (Eph 1:4). Peter echoes this idea, drawing on Leviticus. "Be holy because I am holy" (1 Pet 1:16).

Jesus in the Sermon on the Mount clearly focuses on virtues when he blesses those who are poor in spirit, the meek, those who hunger for righteousness, the merciful, and the pure in heart (Matt 5:1–10). There are also several lists of virtues in the New Testament which again would suggest that character and virtue are important for Christian ethics. Paul, in one of the most telling passages in Scripture related to character transformation, challenges us:

> Therefore, as God's chosen people, holy and dearly loved, clothe yourselves with compassion, kindness, humility, gentleness and patience. Bear with each other and forgive one another if any of you has a grievance against someone. Forgive as the Lord

forgave you. And over all these virtues put on love, which binds them all together in perfect unity. (Col 3:12–14; cf. 2 Pet 1:5–7)

These moral virtues also have implications for the mind. Indeed, I believe they can and should be translated into intellectual virtues, as I will begin to do in the next sections of this chapter and in the chapters that follow.

THE BIBLE ON EPISTEMOLOGY AND INTELLECTUAL VIRTUES

I turn now to a biblical epistemology. Here again there have been some recent significant developments that have paved the way for my treatment of intellectual virtues and vices. A number of philosophers associated with what has come be identified as "Reformed epistemology" have attempted to integrate theological insights and analytical epistemology referred to earlier in this chapter. Alvin Plantinga's work is probably the most robust and well defended example of Reformed epistemology.[48] Plantinga and other Reformed philosophers clearly attempt to represent the Christian tradition in epistemology, but the connection with Scripture remains somewhat tenuous in their writings.[49]

Esther Meek has put her own stamp on Reformed epistemology by challenging the knowledge-as-information outlook that has dominated philosophy and still persists in Reformed epistemology.[50] In her more recent work, *A Little Manual for Knowing*, Meek begins with a treatment of love, admitting that it might seem to be an odd place to start when dealing with epistemology.[51] Meek argues that the traditional approach to epistemology, which focuses on "knowledge-as-information," is wrong in that it treats reality as impersonal bits of material.[52] Instead, reality needs to be understood as a gift which then calls for personal response. Indeed, reality has normative features in that God created reality to be the way it ought to be. We as knowers are therefore called to give our consent to the way things are meant to be. This leads to a "covenantal epistemology," a "dance of overture and response."[53] Therefore, "We love in order to know."[54] Here we begin to see the emergence of intellectual virtues, though Meek does not explicitly refer to them as such. Knowing begins with love, love of the gift of reality and the love of knowledge and truth about reality, as we will see in chapter 2. Knowing also requires humble submission to the way things are, the way God created reality. In other words, intellectual humility is required in a healthy approach to knowing.

More recently, a number of Christian philosophers have tried to develop an epistemology directly from Scripture.[55] Their starting point is the exegesis of biblical texts in an attempt to develop a uniquely biblical epistemology. The accounts of creation and fall are carefully exegeted to see what they say about epistemology. Other texts that speak to epistemology either directly or indirectly, such as the exodus story, the book of Ecclesiastes, and the Gospels, are also considered.

So what does a biblical epistemology look like? Dru Johnson concurs with various writers we have already considered who maintain that knowing is more of a process and always entails someone who is doing the knowing within a particular time and place. Johnson argues that a careful study of the Bible will show that it would be better to talk about "knowing" rather than "knowledge."[56] The Scriptures also rely heavily on sensory terms for descriptions of knowing, and two verbs rise to prominence as indicators of knowing—"listen" and "see."[57] In many cases listening and knowing also mean obeying. For example, in the Sermon on the Mount Jesus says that "everyone who hears these words of mine and puts them into practice is like a wise man who built his house on the rock" (Matt 7:24).[58]

Johnson summarizes the basic structure of knowing in the Bible: "In order to know well, you must listen to trusted authorities and do what they say in order to see what they are showing you."[59] Of significance too is that "the authors of Scripture regularly maintain the connection of the embodied person in his or her community struggling to understand reality over the course of time."[60] Johnson goes on to show how this understanding of a biblical epistemology parallels the structure of knowing in science. "The enterprise of science *seeks to form the novice scientist into a discoverer through social and ritual practices.*"[61] So a biblical epistemology might just be more relevant to the modern world than we realize!

It is this biblical epistemology that brings us closer to what I want to do in this book. One of my central objectives is to articulate what the Bible has to say about intellectual virtues. While these latest developments in biblical epistemology are significant, they tend not to deal specifically with the subject of intellectual virtues.[62] My objective in the next few sections of this chapter is to begin to fill this gap. Of course, the remaining chapters of the book will develop this further. First, I will look at the Great Commandment and its implications for a biblical epistemology and, more specifically, how it relates to intellectual virtues. Then I would like to examine some of the central components of the biblical narrative or worldview to see what they might have to say about intellectual virtues. It should be noted that in doing all this I am drawing on several of Richard Hays's modes of ethical discourse. Consideration of the Great Commandment aligns with broader principles of ethics. And a consideration of the implications of the biblical narrative and worldview for intellectual virtues aligns with the later modes of ethical discourse identified by Hays.

THE GREAT COMMANDMENT AND INTELLECTUAL VIRTUES

When Jesus is asked which of the commandments is the most important, he quotes from the Torah: "Hear O Israel, the Lord our God, the Lord is one. Love the Lord your God with all your heart and with all your soul and with all your mind and with all your strength. The second is this: 'Love your neighbor as yourself.' There is no commandment greater than these" (Mark 12:29–30; Deut 6:4–5; Lev 19:18). It is significant that the Greatest Commandment specifically makes reference to the mind.[63] Sadly, there have been pockets of anti-intellectualism in the church throughout history which are still found in parts of the church today.

But what does it mean to love God with our minds? Here it is significant that Jesus' review of the Great Commandment is prefaced with a reminder that the Lord our God is one. There is no other god. And our God is to be acknowledged as Lord. God is also supposed to be the Lord of our minds. Thus, the frequent reminder in Scripture, "The fear of the Lord is the beginning of knowledge."[64] Again, note the epistemological content of this reminder. We come to know by acknowledging God as the source of all knowledge. This requires intellectual humility, one of the key intellectual virtues.

We are to love God with our whole being, including our minds. Surely this entails that we love God's revelation, both God's special revelation through the Bible and God's general revelation in creation. This means that we will want to grow in our understanding of the Bible and of God's creation. Christians should love to learn. The picture of Jesus as a child listening to the teachers of the law in the temple and asking them questions is a model for us (Luke 2:46). Like Jesus, we should be growing not only in stature, but also in wisdom and understanding (Luke 2:40, 52). The love of knowledge and truth is one expression of our love of God and it is a central intellectual virtue.

What about the second part of the Great Commandment? What does it mean to love our neighbor intellectually? Our neighbor, too, is created in the image of God. Our neighbor, too, has a mind which sometimes (often) comes to conclusions different from our own. So, loving our neighbors will entail that we tolerate them and their ideas, we listen to them, respect their insights, and are willing to learn from them. This is what I will identify in a later chapter as the intellectual virtue of tolerance or forbearance.

We are to love our neighbors as ourselves. This reciprocal dynamic is also expressed in the Golden Rule which Jesus once again presents as a summary of the Law and the Prophets: "In everything, do to others what you would have them do to you" (Matt 7:12). What do we want others to do to us in regard to our minds and our ideas? We want them to respect us and our ideas. Therefore, we, too, need to respect our neighbor even though they disagree with us. Again, the intellectual virtue of tolerance or forbearance. We want our neighbors to treat our own ideas fairly even if they disagree with us. We, too, are called to cultivate the intellectual virtue of fairmindedness. We also want our neighbors who disagree with us not to push their own ideas onto us too strongly. We should do the same when we engage in persuasion and evangelism.[65]

Love is at the heart of the Great Commandment. We are to love God with our minds. We are also to love our neighbors with our minds. Love is at the heart of intellectual virtues. I'm sure Esther Meek would agree with me given her claim that epistemology must start with love.[66]

THE BIBLICAL NARRATIVE/WORLDVIEW AND INTELLECTUAL VIRTUES AND VICES

The first few chapters of Genesis are central to the biblical narrative and the grand themes of a Christian worldview. A careful reading of these chapters will reveal a surprising emphasis on epistemology. We first encounter an ideal way of knowing in the Garden of Eden. Then comes the "fall" of Adam and Eve and with it distorted ways of knowing. Finally, there is a hint of redemption which brings with it the possibility of a restored ideal in knowing, a redemptive epistemology.[67] Each of these three accounts of knowing have important implications for intellectual virtues and vices.

1. Ideal knowing in the Garden of Eden

Genesis begins with God creating a world by uttering commands. Again and again we read, "And God said." And each time something comes into existence, we hear the refrain, "And God saw that it was good." The world came into being by God's word. The same Creator God who called the cosmos into existence in the beginning of time continues to keep the cosmos in existence to the present day (2 Pet 3:5, 7). "For he spoke, and it came to be; he commanded, and it stood firm" (Ps 33:9). All things live and move and have their being by God's sovereign legislative decree (Acts 17:28).

God knew what he was doing when he created the world. Proverbs 8 attributes creation to God's wisdom. A wise Creator designed and ordered the world in accordance with a brilliant plan. "By wisdom the LORD laid the earth's foundations, by understanding he set the heavens in place; by his knowledge the deeps were divided, and the clouds let drop the dew" (Prov 3:19–20).[68] The world is knowable because God created it. John's Gospel begins by connecting the story of creation with Christ and the eternal Word (John 1:1–3). Paul, too, underscores the connection between Christ and creation. Not only were "all things created by him," but "in him all things hold together" (Col 1:16, 17). So, Christ, as the Word made flesh, is at the foundation of creation being knowable.

God's final act of creation involves humankind, "male and female he created them," and they were made in the image of God (Gen 1:27). Adam and Eve were like God in possessing cognitive faculties. God gave them minds to think, although the human capacity for thinking is finite, unlike God's infinite knowledge.[69] Hence the importance of intellectual humility, as expressed so dramatically in the conclusion of the book of Job. God challenges Job with the question: "Who is this that darkens my counsel with words without knowledge? Brace yourself like a man; I will question you, and you shall answer me" (Job 38:2–3). Then, after a flurry of rhetorical questions relating to the power and wisdom of God displayed in creation, Job is brought to a proper understanding of himself as a finite and fallible creature. "Surely I spoke of things I did not understand, things too wonderful for me to know" (Job 42:3).[70]

After blessing Adam and Eve, God gave to this highest order of his creation a mandate to "fill the earth and subdue it," and to "take care of it" (Gen 1:28; 2:15). We are called to be vice-regents of God. This creation mandate includes acquiring an understanding of nature. God created a world that was knowable, and he created human beings that were fit for thinking and learning in all its forms. God gave to Adam and Eve and to us "ears that hear and eyes that see" (Prov 20:12). Indeed, the whole world can be seen as a school for the human race.[71] The first man grew in knowledge by studying God's handiwork and by following God's instructions.

Adam also grew in his understanding of God and himself. The LORD God said, "It is not good for the man to be alone" (Gen 2:18). And then God invites Adam to engage in an exercise that will help Adam to discover this for himself. After naming all the beasts of the field and all the birds of the air, Adam concluded that none of them were really suitable as a companion for him (Gen 2:19–20). And once again, God provided Adam with what he needed, and once again Adam could learn what a delightful companion Eve was.

What was knowing like in the Garden of Eden? Adam and Eve will have been immediately aware of God's presence and his care for them. They also learned by listening to God. God taught Adam and Eve, instructing them to eat from "every tree that has fruit with seed in it," but not to eat from "the tree of the knowledge of good and evil" (Gen 1:29–30; 2:9, 16–17).[72] Interestingly, we are also told that the trees were "pleasing to the eye and good for food" (Gen 2:9). So, Adam and Eve could discover for themselves that the fruit from trees both looked good and was also nourishing. They were created as sentient beings who could not only appreciate beauty but who also could let their curiosity lead them to new discoveries. Here knowing was a process, and clearly Adam and Eve had been created with a desire to gain knowledge and truth. More on this in the next chapter.

God also brought to Adam "all the beasts of the field and all the birds of the air" and gave to Adam the responsibility to name them (Gen 2:19–20). Classifying and making distinctions of all that God had created took time. So, while Adam had a God-given curiosity, this curiosity was under the direction of God. Thus, Adam was called to exercise intellectual humility. He didn't know everything and so he needed to accept God as his teacher.

God created a world that could be known, and he gave man the capacities to know this world, and there was a match between the world God created and man's abilities to know this world. Knowing was covenantal in nature. God gave his blessing to Adam as he followed God-ordained ways of knowing, and he also outlined the consequences that would follow if his guidelines for knowing weren't followed.

The love of knowledge and truth, openness to learn new things, intellectual humility, and intellectual courage—all of these intellectual virtues are practiced in a perfect setting, the Garden of Eden. "Eden" in fact means bliss, delight, or pleasure, with nuances of contentment and prosperity.[73] And it is in this setting that Adam and then Eve came to know more and more as they submitted to the authority of God and as they explored the world that God had created. And they flourished. Knowing in the right way, knowing that is a result of loving the truth and practicing intellectual humility, leads to blessing and to human flourishing or *shalom* (Gen 1:22). "In the Bible shalom means *universal flourishing, wholeness and delight* . . . . Shalom, in other words, is the way things ought to be."[74] This is what God intended for humankind.

2. Distortions of knowing in the Garden

Sadly, the beautiful account of creation and the Garden of Eden is not the end of the biblical story. A "crafty" serpent appears and dares to say to Eve, "Did God really say, 'You must not eat from any tree in the Garden'?" (Gen 3:1). Eve makes the mistake of entertaining this question and Adam does nothing to intervene. Instead of listening to God, they listened to a serpent who was calling into question God's truthfulness and trustworthiness. Adam and Eve were not content to live as finite creatures, limiting their desire to know within the constraints dictated by God. Instead, they wanted to be like God in every way (Gen 3:5). They wanted to know more than they were meant to know. They wanted to know independently of God. They wanted to be autonomous knowers, trusting their own eyes which now were leading them to distorted desires.

The "fall" of Adam and Eve caused them to be afraid when they "heard the sound of the LORD God as he was walking in the garden in the cool of the day, and they hid from the LORD God among the trees of the garden" (Gen 3:8). They no longer wanted to converse with God or listen to him. They were hiding from the truth. Paul describes human beings after the fall as suppressing the truth and not able to draw the proper conclusion about God from what can be seen with their eyes (Rom 1:18–20). Although they knew God, they failed to honor God, so "their thinking became futile and their foolish hearts were darkened. Although they claimed to be wise, they became fools" (Rom 1:21).

Another way to describe the distortions of knowing that emerge as part of the fall of Adam and Eve is to introduce the notion of intellectual vices or intellectual sins. The desire for knowledge and truth is now distorted. Intellectual arrogance replaces the intellectual humility that characterized Adam and Eve before the fall. Instead of listening to God, they now choose to listen to a serpent. Instead of openness to what God might want to say to them, they hide themselves from God. Closed-mindedness makes it impossible for Adam and Eve to appreciate the consequences of their distorted knowing. And the result of all this is that they are driven from the Garden of Eden.

Indeed, Genesis 4–11 gives us a tragic description of a rather destructive trajectory that follows the sin of Adam and Eve. Immediately following the expulsion of Adam and Eve from the Garden of Eden, we have the sad story of Cain and Abel (Gen 4:1–16). There would seem to be something wrong with Cain's offering to God, he gets "very angry, and his face was downcast," and in the end he kills his brother Abel (v. 5). This is hardly a picture of a man who is humble and who wants to think and do what is right. Then we have the story of a people who are united in language and ideology, who want to build a city and the Tower of Babel that would reach to the heavens, thus making a name for themselves (Gen 11:1–9). There is intellectual arrogance here and empire building. And God is not pleased. This story also teaches us that "cognitive malfunction can be corporate as well as individual."[75] Then follows the story of Noah and the flood. "The LORD saw how great man's wickedness on the earth had become, and that every inclination of the thoughts of his heart was only evil all the time" (Gen 6:5). Note especially that it is the "thoughts of the heart" that had become distorted.

This same trajectory and faulty epistemology is reiterated in the New Testament. Paul, for example, gives us a graphic description of the consequences of "a depraved mind" (Rom 1:28).

> Furthermore, just as they did not think it worthwhile to retain the knowledge of God, so God gave them over to a depraved mind, so that they do what ought not to be done. They have become filled with every kind of wickedness, evil, greed and depravity. They are full of envy, murder, strife, deceit and malice. They are gossips, slanderers, God-haters, insolent, arrogant and boastful; they invent ways of doing evil; they disobey their parents; they have no understanding, no fidelity, no love, no mercy. Although they know God's righteous decree that those who do such things deserve death, they not only continue to do these very things but also approve of those who practice them. (Rom 1:28–32)

Here, once again, we see a close link between distorted knowing and distorted desires and behavior. Intellectual vices have negative consequences.

The effects of the fall can be described as epistemologically crippling. There is some dispute among theologians as to how crippling the fall has been. Roman Catholics tend to have more faith in the mind despite the fall, while Protestants tend to highlight the distortions of our epistemic faculties due to our being sinful creatures. However, both sides agree that the fall of Adam and Eve has led to some cognitive malfunctioning. Thankfully, God's grace never allows sin to completely destroy the functioning of our epistemic faculties. But there is more. God has also provided a way to overcome the devastating effects of sin on our minds. Though "all have sinned and fall short of the glory of God," we can be made right with God "through the redemption that came by Jesus Christ" (Rom 3:24). And God's plan of redemption also includes redemption of our minds, to which we now turn.

3. Redemptive epistemology

Thankfully, the fall of Adam and Eve and its disastrous consequences for them and all of humankind after them is not the end of the biblical story. Already in Genesis you have hints of God's rescue plan for a very broken world. Eve's "offspring" would eventually crush the head of the serpent (Gen 3:15). It was through Abraham and his progeny that "all the peoples on earth will be blessed" (Gen 12:1–3). The prophets tell of a coming Messiah who will carry out this plan of redemption. Jesus goes to the cross and takes upon himself the sin of mankind and the brokenness of the world, and is then raised from the dead, signaling victory over evil and all that is wrong in the world. He promises to come again to usher in a new heaven and a new earth when the full plan of redemption will be completed. But we are not there yet. We live in an in-between time where redemption is still in process. This raises the important question as to what redemption might mean for our minds during this in-between time.

Richard Smith introduces the notion of a "redemptive epistemology" to characterize knowing during the time between the fall of Adam and Eve and the new creation.[76] Smith uses the call of Isaiah to illustrate this transformative epistemology.[77] Isaiah first "saw the Lord seated on a throne, high and exalted" (Isa 6:1). He heard the voice of the Seraphim who were calling to one another, "Holy, holy, holy is the Lord Almighty; the whole earth is full of his glory" (v. 3). Isaiah is listening to the voice of God and is acknowledging his sovereignty. Isaiah then cries out, "Woe is me! I am ruined! For I am a man of unclean lips, and I live among a people of unclean lips, and my eyes have seen the King, the LORD Almighty" (v. 5). Here we have repentance, with Isaiah identifying himself with a rebellious and sinful people. After repentance, Isaiah's lips are purified (vv. 6–7), and then he responds in obedience to God's call (v. 8). Isaiah modeled a redemptive epistemology. Listening to God, displaying a godly fear, contritely confessing sin, embracing divine cleansing, hearing God's call, and then responding in obedience.

This story touches on two dimensions of a redemptive epistemology, the personal and the societal. At a personal level Christians find themselves torn. Paul describes Christians as a walking civil war—there is a part of us that wants to do what is right, but there is another part of us pulling us towards evil (Rom 7:14–25). "What a wretched man I am!" (v. 24). Paul makes it very clear that this civil war also affects the mind. Our minds are in tension between thinking in accordance with what the Spirit desires and thinking that is in line with our sinful nature (Rom 8:5). Who will rescue us from this mental battle? "Thanks be to God—through Jesus Christ our Lord!" (Rom 7:25).

Paul goes on to describe what this rescue will mean in the day-to-day life of the Christian. He challenges us to separate ourselves from the "pattern of this world" and to "be transformed by the renewing of your mind" (Rom 12:2). In his letter to the Ephesians, Paul talks about putting off "your old self which is being corrupted by its deceitful desires" and "to put on the new self, created to be like God in true righteousness and holiness," and this includes being "made new in the attitude of your minds" (Eph 4:22–24). What will this look like? Christians are people who recognize that they are fallen and sinful creatures, who are always in need of grace. Instead of an arrogant rejection of God, there will be humble submission to God. Instead of stifling the truth, there will be openness to what God has made plain in Scripture and in creation. Instead of thinking that has become futile, there will now be minds that are being renewed to be in conformity to God's truth as revealed in Scripture and in nature.

The story of Isaiah's call also touches on a second dimension of a redemptive epistemology. Just after Isaiah's response to the call of God, we get a rather pessimistic portrayal of the difficulties he would face in his ministry. He would be speaking to people who have eyes that don't really see, ears that don't really hear, and hearts that are calloused (Isa 6:9–10). Jesus uses this very passage to explain the parable of the sower to his disciples (Mark 4:10–20). And Paul, too, uses this same passage to explain why some people didn't respond to his message (Acts 28:25–27). Christians today also live in a world where many people are in rebellion against God, who as a result have minds that are leading them astray, and whose thinking is corrupted by intellectual vices such as the failure to search for truth, intellectual arrogance, and closed-mindedness.

Again, it is not easy to live in such an intellectual environment. It is not easy to encounter these intellectual vices in others. At the same time, Christians realize that they themselves are tempted by these same intellectual vices. So, Christians find themselves engaged in a battle of the mind, both within and without. Thus, we find Paul using battle imagery, instructing us to "put on the full armor of God," including "the belt of truth buckled around your waist," and a "breastplate of righteousness," and "the sword of the Spirit, which is the word of God" (Eph 6:10–18). Discernment and vigilance are required, and prayerful reliance on God who gives grace to the humble in spirit.

Isaiah introduces another word to describe a redemptive epistemology—healing. He describes an alternative to this pessimistic prognosis of a mind and heart in rebellion against God—the possibility that "they might see with their eyes, hear with their ears, understand with their hearts, and turn and be *healed*" (Isa 6:10b; my emphasis). This theme of healing is in fact repeated several times in the final chapters of Isaiah, which portray a vision of a new heavens and a new earth (Isa 57:18, 19; 58:8). This will be not only a time when "the wolf will live with the lamb" but also a time when "the earth will be full of the knowledge of the Lord" (Isa 11:6, 9). Here we have a restored epistemology that once again reflects knowing in the Garden of Eden before the fall.

A healing of the mind is what we need, given the effects of the fall of Adam and Eve. This healing can also be described in terms of a turning away from intellectual vices and a recovery of intellectual virtues. Instead of intellectual arrogance, there is a submission of the mind to God and to his revelation in Scripture and in nature. Instead of closed eyes, ears, and hearts, there is openness to what God has revealed in Scripture and nature. Instead of suppressing truth, there is an honest searching for truth. Instead of hatred for those who disagree with you, there is love and respect and care taken to represent the other's views fairly. Instead of cowardice, there is intellectual courage to humbly give witness to the truth in the face of opposition.

Healing. That is what we need. Redemption of our minds. And what are the results? Following a God-ordained way of knowing leads to blessing and human flourishing. Again and again in Deuteronomy, which can be read as "the Rosetta stone of redemptive epistemology," we find God pleading with Israel to fear him and to love God with heart and mind "so that it might go well with them and their children forever" (Deut 5:29).[78] And we are repeatedly reminded that failure to follow God's way of knowing leads to the very opposite of human flourishing. This is at the heart of God's covenant with his creation and with humankind. Obedience leads to blessing and disobedience leads to death.[79] This also applies to the mind. Cultivating and practicing intellectual virtues will lead to human excellence and more generally to human flourishing. Cultivating and practicing intellectual vices will lead to unhealthy minds and unhealthy societies.

In a world where there is growing fragmentation and polarization, where sloganeering and demonization dominate our discourse, we need to think more carefully about intellectual virtues and vices. In the chapters that follow, we will be looking more closely at these intellectual virtues and vices, one at a time. This book is not an exhaustive treatment of all intellectual virtues and vices. Instead, I am limiting myself to those that I consider to be most important for our time. It should also be noted that intellectual virtues tend to overlap to some extent. So a careful consideration of the more important intellectual virtues and vices should suffice.

Each of the following central chapters will begin with an exercise in self-examination of the intellectual virtue and corresponding vices under discussion in the chapter. This is in keeping with Paul's advice: "Examine yourselves . . . test yourselves" (2 Cor 13:5). Readers are encouraged to first spend some time completing the questionnaire at the beginning of each chapter and then pondering the questions, speculating why I have included these questions and not others, and even evaluating the questionnaire. Do you feel it is fair and an accurate measure of the intellectual virtue in question? Hopefully the reader will then be in a better position to understand and evaluate the exposition of the virtue and corresponding vices that follow in the chapter. Readers might want to do the questionnaire again after they have read the chapter to see if their self-evaluation remains the same. And again, they might want to evaluate the individual questions and the questionnaire as a whole. If your frustration level is very high, you might even want to write the author of the questionnaire!

2

Love of Knowledge and Truth

They perish because they refused to love the truth and so be saved.
(2 THESSALONIANS 2:10)

Truth is so obscure in these times, and falsehood so well established, that, unless we love the truth, we shall never recognize it.
(BLAISE PASCAL, *PENSÉES* §739)

Before you complete the questionnaire that follows, give yourself a rating (0–10) on your love of knowledge and truth.

QUESTIONNAIRE: A SELF-EVALUATION

For each of the following statements, answer **yes**, **no**, or **unsure/maybe**.

1. I care deeply about growing in knowledge and finding the truth.
2. I welcome criticisms of my beliefs.

3. I readily admit that I am wrong when I discover that I have an incorrect belief.

4. I occasionally spend some time evaluating my core beliefs or the worldview/religion that I hold.

5. I am careful to base my beliefs on evidence and arguments.

6. I spend very little time surfing the internet, perusing what catches my interest.

7. I am very concerned about falling prey to accepting fake news or unsubstantiated conspiracy theories and make it a point to test claims that sound suspicious.

8. I am not at all concerned about impressing people with what I know. I value acquiring knowledge for its own sake.

9. I believe there is such a thing as "truth." I am not a relativist.

10. I delight in sharing what I have come to know with others. Indeed, on important matters, I feel I have an obligation to do so.

Now give a numerical value to each of your answers—**1 for yes; ½ for unsure/maybe; 0 for no**. Then total your numerical values. The total out of 10 gives the percentage grade for your having the intellectual virtue of the "love of knowledge and truth."

Remember this questionnaire has been prepared by a philosopher and not a social scientist, so there is little scientific validity to the grade that you finally get! But the author hopes this exercise has helped you to think about how much you care about knowledge and truth, and how much you try to avoid the vices of intellectual laziness and carelessness.

You might also want to evaluate the questionnaire itself. Do you think the questions asked represent a fair assessment of whether or not someone has the intellectual virtue of the love of knowledge and truth? Can you think of better questions? Reading the chapter will hopefully help you to understand why the author has included the questions he did. You might even want to do the questionnaire again after you have read the chapter. Are the results the same? Has your initial evaluation of the questionnaire changed?

Luke's brief account of Paul's mission to Thessalonica and Berea provides a telling illustration of both the presence and the absence of the intellectual virtue of the love of knowledge and truth (Acts 17:1–15). In both cities Paul exemplifies the love of knowledge and truth by conveying his message in a manner that showed he cared about knowledge and truth. "He reasoned with them from the Scriptures, explaining and proving that Christ had to suffer and rise from the dead" (vv. 2–3). He also argued that the Jesus of history was in fact the fulfillment of the Christ portrayed in the Old Testament (v. 3). In both cases some Jews and Gentiles "were persuaded" by these arguments while others turned a deaf ear to Paul's message and quickly resorted to hostility and violence (vv. 4–5, 12–13). The latter response, growing out of "jealousy" (v. 5), exemplifies the absence of a love of knowledge and truth.

Of particular significance is Luke's description of many in the Berean audience. "Now the Bereans were of more noble character than the Thessalonians, for they received the message with great eagerness and examined the Scriptures every day to see if what Paul said was true" (Acts 17:11). Here were people who carefully and eagerly listened to what Paul said, and who went on to critically evaluate whether Paul's message lined up with the Hebrew Scriptures. And they did this every day, determined to find out if what Paul said was true. If only more Christians today would evaluate the sermons of their pastors! It should further be noted that the Bereans are described as "of more noble character than the Thessalonians." Luke is treating the way in which the Bereans responded to his message as a character trait, a virtue. Indeed, he is hinting at the notion of an intellectual virtue. We have here a paradigm case of the intellectual virtue of the love of knowledge and truth.

BEGINNING MY TREATMENT OF intellectual virtues with the love of knowledge and truth calls for some explanation. Not all scholars agree that the love of knowledge and truth should be treated as a separate intellectual virtue. Some see the love of knowledge and truth as foundational to the other intellectual virtues.[80] Some describe all the intellectual virtues as "unified" by the love of knowledge and truth.[81] Others treat the love of knowledge and truth as a description of the nature of intellectual virtues generally.[82] I don't think it is necessary to resolve this debate for my purposes. In fact, it is rather difficult to distinguish between a description of the nature of intellectual virtues generally and the more specific intellectual virtue of the love of knowledge and truth. We will also find that intellectual virtues overlap with each other.[83] So, whether a general term or a specific intellectual virtue, I believe a focus on the love of knowledge and truth is needed. Either way, the love of knowledge and truth is very important, and so I start with it.

Some explanation is also needed as to why I am limiting myself to knowledge and truth in this chapter. While knowledge and truth are general concepts, there are other qualities of the mind that might be thought of as equally deserving of attention, for example, the love of learning, acquiring justified true beliefs, and growing in understanding and wisdom. However, these additional concepts are closely related to knowledge and truth. Knowledge is often understood as involving justified true beliefs, so the love of knowledge could equally well be described as the love of justified true beliefs or the love of truth. Some writers seem to equate the love of wisdom with the love of truth and again make the love of wisdom foundational or at least integrally related to the other intellectual virtues.[84] In this chapter I will in the main talk about the love of knowledge and truth, though these concepts should be seen as representative of the love of wisdom and understanding, and indeed of all the intellectual virtues as a collective.

HUMAN NATURE AND THE LOVE OF KNOWLEDGE AND TRUTH

It would seem that we are by nature hard-wired to search for knowledge and truth. Ancient Greek philosopher Aristotle described human beings in this way. "All men by nature desire to know. An indication of this is the delight we take in our senses."[85] Babies, quite soon after they are born, give indication of listening carefully to sounds and searching with their eyes. Children are by nature very curious. They want to know. They keep asking why, sometimes driving parents to distraction. This desire to know extends into adulthood, though sadly we don't always show the excitement about knowing that children display.

Aristotle's assessment begs an important question. Why do we desire to know? The biblical story of creation gives us an answer to this question. I have already reviewed the story of creation in the previous chapter and so will be brief here. The first two chapters of Genesis describe God as the Creator of all that exists, including human beings, who are created in the image of God. God created the world by wisdom and understanding and knowledge. And Adam and Eve were created with a desire to know God and the world he created. One can imagine Adam and Eve being "like toddlers exploring the world for the first time hand in hand with their father."[86]

Adam and Eve were created so as to be naturally curious and so they wanted to know more and more about the world they lived in. They also wanted to know more about God and themselves. Indeed, after declaring that it is not good for man to be alone, God gives Adam the assignment to find this out for himself by naming "all the beasts of the field and all the birds of the air," only to discover that none of these were a "suitable helper" for him (Gen 2:18–20). God then creates Eve from and for Adam, and one can only imagine their delight in discovering more about each other.

Irenaeus (130–202) compared Adam and Eve to inquisitive children to highlight the fact that they were designed for growth.[87] "Humanity is an intentionally created-to-know creature."[88] And of course, coming to know the inexhaustible secrets of God's creation never ends for us as finite human beings. "As the whole world is a school for the human race . . . so every individual's lifetime is a school from the cradle to the grave."[89]

One can imagine the progress Adam and Eve made as they were following "the pathway of sensory discovery, situational awareness, self-knowledge, and intuition of the transcendent."[90] This process will have been based on observation, experimentation, and reflection, and all the while the progress they made "was guided *by* God and led *to* God."[91] Here one cannot help but think of how Jesus ("the last Adam") as a boy impressed the teachers in the temple with his knowledge and understanding, and that in a summary statement of his childhood, we are told that he "grew in wisdom and stature, and in favor with God and men" (1 Cor 15:45; Luke 2:47, 52).

Sadly, this ideal of knowing and growing in knowledge comes to an abrupt end in Genesis 3. The story is interrupted by a "crafty" serpent who leads Eve to question what God had said, and soon Adam joins in this parade of deception. My focus here will be on how this "fall" of Adam and Eve affects their and our desire to love knowledge and truth. In part, they were still exercising the intellectual virtue of desiring knowledge and truth. After all, the forbidden tree was described by God as "the tree of the knowledge of good and evil" (Gen 2:17). But they were not content to live as finite creatures, limiting their desire to know within the constraints dictated by God. Yes, they still wanted to gain knowledge, but this desire to know was now distorted. They were obsessed with wanting to know more than God wanted them to know.

The desire for knowledge and truth was and is distorted in other ways. Sin, as Augustine taught us, has a way of deforming our loves.[92] Adam and Eve were now listening to a serpent rather than God. They were entertaining questions about God rather than trusting in God. They were trusting in their own senses and desires rather than letting these be directed by God. They wanted to know independently from God. They wanted to be autonomous knowers, trusting their own senses and their own thinking.

And what about their desire for truth? We find Adam and Eve hiding from God. Instead of open communication with God, they are now afraid of what God might say to them. Indeed, God interrogates them with four questions: "Where are you?" (Gen 3:9); "Who told you that you were naked?" (v. 11); "Have you eaten from the tree that I commanded you not to eat from?" (v. 11); "What is this you have done?" (v. 13). Adam and Eve had a hard time answering these questions. Reflecting the tactics of the serpent, they resorted to "obfuscation, diversion and blame shifting."[93] They were not only hiding from God but also hiding from the truth.[94]

The effects of the fall of Adam and Eve on the desire for knowledge and truth are catalogued throughout the Bible. The book of Proverbs frequently labels those who no longer desire knowledge and truth as fools. "How long will you simple ones love your simple ways? How long will mockers delight in mockery and fools hate knowledge?" (Prov 1:22).[95] The Psalmist, too, labels as "fools" those who "do not understand" that the wicked will eventually perish (Ps 92:6). "Take heed, you senseless ones among the people; you fools, when will you become wise?" (Ps 94:8). And then this assessment of the human mind: "The LORD knows the thoughts of man; he knows that they are futile" (Ps 94:11). The Psalmist also warns us not to be "like the horse or the mule, which have no understanding," and therefore have need to be controlled by bit and bridle (Ps 32:8-9). Interestingly, it is the "fool" who says, "There is no God" (Ps 14:1; 53:1).

Isaiah gives us a poignant description of hearts and minds that are no longer able to seek knowledge and truth because God has given up on them, as it were. "Be ever hearing, but never understanding; be ever seeing, but never perceiving. Make the heart of this people calloused; make their ears dull and close their eyes" (Isa 6:9–10; cf. Ps 81:11–12). This is not exactly a positive description of human knowing, but it is the condition of humanity after the fall. Eyes that don't really perceive what is right before them. Ears that no longer are open to hearing the voice of the LORD. Hearts that suppress the truth. This is what rebellion against God leads to.

This assessment of the human mind is repeated again and again in Isaiah.[96] In the middle of a long passage condemning idolatry, Isaiah says this: "They know nothing, they understand nothing; their eyes are plastered over so they cannot see, and their minds closed so they cannot understand" (Isa 44:18). And this affects every dimension of human knowledge and claims to truth. Our understanding of truth is always partially distorted, and this is always coupled with a desire to hold on to our distorted perceptions of truth and to not bother trying to evaluate them. The desire for knowledge and truth is stifled.

Jesus draws on Isaiah's description of closed hearts and minds in explaining the parable of the sower to his disciples.[97] Jesus also condemns the Pharisees, "the experts in the law, because you have taken away the key of knowledge" (Luke 11:52). The apostle Paul similarly describes human beings after the fall as suppressing the truth and not being able to draw the proper conclusion about God from what can be seen with their eyes (Rom 1:18–20). Although they knew God, they failed to honor God, so "their thinking became futile and their foolish hearts were darkened. Although they claimed to be wise, they became fools" (Rom 1:21). Elsewhere, Paul maintains that "the god of this age has blinded the minds of unbelievers, so that they cannot see the light of the gospel of the glory of Christ, who is the image of God" (2 Cor 4:4). So now we have minds that are closed to some important truths about God.

Paul also identifies various ways in which we can fail to be serious in our search for truth. He repeatedly warns about foolish arguments and controversies that are unprofitable and useless.[98] What Paul no doubt has in mind here is arguing for the sake of arguing, a phenomenon that is all too common today, even in the church. Paul also tells us that a time "will come when men [and women] . . . will gather around them a great number of teachers to say what their itching ears want to hear" (2 Tim 4:3). Paul suggests that in the last days, there will be people who are "always learning but never able to acknowledge the truth" (2 Tim 3:7). Here again we have a confusing mixture of "always learning" and yet a refusal to carry this learning to its logical conclusion. The author of Hebrews identifies another effect of sin. He is frustrated in his desire to share some further theological insights because his readers are "slow to learn" (Heb 5:11).

So what should we conclude about human nature and the desire for knowledge and truth? We both desire and don't desire knowledge and truth.[99] While we still want to know to some degree, there is also within us a tendency not to want to know the truth, especially concerning God and ourselves. We therefore need to fight against that part of our nature that does not love knowledge and truth as much as it should. Hence also the need for the intellectual virtue of the love of knowledge and truth, both for us as individuals and for any group of individuals, including the church.

Thankfully, the story of the fall of Adam and Eve is not the end of the Christian narrative. There is a concluding chapter of redemption and restoration of the ideal that once existed in the garden of Eden. And this redemption includes a restoration of a healthy love of knowledge and truth. More on this later. First, we need to get a better understanding of the meaning of the love of knowledge and truth.

KNOWLEDGE, UNDERSTANDING, AND WISDOM

So far I have been assuming a common sense understanding of the intellectual virtue of the love of knowledge and truth. Obviously, this is not enough. We need to come to a better and more nuanced definition of this intellectual virtue. In order to do this, I want to break down the notion of "the love of knowledge and truth" and consider each part of this phrase on its own. So first I will deal with the meaning of knowledge and its close associates, understanding and wisdom. Then I will deal with truth. And finally, the love component of the intellectual virtue of the love of knowledge and truth.

What is knowledge? I have already touched on this question in chapter 1. The rough consensus of philosophers for several millennia was that knowledge is justified true belief.[100] In other words, people who claim to have knowledge must believe what they claim to know, they must have evidence for what they claim to know, and what is believed must in fact be true. Much ink has been spilled in exposing the problems with this definition since 1963, when an American philosopher wrote a short essay in which he provided examples of beliefs that were true and justified, but that most people would agree should not be classified as knowledge.[101] Other questions arise. How much justification is required for a belief to be elevated to the status of knowledge? What is truth? And what is a belief?

Another problem with this definition is that it treats knowledge and truth as objects, as something we can possess. Hence our frequent use of nouns to label knowing. But, as I have already pointed out in chapter 1, it is now recognized that knowing is more of a process than a product, a process occurring at a particular time and place. Dru Johnson, among others, has argued that it would be better to talk about "knowing" rather than "knowledge" if we are trying to articulate a biblical epistemology.[102] He argues further that this also applies to knowing in science.[103]

While I am sympathetic with Johnson's analysis of knowing in the Bible and in science, I think he goes too far in dismissing the noun usage of knowing. A focus on the process of knowing is not enough. We also need to look at the end goal of this process. There is such a thing as knowing well or seeing correctly. And the Bible does talk about knowledge as something that is achieved in the process of knowing. Indeed, Johnson is forced to admit that the Bible does sometimes describe knowledge as a "product."[104] A careful study of the Bible will show that "knowledge" is often used as a noun.[105]

A few comments specifically about understanding and wisdom might be in order. The notion of understanding would seem to refer to a greater depth and breadth of knowledge. Taking a course in Shakespeare will deepen our understanding of his plays and, at the same time, deepen our understanding of human nature. Science gives us not only knowledge but also "a kind of systematic *appreciation* of things."[106] King Solomon was known for his wisdom and understanding. "God gave Solomon wisdom and very great insight, and a breadth of understanding as measureless as the sand on the seashore" (1 Kgs 4:29).

Aristotle included practical wisdom (*phronēsis*) among the intellectual virtues. Some contemporary writers treat the love of wisdom as a foundational intellectual virtue.[107] Wisdom is typically understood as practical in nature—making good choices that enhance human well-being. But making good choices requires knowledge. It is, therefore, difficult to draw a sharp distinction between wisdom and knowledge. The most common Hebrew term for wisdom (*hochmah*) has a broad meaning and is often combined with other epistemic terms. Proverbs has a lot to say about wisdom, but references to wisdom are often closely linked to references to knowledge and understanding. For example, all three terms are used to describe how the LORD laid the foundations of the earth (Prov 3:19–20). Many other illustrations of such interchangeability could be provided. "For the LORD gives wisdom, and from his mouth come knowledge and understanding" (Prov 2:6). "Wise men store up knowledge" (Prov 10:14).[108]

I conclude that while it might be difficult to give precise definitions of knowledge, understanding, and wisdom, we do have a rough idea of what these terms mean. Given their overlapping meanings, I will in this chapter focus on the love of knowledge and its implicit reference to truth.

TRUTH

We live in a time when it is difficult to talk about truth. As a college instructor, I encountered in my students a fierce resistance to the notion of truth. Allan Bloom begins his masterpiece, *The Closing of the American Mind*, with this commentary on today's students: "There is one thing a professor can be absolutely certain of: almost every student entering the university believes, or says he believes, that truth is relative. If this belief is put to the test, one can count on the students' reaction: they will be uncomprehending."[109] That has been my experience as well. For most students today, "It's true for me," seems to be the end of any argument. Of course, this view of truth is not limited to students. As already pointed out in the preface, we live in a post-truth era. There are outright denials of the very idea of truth. "Truth" is conceived as a social construction or it is reduced to a power construct.

Of course, these reductionistic accounts of truth cannot be sustained for long. Relativists invariably contradict themselves and are forced to admit that some things really are true. Social constructivists invariably want to exempt their own position from being seen as an arbitrary social construction. And those who want to reduce "truth" to a power construct invariably want to say that their claims are true. We simply can't avoid the notion of truth. Nor can we entirely negate the search for truth, as has already been argued earlier in this chapter.

In my many years of teaching and my ongoing deliberations on this topic, I have come to realize that much of the opposition to the notion of truth is based on a failure to make an important distinction between truth as an ideal concept, which is in some way absolute, and the human search for truth, which is in fact relative.[110] I like to illustrate this distinction with a philosophical diagram I have labeled "Ladder of Truth."[111]

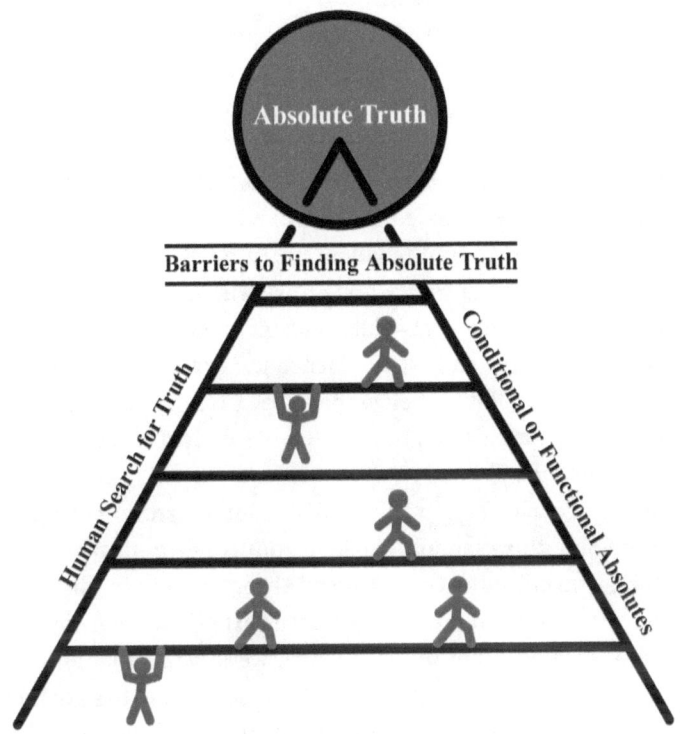

Figure 2: Ladder of Truth

In this diagram, you find truth with a capital *T* placed above a barrier. For Christians, Absolute Truth is of course found in God. Thus, the Psalmist refers to the LORD as "the God of truth" (Ps 31:5; cf. Isa 65:16). Even skeptics and agnostics find it useful to refer to God in order to help us understand the notion of truth and genuine knowledge. Bertrand Russell, for example says, "The free intellect will see as God might see, without a *here* and *now*."[112]

Below the barrier, you find human figures in the here and now, desperately trying to climb the ladder in order to get closer to the Truth. Already as children, we are trying to discover the truth about things. The search for truth, as we have already seen, is simply part of human nature. In fact, we also have a tendency to think that we have arrived at the truth.[113] This very tendency is itself a pointer to the ideal of Absolute Truth. We long for truth with a capital T. But we often find that we get it wrong. This again points to an ideal of truth which serves as a standard by which we measure our mistaken convictions. The concept of error presupposes the concept of truth.

Now I quite agree that we can never presume to have actually arrived at the Absolute Truth. Hence the barrier in the diagram. Here it needs to be stressed that we as human beings can never cross this barrier. Why? As finite creatures we are stuck with having a limited perspective. We only see through a glass darkly—as the apostle Paul puts it in his famous discourse on love (1 Cor 13:12). We are fallible and sinful creatures, so we remain on the ladder of truth below the barrier, trying hard to arrive at Truth. If we are honest, we will be very aware of the fact that we can never arrive at absolute certainty regarding our convictions about what we believe to be true. Hence the notion of "conditional or functional absolutes" found below the barrier. Our certainties are at best provisional. Our claims to truth are always tentative. We can at best only stumble towards the Truth.

One of my favorite quotes that I have often used in college classes when discussing this diagram is taken from American pragmatist William James, who describes the notion of Absolute Truth in this way: "The 'absolutely' true, meaning what no further experience will ever alter, is that ideal vanishing-point towards which we imagine that all our temporary truths will someday converge."[114] I believe James has got it exactly right. We cannot do away with the notion of truth with a capital *T*. That is what we all aspire to, but there are significant barriers to our ever saying with complete confidence that we have got the Truth. We are, therefore, stuck with "temporary truths," and humility demands that we admit the same, though we never give up on our continuing search for Truth. Without an ideal of Truth, without a goal in our search for knowledge and truth, we are left aimlessly floundering in a sea of relativism, which Amos has described so poignantly: "Men will stagger from sea to sea, and wander from north to east, searching for the word of the LORD, but they will not find it" (Amos 8:12). Sadly, it is "the lovely young women and strong young men" who suffer as they "faint because of thirst" (v. 13).

Current skepticism about truth is of course not really new. At Jesus' trial Pilate famously asked Jesus, "What is truth?" (John 18:38). The Bible in fact has a lot to say about truth. The Hebrew word group most often translated as "true" is better captured by the English word "fidelity."[115] In the Hebrew Bible, "true" (*aman*) is always an adjective, though it can be readily conceptualized as a noun: truth (*emet*), or in Greek "*aletheia*," as in Jesus being the way, the truth (*aletheia*), and the life (John 14:6). These Hebrew and Greek words for true can be applied to a wide range of things—reports, statements, actions, people, and even objects like a tent peg (Isa 22:23). When something is true, it does what it ought to do; it is trustworthy.[116] Hence Jesus' frequent prefacing of important statements, "Truly (*alethos*) I say to you," highlighting his statements as trustworthy or as providing apt guidance to his followers.

It should also be noted that the words "believe" or "faith" in the Scriptures come from the same Hebrew word group (*aman*), and are better translated as "trust."[117] Using the word "trust" forces us to look for the object or person to be trusted. Hence John's explanation as to why he wrote his Gospel: "That you may believe [trust] that Jesus is the Christ, the Son of God, and that by believing [trusting] you may have life in his name" (John 20:31). The Gospel of John concludes with a very personal note: "This is the disciple who testifies to these things and who wrote them down. We know that his testimony is true [trustworthy]" (John 21:24).

So what is truth? Truth is an account of reality that is trustworthy. Truth claims match up with reality in some way. Of course, we cannot ever definitively say that we have got the truth. We often err. But even the notion of error presupposes truth. So, we still need the concept of truth, and we also should always be searching for the truth.

THE LOVE OF KNOWLEDGE AND TRUTH

We are now in a position to consider what it means to love knowledge and truth. First, what does love mean here? Jason Baehr describes the love connected with intellectual virtues in terms of a "positive psychological orientation" to knowledge and truth.[118] That is certainly part of the meaning of love in this context. But surely love is more than a psychological orientation. To love knowledge and truth entails that we value these epistemic goods. But even this is not enough. Love here also means that we are committed to finding knowledge and truth. Love needs to be translated into action. Lovers of knowledge and truth will make an effort to arrive at knowledge and truth, and they will experience pain when they discover that they are ignorant about something important or when they are unable to find knowledge and truth.[119] They will persevere in the search for knowledge and truth. They will also be eager to share their knowledge and their understanding of the truth with others.

Here is a brief summary statement of the meaning of this intellectual virtue. **Definition: The love of knowledge and truth** is the disposition to take an interest in knowledge and truth; to experience pain when one becomes aware of one's ignorance or when one is unable to find knowledge and truth; to be excited about the prospect of learning; and to engage in actions that aim at the acquisition, maintenance, transmission, and application of knowledge and truth.[120]

Why is the love of knowledge and truth important? It might seem that this question is redundant. Surely, the value of knowledge and truth is self-evident. Knowledge and truth are intrinsic goods and don't need any further justification. That is why Pope John Paul II entitled his 1993 encyclical *Veritatis Splendor* (The Splendor of Truth).[121] Knowledge and truth have a brilliance in and of themselves. But there is more to be said here.

Knowledge and truth put us in tune with reality. When we search for knowledge and truth, we seek to know the real nature of the universe. And again there is surely intrinsic value in this. Esther Meek likes to remind us that reality is a gift given to us by God.[122] This calls for a response of thankfulness and love both for the gift and the giver of this gift. Knowing therefore quite properly starts with love, a love for knowledge and truth about reality. And the goal can be understood in terms of "relational health between knower and known."[123]

But there is even more. Coming to know the truth about reality, including ourselves, is useful. We need knowledge and truth in order to survive. I want my doctor to be knowledgable about the field of medicine when I come to her office with an ailment. Thankfully, I have an excellent doctor who is careful to search for truth and will even consult with her colleagues when she is unsure about something. And she is even willing to admit when she has made an error. Truth matters. There is pragmatic value in loving knowledge and truth.

Finally, the love of knowledge and truth is part of human nature, as we have already seen. God created us to love knowledge and truth. This is why the love of knowledge and truth is an intellectual virtue. This is an important part of what we were meant to be. This is what makes for human excellence.

THE REDEMPTION OF THE LOVE OF KNOWLEDGE AND TRUTH IN THE BIBLE

We have already examined the Genesis story of creation and what it has to say about human nature in relation to the love of knowledge and truth. God created Adam and Eve with a desire to know and discover truth. Sadly, this desire was partially corrupted by the fall. As a result human beings find themselves both desiring and not desiring knowledge and truth. We are at war within ourselves. Thankfully, this is not the end of the biblical narrative. There follows the wonderful story of redemption and restoration. And this includes a redemption of our minds, a healing of our lack of desire to seek knowledge and know the truth. In chapter 1 we considered the general nature of "a redemptive epistemology," to use a phrase introduced by Richard Smith.[124] Our focus here will be on the redemption of the love of knowledge and truth.

What is perhaps surprising is the repeated exhortations in the Bible to love knowledge and to seek truth. Why these constant reminders? Because we are torn between desiring and not desiring knowledge and truth. Our minds are partially corrupted by sin. Even as Christians, we still are fighting a battle against our "old self" and have a need to put on a "new self," which "is being renewed in knowledge in the image of the Creator" (Col 3:10). Therefore, we need to be exhorted again and again to have our minds healed so as to renew our love for knowledge and truth. What follows is a brief review of biblical encouragements to love knowledge and truth.

The proverbs of Solomon are full of exhortations to search for knowledge, understanding, and truth. Proverbs 2 gives advice to a son or daughter, using an array of metaphors to describe the urgency of searching for wisdom, knowledge, and understanding.

> My son, if you accept my words and store up my commands within you, turning your ear to wisdom, and applying your heart to understanding, and if you call out for insight and cry aloud for understanding, and if you look for it as for silver and search for it as for hidden treasure, then you will understand the fear of the Lord and find the knowledge of God. For the LORD gives wisdom and from his mouth come knowledge and understanding. (Prov 2:1–6)

"Blessed is the man who finds wisdom, and the man who gains understanding" (Prov 3:13). "Wisdom is supreme; therefore get wisdom"

(Prov 4:7). "The discerning heart seeks knowledge" (Prov 15:14). "An intelligent mind acquires knowledge, and the ear of the wise seeks knowledge" (Prov 18:15). "Apply your mind to instruction and your ear to words of knowledge" (Prov 23:12). Even a commercial metaphor is used to highlight the importance of acquiring knowledge and truth. "Buy the truth and do not sell it; get wisdom, discipline and understanding" (Prov 23:23).

The Psalms also frequently talk about delight in the law of the LORD (Pss 1:2; 112:1). Psalm 119 is one long poem describing how important it is to long for, to seek out, to memorize, to meditate on, and to walk in accordance with the truths and the wisdom found in God's laws, statutes, commandments, and precepts. Psalm 33 describes the word of the LORD as "right and true," and calls a blessing on those who honor God and his word.

The same themes are found in the New Testament. I have already drawn attention to Luke's description of the boy Jesus growing in wisdom (Luke 2:47, 52). In his final days, Jesus comes back to the theme of truth again and again. In a final lengthy discourse to his disciples, he informs them that he is going away soon, but he goes on to say that this will be for their good. Sandwiched in between you have this reassuring statement: "But I tell you the truth" (John 16:7). And then Jesus promises to send an Advocate, or the Holy Spirit, who is again described as being related to truth. "But when he, the Spirit of truth, comes, he will guide you into all the truth" (John 16:13; cf. 1 John 5:6).

We have already seen how the apostle Paul identifies various ways in which we can fail to be serious in our search for truth. But that is not what a redeemed epistemology looks like. Instead, we find Paul repeatedly hoping and praying that God's people will grow in wisdom, understanding, and "the knowledge of the truth."[125] At the same time, Paul and also John urge us to "test everything" and so distinguish between "the spirit of truth and the spirit of falsehood" (1 Thess 5:21; 1 John 4:1–6).

Here it is important to note that while most of the above references relate to knowledge and truth about God and his laws, they should not be interpreted as applying only to the religious domain. Indeed, as I argued in the previous chapter, the distinction between "religious" and "secular" knowledge is really foreign to a biblical worldview. All truth is God's truth. Scientific truth is ultimately grounded in God, who created the universe with wisdom. When God asks Adam to name the animals, he is being asked to come to an understanding of the "secular" domain. When God calls humankind to rule over all creation, this surely includes coming to understand God's creation and the norms he has built into creation.

Further, some of the verses quoted earlier from Proverbs clearly apply to all knowledge. Daniel and his three friends are chosen to be trained for royal duties in Babylon and are taught "the language and literature of the Babylonians" (Dan 1:4). Interestingly, God is described as giving to these four young men "knowledge and understanding of all kinds of literature and learning" (1:17). Jesus at one point specifically addresses so-called secular knowledge when he commends the people for knowing how to interpret the appearance of the earth and the sky, but then calls them hypocrites because they do not "know how to interpret this present time" (Luke 12:54-56). So the biblical calls to grow in knowledge and wisdom extend to all spheres of knowledge and wisdom.

The redemption of the love of knowledge and truth can be seen as a restoration of what knowing was like in the Garden of Eden before the fall of Adam and Eve. Indeed, the prophets frequently talk about a future paradise, "a new heavens and a new earth," a restoration of Eden, a re-creation which really involves a "curse reversal."[126] Isaiah, for example, envisages a time when the nations will be streaming to the mountain of the LORD so that they can be taught God's ways and hear "the word of the LORD" (Isa 2:2-4). A little later Isaiah once again talks about a time when "the earth will be full of the knowledge of God," and the result is a restored Eden where God once again dwells in the midst of his people and there is peace and harmony and shalom (Isa 11:9).[127] This is the culmination of a redeemed epistemology.

In the meantime, in this time between Christ's first and second coming, we as Christians must do our very best to love knowledge and truth. Here I like to draw on the imagery of the Psalmist which has inspired countless Christian scholars in all fields of knowledge. "For with you is the fountain of life; in your light we see light" (Ps 36:9). It is as we love knowledge and truth and conduct our search for knowledge and truth in the light of the LORD as found in God's revelation in Scripture and in nature that we come closer to God's ideal for humankind, closer to not only epistemological harmony but also personal well-being. This is what it means to achieve human excellence in knowing. And here we find intellectual shalom, healing, joy, and peace.[128]

THE LOVE OF KNOWLEDGE AND TRUTH IN ACTION

So far I have focused primarily on a subjective description of what it means to love knowledge and truth. I have already suggested that this is not enough. Love needs to be translated into action. So, what are some practical expressions of the love of knowledge and truth? For one, this intellectual virtue will express itself in inquisitiveness and curiosity.[129] I will argue later that curiosity can also become distorted into a kind of idle curiosity which is not really serious about learning and searching for truth. But admitting this should not detract from allowing for a healthy kind of curiosity. Children certainly display healthy curiosity, always stopping to look carefully at a butterfly crossing their path. Children also like to ask questions, their favorite being the question "why"? Adults might have something to learn from children in continuing to learn and pursue truth.

Healthy curiosity will be careful in acquiring knowledge and searching for truth.[130] It will pay careful attention to detail when observing things. It will listen carefully to what others say. It will lead doctors to be conscientious in examining patients. It will lead engineers to check their calculations before submitting a proposal for a project. It will lead students to do their best in school. It will lead parents to read books on how best to raise their children. It will value knowledge and truth for their own sake.

Perseverance is sometimes listed as a separate intellectual virtue.[131] But I prefer to see it as another expression of the love of knowledge and truth. Peter, for example, links growth in knowledge to perseverance (2 Pet 1:6). The need for perseverance arises because sometimes we face obstacles in our search for knowledge and truth. We might find ourselves naturally inclined to be complacent about the love of knowledge and truth. There may even be people who discourage us in the pursuit of learning. I had a grandfather who warned Christian youth about the dangers of going to university. My family was opposed to my switching from a physics to a philosophy major at university. This called for some perseverance on my part.

Lovers of knowledge and truth will be careful to avoid error. They will be suspicious of hasty generalizations. They will do some fact-checking when claims sound a bit dubious. They will avoid conspiracy theories based on speculation. They will consult with doctors about the safety and efficacy of vaccines for COVID. They will be open to new ideas and arguments even when they conflict with their own. Like the Bereans that Paul encountered, Christians who love the truth will evaluate the sermons preached in their churches. They will do some serious study of Scripture, although here we need to be realistic and not expect the layperson to be as studious as the theologian. More on this later.

Lovers of knowledge and truth will be careful to look for evidence for the beliefs that they hold. They will also display an openness to criticisms of beliefs held. Such openness is related to the virtue of open-mindedness, which I want to treat as a separate virtue in chapter 4. Here I simply want to note that being open to criticisms of one's belief is one way of testing whether one is concerned about basing beliefs on evidence. Lovers of knowledge and truth will also be sensitive to adjusting the confidence they display in their convictions to the level of evidence they have for their beliefs. If evidence for a belief is minimal, they will be careful to say that they are not entirely certain about this belief. The greater the evidence, the greater the confidence and certainty surrounding the expression of their beliefs.[132]

There is one important qualification that needs to be made regarding this evidential dimension of loving knowledge and the truth. There are limits to the demand for evidence for a belief, as various Reformed epistemologists have noted. We can't go on providing evidence forever. At some point we need to start with assumptions and even faith. We need to trust our senses. We need to trust our memory. We need to trust our epistemic faculties. We need to trust the testimony of others. There may even be beliefs for which it is inappropriate to demand evidence. One might say that "evidence" is staring us in the face, so we do not need to look any further for evidence. Alvin Plantinga has suggested that our belief in God can be properly basic and thus doesn't require a further search for evidence.[133] In our pursuit of knowledge and truth, it is always "faith seeking understanding," as various writers have reminded us.[134] But despite this qualification, I still believe that the lover of truth will, where appropriate, look for evidence to back up the beliefs that he or she holds.

DISCRIMINATION IN LOVING KNOWLEDGE AND TRUTH

The limit to searching for evidence relates to a more general limitation that needs to be acknowledged in our obligation to search for knowledge and truth. We are finite beings and simply cannot know everything. We only know "in part," as Paul reminds us in a classic description of love found in his first letter to the Corinthians (1 Cor 13:12). Only God knows fully. There may even be knowledge that only God is meant to have. After all, Adam and Eve were told not to eat from the tree of knowledge of good and evil. This raises an important set of practical questions. If I can't know everything, and if my search for truth is inherently limited, and if there is knowledge we as humans are not meant to have, how do I discriminate in my search for knowledge and truth?[135]

Paul draws our attention to a principle of discrimination that relates in some way to the choice that Adam and Eve faced. "Finally, brothers [and sisters], whatever is true, whatever is noble, whatever is right, whatever is pure, whatever is lovely, whatever is admirable—if anything is excellent or praiseworthy—think about such things" (Phil 4:8). We need to be especially committed to thinking about that which is true and good and beautiful. There is no harm in not knowing everything about what is false and impure and ugly. Of course, some Christians might be called to lead the way in helping us to apply this principle of discrimination and therefore will need to know more about what is false and impure and ugly. But for most of us, the central focus and our love should be for the true and the good and the beautiful.[136] This surely has some implications for the books we read, the movies we see, and the YouTube videos we watch.

We also need to distinguish between beliefs that are important and those that are trivial. It is obviously not that important to learn how many names start with the letter "S" in the local telephone directory. But it is important to learn more about my Christian faith, which gives direction and purpose to my life. We need to take greater care in searching for knowledge and truth with regard to what one writer has called "load-bearing beliefs."[137]

Another principle of discrimination relates to our unique identities as persons. Each of us belongs to a family, we belong to a neighborhood, and we are citizens of a particular country. As Christians, we belong to a church. And then there are our individual interests and abilities. Each of these identities will cause us to be discriminating in our search for knowledge and truth.

Let me give a personal example. I am a philosopher. I love to explore ideas in the field of philosophy. I continue to search for further knowledge and truth in the area of philosophy. I am much less interested in searching for truth in other domains like biology, physics, history, computer programming, and plumbing. I believe it would be a mistake to characterize my lack of interest in these other domains of practical and theoretical knowledge as evidence that I am deficient in possessing the intellectual virtue of the love of knowledge and truth. It would also be wrong for me to describe someone who is not interested in philosophy as failing to love knowledge and truth. I believe it is very important for us as academics not to demand of lay-people that they be as interested in pursuing truth as we are. This is intellectual snobbishness. My electrician friend knows a lot more about electrical circuits than I do, and I can't expect him to be as interested in problems in philosophical theology as I am. The reverse is also true. We must allow for differences in personality, interests, abilities, and levels of education.

I am also a Christian and belong to a church. I, therefore, have a particular interest in growing in knowledge and understanding of truth within the Christian faith. As a philosopher with a specialty in the philosophy of religion, I am of course also interested in learning about other religions. But I am particularly interested in learning about my own Christian faith. And I should not be faulted for this preference. Nor should we blame other Christians, or adherents of other religions, for having a preferential interest in gaining knowledge of the particular religion they are committed to. Of course, there are some dangers here, and I will have more to say about these in chapter 4.

As an academic and a philosopher, the demands of loving the truth are more rigorous than for a worker at a factory, for example. And yet, there is surely a minimal level at which all of us should be searching for knowledge and truth. All of us live in the same world and need to learn to cope with the requirements of living in this world, so we need to search for knowledge and truth that will help us to live in this world. All of us ask "big picture" questions, so all of us should spend some time trying to find answers to the meaning of life and our place in the world. All of us are part of a family, so we need to do our best to learn how to further the well-being of our family. All of us are also part of a society and a political structure, and therefore we have an obligation to learn how to live together and how best to further the political life of our country. Blind allegiance to a political party or leader is not characteristic of someone who loves the truth.

It is not possible to give a precise definition of these qualifications and limitations to the love of knowledge and truth. They might vary with individuals and circumstances. Wisdom is called for in determining what the love of truth means for each of us. And charity is called for when I see a fellow Christian who does not measure up to my own dedication to the love of truth. And yet, it behooves all of us to assess whether we are doing justice to the call to love knowledge, understanding, wisdom, and truth.

HELPING OTHERS SEARCH FOR TRUTH

There is another practical dimension of the intellectual virtue of the love of knowledge and truth that deserves brief treatment. So far I have focused on the obligation each of us has to search for knowledge and truth for ourselves. But the question arises as to whether we also have an obligation to help others in their search for knowledge and truth. The summary description of the love of knowledge and truth as an intellectual virtue earlier in this chapter made reference not only to the acquisition and maintenance of knowledge and truth but also to the "transmission" of knowledge and truth. We are, after all, social beings, so a love of knowledge and truth would seem to extend to helping others to find knowledge and truth as well.

Of course, here an objection immediately comes to mind. Shouldn't we just mind our own business? If everyone searches for knowledge and truth for themselves, then there is no need to help others to acquire this intellectual virtue. The problem with this quick dismissal of our obligation to others is that it rests on an individualism that cannot be sustained. We today like to see ourselves as autonomous, as individuals who can think for ourselves and find truth for ourselves. Indeed, some philosophers treat "epistemic autonomy" or "epistemic self-reliance" as another intellectual virtue.[138] The problem here is that none of us are quite as autonomous as we think.

We are by nature interdependent. Our search for knowledge and truth depends on others, starting from our birth. Most of our beliefs are acquired from our parents, our teachers, and members of our immediate community. Of course, they don't only pass on true beliefs, so there comes a point where we need to test the beliefs that we inherit. But even this testing is best done in cooperation with others. So we need the help of others in our search for knowledge and truth. We rely on the testimony of others for much of our knowledge. We necessarily think within communities. We also need the encouragement of others to keep the flame of loving the truth alive in ourselves.

Let me give a concrete example of our obligation to help others in their search for truth. Suppose I have a lump in my chest, and suppose you have had a similar earlier experience which resulted in your discovery that you had a form of cancer. Most of us would agree that you owe it to me as a friend to try to persuade me to see a doctor to help me find the truth about the lump in my chest. This simple example illustrates that the love of knowledge and truth carries over to helping others to find knowledge and truth. I am sure the reader will be able to give many other examples to illustrate this point.

There is another very important question that needs to be raised here, and that has to do with *how* we fulfil this obligation to help others love knowledge and truth. I suggest that it is concerns about the "how" question that lead many to reject the rather self-evident claim that we ought to encourage and help others to search for truth. The "how" question of course raises some important ethical issues. My desire to help you in your search for truth is circumscribed by your willingness to want and accept my help. Your dignity as a person comes into play. I cannot ride rough-shod over you in my desire to help you find truth. I need to respect your freedom as an individual. I also need to offer this help in a spirit of humility. There are other ethical considerations that come into play here which I have dealt with elsewhere.[139] Here I am mainly concerned to highlight two points. We have an ethical obligation to help others to love the truth, and this obligation must be carried out in an ethical manner.

CONTEMPORARY FAILURES IN LOVING KNOWLEDGE AND TRUTH

There are a number of ways in which we can fail to love knowledge and truth. Indeed, at some point these failures might even be described as vices. There is, first of all, the failure of indifference or complacency with regard to the search for knowledge and truth. Nathan King tells the humorous story of a professor who asked her student, "What's the difference between ignorance and indifference?" The student replied, "I don't know and I don't care"—which is exactly right.[140] King goes on to compare the lack of a desire for knowledge and truth with the lack of a healthy desire for food. There is something unhealthy about a disposition that is indifferent or complacent about searching for knowledge and truth. Sadly, such indifference is all too common today.

One expression of insufficient concern about truth is the widespread failure of people to examine their own cherished beliefs when given an opportunity to do so, or when they are careless in doing such a self-examination.[141] Adam Grant has documented such failures in his recent book with the appropriate title *Think Again: The Power of Knowing What You Don't Know*. He recommends that we schedule a life check-up once or twice per year just as we schedule health check-ups with our doctors. "It's a way to assess how much you're learning, how your beliefs and goals are evolving, and whether your next steps warrant some rethinking."[142]

We can also fail to grow in our understanding of the Christian faith. There are any number of surveys showing an alarming rate of biblical ignorance and even illiteracy among Christians.[143] It would seem that all too many Christians today are intellectually lazy, not reading or studying the Bible, not able or willing to challenge established opinion in the church, or simply succumbing to the latest fads in Christian thinking. Then there is the all-too-common phenomenon of suspension of belief, which becomes a convenient excuse not to seek the truth.[144] Clearly there are some Christian doctrines where suspension of belief might be appropriate. But suspension of judgment isn't always a good thing. There are surely some central Christian claims that call for commitment, not a lazy appeal to a supposed ideal of agnosticism.

Then there is the widespread failure to be concerned about evidence or the lack thereof for one's beliefs. While there are limits to demanding evidence for beliefs, as I have already argued, there is still a place for demanding that our beliefs are based on evidence. It is just wrong to say, "Well it's true for me and that is the end of the matter." It is also wrong to jump to hasty conclusions. Dismissing counter-evidence to our own beliefs is another sign of not loving the truth. Another indicator is the tendency of some people to pass hasty judgment on a speech that goes counter to their own beliefs. Even before the speaker is finished speaking, they have pronounced their verdict, "Wrong," and go about formulating a refutation when they should instead be engaged in careful listening. They might even have something to learn from the speaker they disagree with.

There is of course the opposite failure of being too conscientious, careful, and thorough in our pursuit of knowledge and truth.[145] Nathan King describes this as "intellectual scrupulousness"—an obsession with avoiding mistakes.[146] We need to be realistic. It would seem that there is here an Aristotelian mean between extremes. We can be too careful, but we can also not be careful enough. American pragmatist William

James, in his defense of taking risks in believing, said excessive intellectual carefulness "is like a general informing his soldiers that it is better to keep out of battle forever than to risk a single wound."[147] We can't be pursuing knowledge and truth all the time. We need to live. And this will require that we take risks, not being entirely certain about the truths we are committed to, though all the while willing to explore our tentative conclusions further if circumstances and time permit.

There is also the vice of idle curiosity. Here it is important to note the qualifier "idle." As already stated, there is a healthy kind of curiosity. Indeed, healthy curiosity can be seen as an expression of the love of knowledge and truth. But there is also an unhealthy kind of curiosity. Augustine warns about this distortion of the love of knowledge and truth, a "futile" kind of curiosity (Latin: *curiositas*) which "masquerades under the name of science and learning."[148] He goes on to warn that this unhealthy thirst for knowledge about everything leads people to go out of their way to view a mangled corpse by the roadside, to become obsessed with gladiator games, to absorb gossip, and to demand signs and wonders in religion.

A biblical example of unhealthy curiosity is Herod "the tetrarch," who seems to have inherited his father's suspicions about Jesus. In the Gospels, Herod the tetrarch is known for the imprisonment and execution of John the Baptist and his brief encounter with Jesus after he was sent to him by Pilate for judgment. "When Herod saw Jesus, he was greatly pleased, because for a long time he had been wanting to see him. From what he had heard about him, he hoped to see him perform some miracle" (Luke 23:8). Here we have an idle curiosity, not at all interested in knowing the truth about Jesus. And when Herod plied Jesus with "many questions," Jesus appropriately "gave him no answer" (v. 9).

How does this vice of idle curiosity express itself today? Think of crowds gathering to witness an accident or other tragedy. And what about the endless amount of time we can spend surfing the internet for disconnected pieces of information or tracing threads of conversations about unimportant details, often numbering in the hundreds.[149] How much of our watching of movies and binging on Netflix is due to idle curiosity? Or our spending hours reading the newspapers or watching the latest evening news on television.[150] Then there is our fascination with exploring foreign ideas. Paul describes the Athenians as spending their time "doing nothing but talking about and listening to the latest ideas" (Acts 17:21). Sadly, I find this phenomenon occurring even in churches today, what with the exploration of other religions and even the conducting of smudging ceremonies in adult Sunday School classes. Surely, the focus in a Christian church should be on growing in knowledge and understanding of Christian theology and truth. The church is not a university where pluralism is the norm (or at least should be).

This chapter on the more general intellectual virtue of the love of knowledge, wisdom, understanding, and truth can be summed up in the words of the Teacher as found in the final chapter of the book of Ecclesiastes: "Not only was the Teacher wise, but also he imparted knowledge to the people. He pondered and searched out and set in order many proverbs. The Teacher searched to find just the right words, and what he wrote was upright and true" (Eccl 12:9–10). The Teacher also reminds us that the words of the wise that result from searching the truth have their ultimate source in "one Shepherd," who is none other than the Creator whom we are encouraged to remember, even in our youth (12:11, 1). And then comes a note of realism: "Of making many books there is no end, and much study wearies the body" (12:12). It is not easy to be a lover of knowledge and truth, but we need to keep at it, while at the same time recognizing that as finite beings we can't read all the books that have been written. The author of this book thanks the reader for thinking that his book merits reading!

3

Intellectual Humility

Do you see a man wise in his own eyes? There is more hope for a fool than for him.

(PROVERBS 26:12)

For whoever exalts himself will be humbled, and whoever humbles himself will be exalted.

(MATTHEW 23:11)

Before you complete the questionnaire that follows, give yourself a rating (0–10) on humility generally and on intellectual humility more specifically.

QUESTIONNAIRE: A SELF-EVALUATION

For each of the following statements, answer **yes**, **no**, or **unsure/maybe**.

1. I find it easy to admit that I might be wrong about my beliefs.

2. I feel strongly that my beliefs need to match a reality that lies outside of me and whatever I believe.

3. I recognize that I am very dependent on others in finding knowledge and truth.

4. I am not very worried about sometimes appearing to be rather stupid.

5. I am very open to having others criticize my beliefs.

6. I regularly listen carefully to others, trying to understand their position, trying to learn from them, even if they express a position very different from what I hold.

7. Although I recognize the importance of helping others to discover knowledge and find truth, I don't feel obsessed about convincing others about my own convictions.

8. I always express some caution when I am expressing viewpoints in fields that I know little about.

9. I am quite willing to read old books on a subject and am careful not to dismiss traditional ideas simply because they are old.

10. I always try very hard to avoid showing off my knowledge and wisdom.

Now give a numerical value to each of your answers—1 **for yes;** ½ **for unsure/maybe; 0 for no.** Then total your numerical values. The total out of 10 gives the percentage grade for your having the virtue of "intellectual humility."

See the end of the questionnaire in chapter 2 for some additional comments about the validity of this exercise.

A recent biography of Eugene Peterson recounts an incident in his education which illustrates so well the nature of intellectual humility. Peterson was enjoying the intellectual stimulation of graduate studies at Johns Hopkins University and, in particular, the genius of one of the world's most prominent biblical archeologists and Semitic scholars, Dr. William Albright. In one lecture, Albright was sharing a recent discovery he had made regarding the story of Abraham commanded by God to sacrifice Isaac.

> Albright rushed into class, breathless to share his ground-breaking discovery. Feral with new knowledge, he attacked the room-wide blackboard, scratching strange linguistics from one wall to the other. He poured Ugaritic, Arabic, Assyrian, Aramaic, and Hebrew onto the black space, basking in his monumental triumph. *He had found it.*
>
> Eugene and the rest of the class reeled, trying to keep up with this explosion of genius. But then, the unthinkable—Prescott Williams, one of Eugene's friends, interrupted. "But, Dr. Albright . . ."
>
> The class sat spellbound. *Impossible*—one of their own disagreeing with the master. But Albright listened, stone still and pondering as Prescott politely walked through his objections to the argument. Then the room fell silent. The professor picked up his eraser and slowly wiped vast swaths across the blackboard. "Forget everything I said," he stated simply. "Prescott is right."[151]

WHEN PLANNING THIS BOOK, I wrestled with the question as to which intellectual virtue I should start with. I wanted to begin with the most important virtue. But which intellectual virtue is the most important? In the end I decided to start with the love of knowledge and truth. But a good case can be made for starting with intellectual humility as the most important.[152] The Bible has a lot to say about humility generally and also, more specifically, about intellectual humility as will be shown later. The fall of Adam and Eve can be described in terms of intellectual arrogance. Again and again in Scripture, woes are pronounced on those who are wise in their own eyes and blessings are pronounced on those who are humble in spirit and admit that they are not all-knowing.[153] So we had better listen carefully to what the Bible has to teach us about the virtue of intellectual humility.

How humble are you and I? Of course, this question puts us into a catch-22 situation. If you give yourself a high score on humility, then you are probably not very humble. But it is also possible to give yourself too low a score on humility, which can be interpreted as another sign of pride. It is simply difficult to assess one's own humility. So perhaps we should allow others to evaluate us with regard to this virtue. Better still, perhaps we should forget all about trying to rate ourselves on the humility-scale. Trying to answer the question entails self-absorption and is already a sign of undue pride. And yet, this is an important question. The Bible repeatedly talks about the need for humility, and pride is often condemned. So we need to address this question. I trust the questionnaire has helped you to approach this question a bit more objectively. And if there was a significant difference between your initial rating and the tally after you completed the questionnaire, then perhaps at the very least you will be motivated to read on.

HUMILITY AND PRIDE IN THE BIBLE

I begin with a brief review of what the Bible has to say about humility and pride, without the qualifier "intellectual." In fact, the concepts of pride and humility occur rather often in the Scriptures. There are literally hundreds of references to words that relate to the concepts of humility and pride: words like humble, contrite, meek, lowly, and "a servant-like attitude" for the concept of humility, and arrogance, proud, conceit, haughty, and boasting for the concept of pride. Of course, this raises the question as to why humility is considered a virtue. I will consider this question later in this chapter. My purpose here is simply to highlight the fact that the virtue of humility is an important biblical concept.

The story of Israel in the Old Testament gives us a fascinating testimonial of humility in the person of Moses. The immediate context of this story is Miriam and Aaron, the sister and brother of Moses, challenging Moses's authority. Unfortunately, the LORD was listening, and later we are told that "the anger of the LORD burned against them." Then follows this statement: "Now Moses was a very humble man, more humble than anyone else on the face of the earth" (Num 12:3). This of course raises the question as to why Moses is described as being very humble. He was after all a powerful leader who had been raised and educated in Pharaoh's court with all its privileges. And yet, he is described as being a humble man. Why? Because he identified with the suffering of his people. Because he gave up all the privileges associated with being a member of Egyptian royalty in order to help his people. Because when an angel of the LORD appeared to him in a burning bush, he "hid his face, because he was afraid to look at God" (Exod 3:6). Because when God called him, he was aware of his weaknesses. But ultimately, he responded in obedience to God. That is what a humble man looks like.

Humility is repeatedly described as a virtue in the Old Testament. "For this is what the high and exalted One says—he who lives forever, whose name is holy: 'I live in a high and holy place, but also with the one who is contrite and lowly in spirit, to revive the spirit of the lowly and to revive the heart of the contrite'" (Isa 57:15). And then there is that beautiful summary of what is good and what the LORD requires of us: "To act justly and to love mercy and to walk humbly with your God" (Mic 6:8).

Two of the beatitudes in Jesus' Sermon on the Mount touch on humility. "Blessed are the poor in spirit for theirs in the kingdom of heaven. . . . Blessed are the meek for they will inherit the earth" (Matt 5:3, 5). Jesus drew attention to children to illustrate what humility looks like. "I tell you the truth, unless you change and become like little children, you will never enter the kingdom of heaven. Therefore, whoever humbles himself like this child is the greatest in the kingdom of heaven" (Matt 18:3-4). Then there is Jesus' death on the cross, one of the most shameful ways to die, which eventually led to a revolution in the way in which disciples thought of greatness—see, for example, Paul's hymn to humility in Phil 2:5-11. Peter, who had learned some painful lessons about humility, expands on this theme. "Clothe yourselves with humility towards one another, because 'God opposes the proud but gives grace to the humble.' Humble yourselves, therefore under God's mighty hand, that he may lift you up in due time" (1 Pet 5:5-6).

By contrast, pride is often condemned in Scripture. Indeed, there are even more condemnations of pride than there are commendations of humility in the Bible. Many of these references are found in the Psalms and Wisdom literature. The very first psalm calls blessings on the man or woman who does not "stand in the way of sinners or sit in the seat of mockers," i.e., the seat of the scornful and proud (Ps 1:1). "Pride goes before destruction and a haughty spirit before a fall" (Prov 16:18). Isaiah touches on the issue of pride repeatedly. Here are just a few verses of blistering judgment on Judah and Jerusalem early in the book: "The LORD Almighty has a day in store for all the proud and lofty. . . . The arrogance of man will be brought low and the pride of men humbled" (Isa 2:12, 17). In a prophecy against Babylon, the LORD says this: "I will put an end to the arrogance of the haughty and will humble the pride of the ruthless" (Isa 13:11).

Similar condemnations of arrogance are found in the New Testament. For example, Jesus gives us a long list of evils that come "from within, out of men's hearts," one of which is "arrogance," an evil that makes persons "unclean" (Mark 7:20–23). Paul is worried that when he comes to visit the church in Corinth he will find "arrogance" alongside quarreling, jealousy, outbursts of anger, factions, slander, and gossip (2 Cor 12:20). Perhaps these evils are in fact interrelated. James draws on Proverbs when he says, "God opposes the proud, but gives grace to the humble" (Jas 4:6; Prov 3:34; cf. 1 Pet 5:5). John lists "boasting" as coming from the world and its desires (1 John 2:16).

The above review has dealt with humility and pride generally. These Bible verses do not refer specifically to intellectual humility and pride. But we must be careful not to think that these general references to pride and humility preclude application to the mind or the intellect. After all, pride and humility have to do with the whole person, and so all these passages can be interpreted as making an implicit reference to intellectual pride and humility.

This all-encompassing meaning of pride and humility is further reinforced when we look at the biblical concept of the heart or spirit. The Scriptures frequently refer to the heart as the center of humility and pride. For example, Psalm 51:17—"The sacrifices of God are a broken spirit; a broken and contrite heart, O God, you will not despise." The wicked are described as having "callous hearts" and mouths that "speak with arrogance" (Ps 17:10). I have already mentioned Jesus' list of evils that come "from within, out of men's hearts," one of which is arrogance (Mark 7:20–23). Jesus encourages the weary and burdened to learn from him, "For I am gentle and humble in heart" (Matt 11:28). Here we need to keep in mind that when the Bible refers to the heart it is talking about the center of our being. So, the heart includes the mind. Hence "proud of heart" includes the notion of intellectual pride.[154]

INTELLECTUAL HUMILITY AND PRIDE IN THE BIBLE

I now want to look specifically at the notions of intellectual humility and pride. Here we face an immediate problem. The phrases "intellectual humility" or "intellectual pride" are nowhere to be found in the Bible. This should of course give us pause. There is always a danger in foisting modern concepts on the Bible. At the same time, we must be open to the possibility that the Scriptures might contain equivalent expressions. I now want to show that there are indeed many Bible passages that make reference to the meaning captured in the phrases "intellectual humility" and "intellectual pride." Here I am assuming that we all have a rough idea of the meaning of these concepts. A more careful definition will be provided later.

I start again with the Genesis account of creation and the fall of Adam and Eve. An intelligent Creator God speaks creation into being and this creation is declared good. God also creates man and woman in his image, though it is important to note that they are still created beings and so are dependent on God like the rest of creation. We are finite beings in that God created us with limitations. We are limited by space and time. We have limited energy and power. Our knowledge and perspectives also always have limits. Our limits, our creaturehood, and our ongoing dependence on God call for humility in how we think about ourselves, i.e., intellectual humility.

Adam and Eve are commanded to fill the earth and subdue it and care for it (Gen 1:26; 2:15). This calls for humble submission. And then Adam and Eve are told that they can eat of every tree in the garden, "but you must not eat from the tree of the knowledge of good and evil" (Gen 2:17). This is the first time that the word "knowledge" is used in the creation account. Adam is given another assignment. He is asked to name all the living creatures that God had made. Clearly this task requires some creative thinking. So in Genesis 1 and 2 you have a healthy balance between Adam listening to God and doing some thinking under the direction of God. This is what intellectual humility looks like. Indeed, this is God's ideal for the human mind.

Sadly, the situation changes in Genesis 3, when Eve and then Adam listen to a new authority, a serpent (Satan), who dares to challenge what God has said about the tree of the knowledge of good and evil and the predicted effects of eating its fruit: "When you eat of it your eyes will be opened, and you will be like God, knowing good and evil" (Gen 3:5). Then follows a reversal of the healthy balance in listening and thinking that existed up until this time. Eve sees that the fruit on this forbidden tree is "good for food and pleasing to the eye, and also desirable for gaining wisdom" (Gen 3:6).

While not all commentators agree on how to interpret the fall, I want to suggest that a central component of the fall is intellectual pride. Eve and then Adam refuse to listen to God. They choose to listen to Satan instead and trust in their own senses in assessing the fruit of this tree to be desirable.[155] Indeed, Satan was right. Eating of this tree would make them like God in a new way. They were already created in the image of God, but they wanted to be even more like God. They were usurping their status as created and dependent beings who needed to listen to God. This is intellectual pride. And it is sin.

We have already seen that Psalms and Proverbs often address the issue of humility and pride generally. But it is quite evident that sometimes specific reference is made to the notions of intellectual humility and intellectual pride. In Psalm 25 we read that God "guides the humble in what is right and teaches them his way" (v. 9). This is intellectual humility, where the humble allow themselves to be taught by God. In Psalm 75 the sovereign God addresses the arrogant: "To the arrogant I say, 'Boast no more,' and to the wicked, 'Do not lift your horns . . . do not speak with outstretched neck'" (vv. 4, 5). The language used here is metaphorical, referring to powerful animals that are pushy, thrusting, self-willed; in a word, arrogant. The outstretched neck is similarly that of a headstrong animal, refusing to be bridled or tamed. So, the Psalmist is referring to people who refuse to listen to the voice of God, who refuse to submit to God, and whose speech is arrogantly defiant of God. By contrast, Psalm 131 speaks of intellectual humility. "My heart is not proud, O LORD, my eyes are not haughty; I do not concern myself with great matters or things too wonderful for me" (v. 1). This psalm describes an intellect that acknowledges its limitations, and is therefore humble. There are also repeated condemnations of a haughty spirit and intellectual pride in Proverbs. "Do you see a man wise in his own eyes? There is more hope for a fool than for him" (Prov 26:12).[156]

Among the prophets, Isaiah repeatedly addresses the issue of humility and pride. Already in chapter 5 Isaiah talks specifically about intellectual humility and pride: "Woe to those who are wise in their own eyes and clever in their own sight" (Isa 5:21). The fall of Babylon is described in Isaiah 47, but note how this is related to intellectual pride: "Your wisdom and knowledge mislead you when you say to yourself, 'I am, and there is none besides me'" (v. 10). Isaiah ends with an expression of hope, and it is surely of some significance that this hope of a new heavens and a new earth includes a transformed people who display intellectual humility: "But this is the one I esteem, he who is humble and contrite in spirit, and trembles at my word" (Isa 66:2).

The prophets Ezekiel and Daniel give us a contrasting picture of intellectual pride and intellectual humility. Listen to what Ezekiel says to the king of Tyre: "In the pride of your heart you say, 'I am god; I sit on the throne of a god in the heart of the seas.' But you are a man and not a god, though you think you are as wise as a god" (Ezek 28:1–2). By contrast, Daniel is told in a vision: "Do not be afraid, Daniel. Since the first day that you set your mind to gain understanding and to humble yourself before your God, your words were heard, and I have come in response to them" (Dan 10:12).

These same themes also appear in the New Testament. In the Magnificat of Mary, the mother of Jesus, she draws on Hannah's psalm of praise when she declares that God "has scattered those who are proud in their inmost thoughts . . . but [he] has lifted up the humble" (Luke 1:51–52; 1 Sam 2:1–10). Note that it is the thinking of the proud that is being judged here. I have already drawn attention to Jesus' frequent reference to children as exemplars of humility. Sometimes Jesus specifically draws our attention to the intellectual humility of children. "I praise you Father, Lord of heaven and earth, because you have hidden these things from the wise and learned and revealed them to little children" (Luke 10:21).[157] The child is a model of intellectual humility.

Probably the most extended treatment of intellectual pride in the Bible occurs in Paul's first letter to the church at Corinth. After dealing with the problem of divisions in the Corinthian church, Paul moves on to develop a theme that keeps recurring in his letters. He highlights the foolishness of the message of the cross and at the same time challenges the wisdom of this world (1 Cor 1:18—2:16). The word "wisdom" or *sophia* occurs twenty times in these two chapters. It is Paul's overriding concern. But what exactly does he mean when he says that from the perspective of Greek wisdom or the wisdom of the world, the message of the cross is foolishness?

Paul Gooch suggests that while we cannot be entirely sure, there are some clues in the text which suggest that the apostle Paul is addressing four concerns, all of which relate to intellectual pride and intellectual humility.[158] First, Paul is concerned about a certain approach to rhetoric that the Greek sophists were famous for. Rhetoric isn't bad in itself, but it is all too easy for rhetoric to degenerate into showmanship, into trying to impress people with your eloquence. Hence Paul's words, "When I came to you, brothers, I did not come with eloquence or superior wisdom as I proclaimed to you the testimony about God" (1 Cor 2:1). Secondly, Paul is concerned about the endless arguing and debating that the Greeks were famous for. Hence the question, "Where is the philosopher [debater] of this age?"[159] Thirdly, Paul is concerned about pretensions in our abilities to know God when there are obvious limits to human knowledge. This concern comes out especially in the second chapter. "No one knows the thoughts of God" (1 Cor 2:12). "For who has known the mind of the Lord?" (v. 16). But the primary concern of Paul is the conceit of human wisdom. Again and again in these chapters, Paul comes back to the theme of boasting. "God chose the foolish things of the world to shame the wise . . . so that no one may boast before him. . . . Therefore, as it is written: 'Let him who boasts boast in the Lord.'"[160] And that is why he keeps talking about the foolishness and weakness of God, even to the point of exaggeration. It is a way of shaming the proud pretensions of human wisdom.

DEFINITIONS OF INTELLECTUAL HUMILITY AND INTELLECTUAL PRIDE

There are a number of confusions surrounding the nature of intellectual humility.[161] My own background was such that I was led to believe to be humble meant I had to think of everyone else as smarter than I was and as knowing more than I did. Perhaps this is not that unusual. C. S. Lewis observed that for many human beings, humility means "pretty women thinking they are ugly and clever men trying to think they are fools."[162]

Some Christians might think this is in keeping with what Paul says when he urges the following: "In humility consider others better than yourselves" (Phil 2:3). But this exhortation needs to be read in context. Paul is talking about selfish ambition and a preoccupation with self-interest. Instead, our attitude should be that of Christ Jesus, who humbled himself and became a servant of others. So, Paul is not saying that we need to think of others as smarter than we are. Indeed, there is surely something dishonest about this kind of reasoning. And when applied to our intellectual capacities, it can cripple our ability to learn and grow.[163] As G. K. Chesterton warned, adopting this understanding of humility can put us on the road "to producing a race of men too mentally modest to believe in the multiplication table."[164]

Unlike the false humility described by Lewis and Chesterton, genuine humility involves having a proper assessment of oneself. Here

Aristotle's description of virtues as a golden mean between extremes is helpful. Authentic humility is a mean between having too low an opinion and too high an opinion of oneself.

So, how should we define intellectual humility? This is harder than it might seem at first. Indeed, one philosopher has identified eight different conceptions of intellectual humility.[165] Another writer strangely defines intellectual humility as having "a disposition to underestimate one's intellectual strengths, accomplishments, social status, and entitlements."[166] This is surely problematic and illustrates what I have already identified as a confusion of intellectual humility with having too low an opinion of oneself.

There is also a tendency to define intellectual humility in negative terms. For example, Roberts and Wood begin their chapter on intellectual humility with an extended list of contrasting vices and their descriptions.[167] Indeed, they argue that because of the "negative character" of intellectual humility, it "is especially important" to describe and "to define" this virtue in connection with its vice counterparts.[168] Now I agree that a study of intellectual virtues should include a study of their corresponding vices. But I believe it is important to try to define intellectual humility in positive terms.

So here is my attempt. **Definition: Intellectual humility** involves an honest assessment of one's intellectual abilities, not too high and not too low, acknowledging that these abilities are a gift from God; a deep desire always to submit to the truth, accompanied by an ongoing willingness to admit that one doesn't know it all and that one might be wrong; an abiding readiness to listen and learn from others and to join with others in gaining knowledge and finding truth; and when we as individuals, parents, or teachers influence others, an awareness of the awesome responsibility of doing so, combined with a commitment always to allow those being taught to make up their own minds.

Intellectual pride or arrogance, by contrast, involves having too high an assessment of one's intellectual abilities; a tendency to overemphasize autonomy and hence an unwillingness to submit to the truth, accompanied by an ongoing unwillingness to admit that one doesn't know it all and that one might be wrong; an abiding failure to listen and learn from others and to join with others in gaining knowledge and finding truth; and when we as individuals, parents, or teachers influence others, an attitude of presumption with regard to doing so, combined with an inordinate desire to dominate and shape the minds of others.

These are rather clumsy definitions, but I believe this clumsiness is unavoidable. Intellectual humility is a complex notion. Later in this chapter I will try to unpack the meaning and some of the practical implications of each of the components of the above definition. Here I limit myself to providing some illustrations and biblical exhortations that relate to each of the elements of the above definition of intellectual humility.

I have already touched on the first component involving a proper assessment of one's intellectual abilities. The story of Daniel provides a good illustration of someone who has neither too high nor too low an opinion of his intellectual abilities. Daniel had received the best that Babylon had to offer by way of education. But when Daniel finds himself in Nebuchadnezzar's court, facing execution because none of the king's astrologers were able to interpret the king's dream, Daniel prays for help:

> Praise be to the name of God for ever and ever; wisdom and power are his.... He gives wisdom to the wise and knowledge to the discerning.... I thank and praise you, O God of my fathers; You have given me wisdom and power, you have made known to me what we asked of you, you have made known to us the dream of the king. (Dan 2:20-23)

When he finally appears before King Nebuchadnezzar, Daniel reminds the king that his ability to reveal the dream comes from "a God in heaven who reveals mysteries," and that "it is not because I have greater wisdom than other living men" (Dan 2:28, 30). This is surely a model of intellectual humility. Sadly, King Nebuchadnezzar has some hard lessons to learn about his own arrogance.

The second requirement of intellectual humility is that we bow before the truth and are willing to admit that we might be wrong. This can be interpreted as a "secular" version of the first requirement. If you don't want to bow before God, you should at least bow before the truth and be humble enough to admit that you don't always get it right. Christians, of course, should bow both before God and before the truth. As Esther Meek has reminded us, reality needs to be seen as a gift from God and therefore calls for a response of humble gratitude and submission.[169]

The Gospel of John provides us with an example of a proud refusal to acknowledge the truth. The question of Jesus' identity is a theme running through John's Gospel. Early in the Gospel account Jesus challenges those who could not accept his testimony that he had come from God the Father. "You diligently study the Scriptures," Jesus said, and yet these are the very Scriptures "that testify about me" (John 5:39). What was the problem? "How can you believe if you accept praise from one another," Jesus said (v. 44). It was concern for their reputation that led many Jews and Jewish leaders to reject the truth that was so evident in the Scriptures they were studying. It was intellectual pride that made them refuse to bow before the truth.

Closely related to the humility exemplified in bowing before God and before the truth is the requirement that one is willing to admit that one does not know it all. All human knowing is limited. We are not omniscient like God. We are finite beings with finite minds. Paul, in his famous description of love, reminds us that we only know in part (1 Cor 13:9). In this present age, "we see but a poor reflection" or "we see in a mirror dimly" (NRSV), and much of life seems full of riddles, as the Greek word used here suggests. It is only in the hereafter that we will know and understand fully (v. 12).

The story at the beginning of this chapter provides another telling illustration of what intellectual humility looks like. It takes a lot of humility for a renowned Old Testament scholar to listen to a student and then to erase the notes he has written on the blackboard during his lecture, announcing that he was wrong and his student was right. Small wonder that Eugene Peterson never forgot this incident. "The people who stand out in my life," he reflected, "are the people who don't flaunt what they are doing and aren't stuck on who they are."[170] This example also illustrates the last component of my definition of intellectual humility, which relates to the context where teachers and preachers are influencing others. Teachers and preachers must be careful not abuse their authority.

The above definition of intellectual humility also makes reference to the art of listening. I have already highlighted the importance of listening to God and to God's prophets in my earlier review of the Bible on intellectual humility, but a few more comments are in order. James urges Christian brothers and sisters to take special note of this: "Everyone should be quick to listen, slow to speak and slow to become angry" (Jas 1:19). Ah yes, we are all too quick to speak, and we all have problems with listening carefully to what others have to say. Even before someone has finished speaking, we are all too often formulating objections to what is being said.

I experienced this during the pandemic (2020–2022) when I was preaching in a church and the service was live-streamed. Towards the end of my sermon, I tried to make a point of application by asking a question that I hoped would make listeners think. I was told later that seconds after I had made my point, comments were being posted on the chat to the effect that what I had said was very problematic. No reasons were given, though it would seem that I had somehow violated some contemporary speech code. But I had only asked a question which was intended to make people think. Obviously, these listeners hadn't given themselves time to ponder the question I had raised. Persons who are intellectually humble are good listeners. They believe they might have something to learn from the next person, even a person they might disagree with.

JUSTIFICATION OF INTELLECTUAL HUMILITY

Not everyone will agree that humility is a virtue. Humility was not a virtue in the Greco-Roman world. In fact, the word meant something like "crushed" or "debased." It was associated with failure and shame.[171] Aristotle insisted that honor and reputation were among the most pleasant things one could contemplate and attain for oneself.[172] This same understanding of humility resurfaces in the Enlightenment. Friedrich Nietzsche (1844–1900), son of a Lutheran clergyman, poured scorn on the Christian virtue of humility, associating it with a "slave morality," and contrasted this with his own "master morality." He advocated autonomy, pride, the will to power, and the noble man. Even today autonomy and power are considered to be ideals towards which we should strive. These contrasting ideals force us to ask why Christians view humility so differently.

Clearly, as we have already seen, the Bible holds up humility as a moral ideal. Jesus seems to have delighted in turning the ancient and worldly notions of greatness upside-down. After reminding us of "rulers" and "high officials" who like to "exercise authority" and "lord it over" others, Jesus says, "Instead, whoever wants to become great among you must be your servant, and whoever wants to be first must be your slave—just as the Son of Man did not come to be served, but to serve, and to give his life as a ransom for many" (Matt 20:26–27). It is Jesus' crucifixion, the most shameful way to die imaginable, that established humility as a virtue in Western Christian culture. Paul captures this so eloquently.

> Your attitude should be the same as that of Christ Jesus: Who, being in very nature God, did not consider equality with God something to be grasped, but made himself nothing, taking the very nature of a servant, being made in human likeness. And

being found in appearance as a man, he humbled himself by becoming obedient to death—even death on a cross! (Phil 2:5–8)

In my earlier review of the story of creation, we have seen that intellectual humility as a virtue also derives from the biblical understanding of what it means to be human. We are not God. We are creatures of God; therefore we have limitations built into our very being. This theme has been so well captured in Kelly Kapic's recent insightful book entitled *You're Only Human: How Your Limits Reflect God's Design and Why That's Good News*. We are limited beings, therefore very dependent on God. We are not self-made individuals nor self-sufficient. "Everything about our existence points back to *gift*."[173] We are finite, fallible creatures who only know in part (1 Cor 13:12). We are further very dependent on others, and most of our knowledge comes second hand. All of these characteristics of human nature call for intellectual humility.

Added to this is the fact that we are also sinful creatures, thus our reasoning is always somewhat tainted. This again calls for intellectual humility. But as Kapic rightly reminds us, there is a danger here of Christians building their idea of humility primarily on their doctrine of sin. Kapic asks the all-important question whether human beings were meant to be humble before the fall. Yes, indeed!

> God created human persons to be dependent on God, others and the earth. Part of the good creation is our creaturely dependence. This means that humility doesn't just say "I'm sorry" and "Can you forgive me," but it says "I don't know" and "Can you help me."[174]

Given this understanding of human nature, it should not surprise us that there is empirical justification for seeing intellectual humility as a virtue. In the long run just about everybody will be better off epistemically if all people have the virtue of intellectual humility.[175] This is not to suggest that intellectually arrogant people might not sometimes contribute to epistemic goods as well or, in some unusual circumstances, the pursuit of knowledge and truth might sometimes benefit from arrogant scholars. But, in most normal circumstances, intellectual humility pays off. Why is this? Because humble persons are freer to pursue truth if not impeded by vanity and arrogance. Because humble persons won't be distracted by wanting to impress others. Because humble persons will be open to being criticized and so can advance the pursuit of truth. Because humble persons will be able to cooperate with others and learn from them in their common search for truth. Because intellectually humble people will be more generous and ready to share knowledge and truth with others so that they can benefit from their insights. Because humility creates healthier human relationships.

In other words, intellectual humility leads to human flourishing, both individually and collectively. "Humility is the path of liberty and joy. It means not having to constantly compete with everyone, but instead learning to delight in others and celebrate them. It is the path of wonder, gratitude, and healthy relationships."[176] Knowing that is grounded in love and intellectual humility leads to peace, joy, and shalom.[177]

UNPACKING THE MEANING AND PRACTICAL IMPLICATIONS OF INTELLECTUAL HUMILITY

So far, my analysis of intellectual humility and intellectual pride has been largely theoretical. What does the Bible say about this virtue and this vice? How do we define these concepts? How do we justify intellectual humility? In dealing with these questions, I have already hinted at some practical implications of intellectual humility and intellectual arrogance. It is impossible to separate theory and practice completely. But I now want to be more deliberate in working out some of the practical implications of intellectual humility and intellectual pride.

1. Fear of the LORD

A fundamental characteristic of a Christian with intellectual humility is that he or she bows in worship and submission before God. Early in Proverbs we have a saying on which the book of Proverbs hangs and which is found repeatedly in the Scriptures. "The fear of the LORD is the beginning of knowledge" (Prov 1:7).[178] The word "fear" in this context means reverence of the LORD or an attitude of submission to the LORD. Of course, reverence and submission require humility. What is interesting here is the connection made between the fear of the LORD and knowledge. The fear of the LORD is the beginning of knowledge. In other words, we are talking about intellectual humility. The preceding verses also make reference to wisdom, understanding, insight, and prudence (Prov 1:2, 3). So intellectual humility is a key to finding knowledge, wisdom, and understanding.

An attitude of humility and worship of God should also follow the gaining of knowledge and understanding. After struggling with the theological problem of the place of Jews and Gentiles in God's kingdom, Paul ends his deliberations with an expression of worship.

> Oh, the depth of the riches of the wisdom and knowledge of God! How unsearchable his judgments, and his paths beyond tracing out! "Who has known the mind of the Lord? Or who has been his counselor?" "Who has ever given to God, that God should repay him?" For from him and through him and to him are all things. To him be the glory forever! Amen. (Rom 11:33–36)

Discovery of truth will lead the Christian who is intellectually humble to worship God who is the source of all truth. Perhaps a prayer of thanksgiving would be in place when we gain a new insight from our reading or conversations with others.

Here it is important to note that we should not limit the need for intellectual humility to religious knowledge and truth. In Proverbs we learn that it is by wisdom that "the LORD laid the earth's foundations, by understanding he set the heavens in place" (Prov 3:19). So, if we want to understand the principles of order that underlie all of creation, we need to start with an attitude of reverent fear of the LORD. The Psalmist, too, reminds us that God established the earth by his word, which is eternal. "Your laws endure to this day for *all things* serve you" (Ps 119:89–91; my emphasis). Science involves the discovery of how God established the world and its laws. Therefore, science requires intellectual humility. And for Christians, discoveries in science should conclude with worship of our infinite and all-knowing Creator-God.

2. How much do we know?

Another dimension of bowing before God is a willingness to admit that we don't know it all. Again, Proverbs is a guide. "Trust in the LORD with all your heart and lean not on your own understanding; in all your ways acknowledge him and he will make your paths straight. Do not be wise in your own eyes" (Prov 3:5–6). Oh, how these words are needed in a culture where we have made an idol of autonomy and independence. By contrast, Proverbs tells us not to lean on our own understanding. We are finite and fallible creatures. Our knowledge is really quite fragmented. We only know in part. There is always more to learn. Only God knows it all. Therefore, we bow before his infinite knowledge and wisdom.

The story of Job can be read as a long lesson on the importance of realizing that human knowledge is very limited. In the end, the LORD confronts Job: "Who is this that darkens my counsel with words without knowledge?" (Job 38:2). Job's response: "Surely I spoke of things I did not understand, things too wonderful for me to know" (Job 42:3). Socrates also captured this kind of intellectual humility when he concluded that the wisest person recognizes how little he really knows.[179] More recently, philosophers have recognized that owning one's intellectual limitations is a key ingredient in intellectual humility.[180]

3. Submission to the authority of God's word

Christians who are intellectually humble submit to the authority of God's word. We have a God who has revealed himself in Christ and in Scripture. Intellectual humility entails hermeneutical humility as we approach the Bible. Our posture as we read the Bible should not be one of sitting in judgment over God's word but rather of letting the word judge us. James exhorts us to "humbly accept the word planted in you" (Jas 1:21).

This is hard to do in today's intellectual climate, saturated with postmodern deconstructionism—which denies the very idea of a text like the Bible having objective meaning. Here we do well to heed the advice of Kevin Vanhoozer, in his masterful work *Is There a Meaning in This Text?* Vanhoozer argues that we are facing a literary crisis in our day which is rooted in a broader philosophical crisis concerning realism, rationality, and ethics. Contemporary deconstructionists follow Feuerbach and Nietzsche in explaining belief in God and the meaning of the biblical text in terms of human projection and the will to power. With these assumptions, all that remains of meaning in a text is what the human ego brings to it. We are only projecting our own meaning into the text.

Christians who are intellectually humble believe there is meaning in the biblical text independent of our attempts to interpret it. We also believe that there is an author of the biblical text, ultimately a divine author, and what we need to do is to try to get as close as possible to what the divine and human authors' intentions were in writing what they did. Therefore, hermeneutical humility is essential as we approach the Bible.

Sadly, intellectual pride is all too common among Christians, both conservative and liberal. Pride "encourages us to think that we have got the correct meaning before we have made the appropriate effort to recover it. Pride typically does not wait to listen; it knows. . . . Pride neglects the voice of the other in favor of its own."[181] Vanhoozer argues that interpretative pride is the preeminent temptation of the fundamentalist insofar as he or she craves certainty. But those on the radical liberal left are equally prone to pride insofar as they adopt a stance of critical thinking and skepticism and have cultivated the supposedly sophisticated approach of reading the Bible with "a hermeneutic of suspicion."[182]

4. Humble readers

The principle of listening carefully to what a biblical author is saying needs to be applied to all our reading. Are we humble readers? Do we read an article or a book with an attitude that we have something to learn from the author? Or are we scornful readers, priding ourselves in being able to take a critical stance on what we read? Sadly, our educational system is obsessed with teaching critical thinking. Now I as a philosopher would be the first to admit that there is value in critical thinking. But we need more emphasis on humble thinking.

Heidi Oberholtzer Lee gives us some helpful advice about what it means to teach students to read with intellectual humility:

> Reading with humility, by which I mean reading generously and hospitably, taking into account one's own limitations and granting that others, whether the text, its author, or fellow interpreters and critics, might have insights to offer us, enhances our ability to learn. Further, it serves as an important corrective to teaching "critical thinking" as simply being critical, speaking only negatively, about a text. Critical thinking can, in fact, be taught more effectively through helping students to approach a text with humility, learning to listen to, value, and engage with others' perspectives in a way that sharpens the mind.[183]

5. Submission to truth

Persons who are intellectually humble acknowledge that there is Truth with a capital *T*. Our task as human beings is to search for truth to the best of our ability and then to accept what we have found to be true. As mentioned in chapter 2, we have a lot of trouble with the notion of truth today. Most people today understand truth to be socially constructed or a power construct. I also stressed the importance of distinguishing between the human search for truth and the ideal of Truth with a capital *T*, so I will not say more here except as it relates to intellectual humility.

Let me illustrate. We have a wonderful, beautiful, intelligent granddaughter, and her grandpa is rather proud of her. But she had one fault when she was three years old. She was a postmodern constructivist when it came to truth. She really believed that she could create truth. She believed that when she called a certain type of prairie grass "foxtail," then it really was foxtail. And if she planted some blades of this grass in a pot with soil, then it would grow, and no amount of argument would convince her otherwise. It is easy to recognize the error of a three-year-old. What puzzles me is that we don't recognize that we as adults often make the same error, when we adopt a position of postmodern constructivism. We as human beings cannot create truth out of thin air. Truth is not something that is socially constructed. Truth is not made by human beings—it is discovered. We do not create truth. We discover truth. To adopt a position of social constructivism is to be intellectually arrogant.

Sadly, this kind of arrogance permeates much of our academic world today. Even more sadly, this ethos is also infecting today's church, where confessions of faith are trampled on and ignored, even by preachers. Many Christians today feel free to create their own brand of Christianity.[184] And then there is the widespread abuse of power and the failure to see how power distorts our thinking. How often are decisions in the church shaped in the main by the rich and the powerful? Having power can make us lose intellectual humility which in turn makes it difficult for us to see reality clearly and discern truth. We have something to learn from Paul's frequent emphasis on power in weakness.[185]

6. Admission of error

There is a corollary closely related to the call for submission to truth. Intellectual humility is exemplified by a disposition that is quite ready to admit that we might have got it wrong. We are fallible creatures and often fall into error. Intellectual humility requires that we acknowledge our fallibility. Philosopher Thomas Nagel, though not a Christian, highlights this dimension of intellectual humility while at the same time recognizing that we are searching for truth. Nagel argues that there is within each of us an impulse to transcend our particular personal point of view. This occurs because we recognize that it is merely a point of view, a perspective, and not simply an account of the way things really are. This recognition causes us to aspire to an objective vantage point—"the view from nowhere," Nagel calls it.[186]

In other words, each of us, if we are honest, are aware of the possibility that our particular perspective might be wrong, so we aspire to a view uncontaminated by any perspectival factors. Or, as Nagel puts it in his more recent work, the last word is not that this is justified "for me" or "for us." Instead, it is an affirmation of objective truth that any reasoner is obliged to recognize. The last word does not belong to human beings.[187] Persons who have a disposition of intellectual humility admit that they don't have the last word. They admit that they might be wrong. Indeed, it might be well for each of us occasionally to verbalize this after we have made an argument for a position that we hold. "But I might be wrong."

7. How smart am I?

Persons who are intellectually humble have a proper estimation of their own intellectual abilities, not too high and not too low. They are also not overly concerned about making an impression about being smart in front of other people. I have already touched on the first part of this practical implication of intellectual humility earlier in this chapter. But this point is so important that it deserves still more attention. Intellectual humility is a mean between the two extremes of having too low and too high an estimation of one's intellectual abilities.

Paul, in a discussion of the church as consisting of various parts, each with different gifts, gives this advice: "Do not think of yourself more highly than you ought, but rather think of yourself with sober judgment, in accordance with the measure of faith God has given you" (Rom 12:3). Applying this to the virtue of intellectual humility, we should not think of ourselves as more intelligent than we are, but it would be equally wrong to think of ourselves as less intelligent than we are. Instead, we need to think of our intellectual abilities with sober judgment, in accordance with the faith God has given to us.

The reference to God here is important. Paul, in his extended treatment of intellectual pride in his first letter to the Corinthians, asks a series of penetrating questions: "For who makes you different from anyone else? What do you have that you did not receive? And if you did receive it, why do you boast as though you did not?" (1 Cor 4:7). Our intellectual abilities are a gift, and so there is no place for bragging about them. Philip Dow suggests further that we will achieve a proper appraisal of our intellectual capacities and limitations only if we compare ourselves with an all-knowing and infinitely intelligent God. The danger is that we keep comparing ourselves with other human beings, and then we will always have a deceptively high or low opinion of our intellectual abilities, depending on who we are comparing ourselves with.[188]

Reference to God also helps to deflect from being overly concerned about making an impression in front of other people. Smart people are in danger of showing off their smarts. On the other hand, it is all too easy for others to think that a person giving a brilliant argument for his or her position is showing off, when this might not at all be the case. Jesus warned about the danger of showing off one's "acts of righteousness" before men (Matt 6:1–4). The solution: Do not announce your acts of charity with trumpets. Indeed, don't even "let your left hand know what your right hand is doing, so that your giving may be in secret" (vv. 3–4).

How does this apply to showing off our intellectual abilities? The problem here is that our intellectual abilities inescapably come to the fore in exchanges with people, in lectures, discourses, and conversations. So how does one avoid showing off one's intellectual prowess in these situations? It is largely a matter of the inner person. It would be wrong for a smart person to try to give the appearance of not being smart by deliberately giving a bad argument. At the same time, giving a brilliant argument should not be given in such a way as to set oneself up to be admired by others, as Jesus warned in another context (Luke 16:15). Interestingly, in this same context Jesus also reminded the Pharisees that "God knows your hearts." Again, we are dealing here primarily with an inner attitude.

Roberts and Wood helpfully identify some emotional markers of intellectual vanity or arrogance: anxiety about how intelligent one appears, excessive joy about appearing to be intelligent, excessive embarrassment or shame at appearing stupid, and disdain for others who are not as bright as us.[189] The word "excessive" is important here because a little bit of vanity is probably acceptable. People with a healthy level of self-esteem might still be a little bothered by others slighting them in public settings. They are hurt by smaller things that are embarrassing (e.g., a man lecturing with egg on his tie) or by other people not taking them seriously, thinking that they are not worth paying attention to. But vain people are *very much* bothered by these things and *very elated* about successful appearances. The vain person is preoccupied with his status-relevant appearances. "He demands to be very well thought of, wishes to be adulated, adored, and honored; and feels nervous and unfulfilled unless he is getting this extraordinary sort of attention."[190]

Navigating these waters is tricky. It is possible for a person to cover up vanity—for example, the Bertram sisters in Jane Austen's *Mansfield Park*, whose "vanity was in such good order that they seemed to be quite free from it."[191] It is also possible to appear humble when really you are vain—for example, the self-effacing person says, "I am no good," or "I am unworthy," or "How stupid I am!" The problem here is that such a person is really drawing attention to himself and might not at all believe what he is saying. Paul also gives us an example of what he calls "false humility" (Col 2:18, 23). By contrast, the reader might want to look again at the example of Old Testament scholar Dr. Albright, described earlier in this chapter. Here we have a delightful example of genuine intellectual humility.

Confession is good for the soul, so let me become more personal. I pay close attention to reviews of my articles and books. I collect them, print them out, and then highlight positive comments and scribble in rebuttals of any unfair negative comments. Am I being vain? Probably. I also have an ego-file in which I have over the years collected cards of appreciation, positive student evaluations, and notes describing incidents that made me feel good about myself. This probably sounds like vanity, but I like to comfort myself with the fact that I haven't opened this file too often. Teaching can sometimes be discouraging, so occasionally I have found it helpful to peruse my ego-file to get some encouragement.

8. Interdependence

Persons who possess the virtue of intellectual humility readily admit their dependence on others in gaining knowledge. We are not as autonomous and independent as we think. Much, indeed most, of what we know comes second hand. Think of children absorbing what parents and church family teach them. Then there are the years of schooling. Even in graduate school, students learn from other authorities and are mentored by their supervisors. Persons who are intellectually humble also recognize that working cooperatively with others is necessary in acquiring knowledge.

Of course, we can be too dependent on others in our search for knowledge and truth. That is why the development of autonomy is often seen as the goal of education, and why autonomy is sometimes identified as an intellectual virtue.[192] But, as I have argued elsewhere, the liberal ideal of autonomy needs qualification.[193] Complete independence is impossible. We are, after all, social creatures and very much dependent on others, including in the intellectual domain. What we therefore need is an ideal of "normal autonomy" or "relational autonomy" which recognizes our interdependence.[194]

Of course, there is still something to be said for being able to "think for yourself."[195] But there are problems with this mantra which is used all too frequently in our day.

> To think independently of other human beings is impossible, and if it were possible it would be undesirable. Thinking is necessarily, thoroughly, and wonderfully social. Everything you think is a response to what someone else has thought and said. And when people commend someone for "thinking for herself" they usually mean "ceasing to sound like people I dislike and starting to sound more like people I approve of."[196]

I am, therefore, not including autonomy as an intellectual virtue in this book. Indeed, philosophers who do so invariably spend a lot of time making qualifications. They are forced to admit that we can't be completely autonomous, that we are dependent on others in our thinking.[197] Thankfully, there are philosophers who try to maintain a balance between autonomy and interdependence, thus providing a better account of what the human search for knowledge and truth should look like.[198]

For another application of the principle of interdependence, I return to a point made earlier about children learning from their parents. The Scriptures remind us repeatedly that children should honor their parents (Eph 6:1–3; Deut 5:16). I believe this exhortation also applies to adult children. Here an interesting and important question arises. What does it mean for adult children to honor their fathers and mothers regarding the beliefs they have inherited in their upbringing? I want to suggest that a key indicator of intellectual humility is an attitude of honoring one's upbringing. This does not mean that we agree with everything that our parents taught us. We all need to move beyond our childhood ideas. Indeed, the Scriptures urge us to put childish thinking behind us.[199] But we should still respect what we were taught as children.

Peter Caws and Stefani Jones are the editors of an interesting book in which eleven philosophers share stories of their religious upbringing and then engage in philosophical and moral reflection on their experience.[200] A variety of mainly Christian family backgrounds are represented, and they vary in degrees of narrowness and strictness. Each of these philosophers, in one way or another, "broke free" from the religious upbringing that was "imposed" on them as children. And each of them are very critical of their upbringing. Nearly all the contributors use the term "indoctrination" to describe their religious upbringing. And most of the essays consider any sort of indoctrination, however mild, to be morally blameworthy.[201] Why? Because they believe that their parents and their religious communities failed to encourage and facilitate their growth towards autonomy. Their upbringing failed to open future possibilities. And of course, now as adults, they see themselves as so much more enlightened!

What is interesting is that the editors of this anthology and some of the contributors are forced to admit that some indoctrination may be inevitable in any kind of upbringing. Thus, they concede that there might be a kind of "mild" indoctrination that is even benign. One of the contributors, Raymond Bradley, concedes that despite his objections to growing up in a fundamentalist Baptist environment, it nonetheless "gave me something tough to chew on, something to cut my teeth on intellectually."[202] Indeed, intellectual growth requires a foundation of first being initiated into a stable primary culture. The development of autonomy and critical openness requires a "narrow" and "strict" upbringing. It is somewhat surprising that all of these writers, despite their being supposedly indoctrinated as children, grew up to become philosophers! Maybe their religious upbringing contributed positively to this outcome.

Being excessively critical of our upbringing is an expression of the intellectual vice of intellectual arrogance. We need to cherish our backgrounds even if we have grown beyond them intellectually. We shouldn't disparage our upbringing but instead build on it. We don't "recover" from our narrow religious backgrounds, as I have heard too many "enlightened" Christians say. Instead, we should treasure our backgrounds even as we have moved to a more nuanced expression of our childhood faith.

There is a further important application of the principle of honoring our parents. It is not only our parents that we need to honor, but also our grandparents and our great-grandparents. Each generation needs to honor the intellectual contributions of the previous generations. Indeed, we are always building on the shoulders of our ancestors. Therefore, honoring our parents entails that we honor tradition. Again, this does not entail that we always need to agree with tradition. Here we need to distinguish between traditionalism and honoring tradition. Traditionalism involves being enslaved to tradition, accepting tradition without question. Proper honoring of tradition means that we honor the insights of our ancestors and acknowledge our indebtedness to tradition while at the same time allowing for respectful critique. Sadly, all too many people today, including Christians, succumb to what C. S. Lewis describes as "chronological snobbery," the belief that we are so much more enlightened than the dark ages of the past.²⁰³ We need to remember that we, too, might have our own blind spots. Indeed, present ideas might just represent a departure from the truth, a point made repeatedly in the Bible.²⁰⁴ Progress is not inevitable. To think in this way is characteristic of those who have a disposition of intellectual arrogance.

9. Influencing others and teaching

One dimension of our dependence on others in gaining knowledge involves parents, teachers, and professors helping children and students to learn. We as learners cannot avoid being dependent on teachers. And this brings us to another important ingredient in my definition of intellectual humility. Parents and teachers who are intellectually humble, while willing to influence others, aren't overly concerned about persuading others. They acknowledge that they might even have something to learn from others and are always wanting to allow their children and students to make up their own minds.

Here it is important to acknowledge that we are all in the business of influencing others. Sadly, there is a lot of public unease about influence and persuasion today.²⁰⁵ But influence and persuasion are inescapable. It has been well said that man is, "among other things, a persuading and persuaded animal."²⁰⁶ Persuasion is not wrong in itself. It is only unethical persuasion that is wrong. And one key ingredient of unethical persuasion is the presence of intellectual arrogance. What is so desperately needed in our time is humble persuasion. Elsewhere, I have also argued for "humble evangelism" and "humble apologetics."²⁰⁷

Another way in which persuasion can become unethical is when the desire to influence and persuade is taken to an extreme. Parents and teachers can be too obsessed with influencing and persuading their children or students. I want to suggest that intellectual arrogance is the besetting sin of teachers and academics, especially philosophers! Listen to Richard Rorty, whose forbearer was the skeptic and atheist Friedrich Nietzsche. Rorty maintains that college professors ought "to arrange things so that students who enter as bigoted, homophobic, religious fundamentalists will leave college with views more like our own." With no hint of his usual irony, Rorty writes that "students are lucky to find themselves under the benevolent *Herrschaft* of people like me, and to have escaped the grip of their frightening, vicious, dangerous parents."²⁰⁸ This is intellectual arrogance at its worst.

Teachers need to teach with humility. The epistle of James has some interesting things to say about teachers. "Not many of you should presume to be teachers, my brothers, because you know that we who teach will be judged more strictly" (Jas 3:1). Then follows an extended treatment of the use of the tongue which is all too prone to making "great boasts" (v. 5). I believe James is here arguing for intellectual humility on the part of teachers. We are reminded that our words will be held up to judge us as teachers. That should keep us humble. Teachers make extensive use of their tongues, tongues that are tempted to boast. Beware of this, teachers.

Educational philosopher R. S. Peters has famously said, "The teacher has to learn to be in authority and to be an authority without being authoritarian."[209] This is hard to do. Teachers have authority, and we must be very careful not to abuse this authority. We cannot help but influence our students. But such influence must be done with intellectual humility. Humble teachers do not have an inordinate concern to be the determiner of the opinions of their students.[210] They are there to help students to learn but always give them the freedom to disagree with them and to make up their own minds as they mature. Of course, the phrase "making up your own minds" needs some qualification because we are never completely on our own in our thinking, as has already been pointed out.

Jesus introduces another important dimension of intellectual humility in relation to teaching. After condemning the teachers of the law and the Pharisees for making public displays of their religiosity, Jesus astonishingly condemns the practice of giving certain people titles like "Rabbi" or "Father" or "Teacher," because "you have one Teacher, the Christ" (Matt 23:8–10). I continue to marvel at how this instruction of Jesus is ignored in the church today when Catholics address their priests as "Father" and Protestants address their leaders as "Pastor so and so." Jesus is clearly trying to level the playing field in the realm of ideas—"you are all brothers [and sisters]" and fellow students with only Christ who deserves the title of "Teacher." Interestingly, Jesus goes right on to talk about humility. "The greatest among you will be your servant. For whoever exalts himself will be humbled, and whoever humbles himself will be exalted" (Matt 23:11). The teacher as servant. What does that look like? I think Jesus' words have much to teach us about intellectual humility and pride for any of us involved in teaching and preaching and scholarship.

10. Intellectual humility and conviction

A note of caution by way of concluding these practical applications of the virtue of intellectual humility. We might be tempted to think that intellectual humility requires an absence of strong beliefs and convictions. I don't think this is the case. All of us have beliefs and convictions that we hold to rather firmly. Indeed, it is impossible to get on in life without having strong beliefs and convictions. But convictions can still be held with humility. There is such a thing as "confident humility," a favorite expression of Adam Grant in his best-selling book *Think Again*.[211] I will say more about this in the next chapter, where I develop the notion of proper confidence regarding our convictions.

I conclude this chapter with a call for introspection. Jesus warned us about the danger of our being very adept at finding a speck in someone else's eye while failing to see the log in our own eyes (Matt 7:3). This also applies to arrogance and intellectual arrogance. It is all too easy to hate intellectual arrogance when we see it in others while failing to see it in ourselves.[212] So the reader might want to do the questionnaire at the beginning of the chapter once again. And make sure that you are honest in answering the questions.

4

Commitment and Openness

> Now faith is being sure of what we hope for
> and certain of what we do not see.
>
> (HEBREWS 11:1)

> He who has an ear, let him hear what the Spirit says to the churches.
>
> (REVELATION 2:7, 11, 17)

Before you complete the questionnaire that follows, give yourself a rating (0–10) on being committed and at the same time open to reconsidering your beliefs.

QUESTIONNAIRE: A SELF-EVALUATION

For each of the following statements, answer **yes**, **no**, or **unsure/maybe**.

1. I am always very careful not to jump to conclusions too quickly, and I always weigh alternatives carefully before coming to a settled conclusion.

2. Although I recognize the danger of making hasty conclusions, I acknowledge the importance of having convictions that are relatively stable.

3. Think of a strong conviction that you have. Can you identify some things that you admit would count as **possible** evidence against your conviction?

4. While acknowledging the importance of allowing for possible counter-evidence against my beliefs, I realize that it is not possible to be constantly reevaluating my deepest beliefs.

5. I make it a point occasionally to read articles and books that articulate political, social, and religious viewpoints that run counter to my own convictions.

6. While acknowledging the importance of breadth and diversity in what I read, I recognize that there is nothing wrong with spending more time reading articles and books that confirm my own convictions.

7. I am always eager to learn new things and am willing to cast aside cherished beliefs if new and better possibilities are on offer.

8. At the same time, I never reject cherished beliefs simply because they are traditional.

9. I value the need to think critically about the beliefs I hold.

10. At the same time, I am very much aware of the danger of being be too preoccupied with criticism and doubt.

Now give a numerical value to each of your answers—1 **for yes**; ½ **for unsure/maybe; 0 for no**. Then total your numerical values. The total out of 10 gives the percentage grade for your having the intellectual virtue of committed openness.

See the end of the questionnaire in chapter 2 for some additional comments about the validity of this exercise.

It was one of those lectures where everything seemed to go right. I felt I was communicating. The students were listening. Good questions were being asked. It was philosophical dialogue at its best. What was the topic? It was an introductory course on ethics, and I was arguing for moral absolutes. I also introduced the idea that objective moral absolutes might ultimately require a transcendent law-giver. After class, one of my favorite students came to talk to me. Yes, professors do have favorites and there are good reasons for this. This girl was bright, always alert in my classes, and obviously interested in what was being discussed. She came to me after this class, and asked one simple question: Can one be an absolutist without being narrow-minded? What a profound question, and I knew enough about this girl to understand why she was asking it. She had come from a fairly liberal church background, but for some reason had attended a rather conservative Bible school in the Canadian prairies. She had already come to see me in my office several times and had repeatedly told me about the seeming narrowness of this school. And that is why she was enjoying taking my philosophy class now. She had the freedom to think.

Can we as Christians believe in absolute moral values without being narrow-minded? This important question can be expressed in different ways. Can we as Christians believe in absolute truth and yet be open-minded? Believing involves some kind of commitment to a belief. So here is another variant of the question. Is it possible for us as Christians to be committed to Jesus and to the truth of the Scriptures and yet be open-minded? I believe the Bible gives an affirmative answer to this question. I want to make a case for "committed openness" in this chapter.

One writer has observed that open-mindedness appears at the top of nearly every list of intellectual virtues.[213] Indeed, there is near consensus that open-mindedness is a paradigm intellectual virtue. In every day discourse, open-mindedness is a condition to aspire to and closed-mindedness a condition to fear. Alan Jacobs tells the famous story of the great economist John Maynard Keynes, who was once accused of having flip-flopped on some policy issue. Keynes's biting reply: "When the facts change, sir, I change my mind. What do you do?"[214] The story may belong to legend, but it illustrates so well the commonly held belief that closed-minded adherence to a position or ideology is bad, and that open-mindedness is an ideal that all of us should aim for.

MISCONCEPTIONS ABOUT OPEN-MINDEDNESS

Unfortunately, there are a number of misconceptions surrounding open-mindedness in the popular understanding of this intellectual virtue. Sometimes the ideal of being open-minded is thought to entail that one must be constantly reevaluating one's convictions and changing one's mind. This has prompted the somewhat cynical response, "Don't be so open-minded that your brains fall out."[215] Open-mindedness can be taken to an extreme. We simply can't be reevaluating our beliefs all the time. We need settled convictions to get on with life. This would suggest that open-mindedness cannot stand on its own. We need somehow to combine open-mindedness with firmness about at least some of our beliefs.

G. K. Chesterton, in his *Autobiography*, gives us a telling description of a variant of the above misconception of open-mindedness. Chesterton describes H. G. Wells as a man who "reacted too swiftly to everything," who was "a permanent reactionary," and who never seemed able to reach firm or settled conclusions of his own. Chesterton goes on: "I think he thought that the object of opening the mind is simply opening the mind. Whereas I am incurably convinced that the object of opening the mind, as of opening the mouth, is to shut it again on something solid."[216] Paul aptly describes this problem in terms of men and women who are "always learning but never able to acknowledge the truth" (2 Tim 3:7). What is needed is a concept of open-mindedness that aims for commitment and truth.

Closely related to the above problem is the equating of open-mindedness with empty-mindedness. The problem here is that there are no empty minds. A child grows up in a particular home and in a particular environment that shapes his or her thinking. As various postmodern writers have shown, thinking and knowing is always part of a tradition. Indeed, the mind can function only "by indwelling a tradition of language, concepts, models, images, and assumptions" which function as a lens through which we try to understand reality.[217] We all have convictions and perspectives, and a coherent definition of open-mindedness must do justice to this fact. But while we have convictions, we must at the same time be open to reevaluating them. This is what is right about open-mindedness.

The notion of empty minds is closely related to the ideal of neutrality, a myth which is sadly all too common in the field of education. Educational philosopher Peter Gardner describes neutrality in this way: "To be open-minded about an issue is to have entertained thoughts about that issue but not to be committed to or to hold a particular view about it."[218] Sadly, agnosticism on theological issues is sometimes seen by Christians as a preferred stance to take. Yes, there are occasions when I might not have a particular conviction on a subject. But I can't get through life without having convictions about many things. And even if I have convictions, I can still be open-minded about them. All that is required is that I am open or willing to change my mind. So, it is a mistake to associate neutrality or agnosticism with open-mindedness.

Another misconception surrounding open-mindedness is its close association with being critical. Indeed, the two notions are often combined to form the concept of "critical openness."[219] There is a lot of emphasis on critical thinking in education today. Training in critical thinking is seen as a key to creating an open mind. Bertrand Russell gives this advice: "When you come to a point of view, maintain it with doubt. This doubt is precious because it suggests an open mind."[220] But it is not at all clear what Russell means here. What does it mean to "come to a point of view"? What does "doubt" mean? And is not doubt fundamentally incompatible with having a point of view? I also believe Russell errs in equating doubt with having an open mind. Further, doubt and critical openness can be taken to an extreme. Hyper-criticism is in fact an intellectual vice about which I will have more to say at the end of this chapter.

These misconceptions and difficulties surrounding the popular notion of open-mindedness have led some writers to suggest that we should simply discard open-mindedness as an intellectual virtue. For example, Alan Jacobs suggests that the notions of open-mindedness and closed-mindedness are "nonsensical and misleading."[221] Jason Baehr seems to agree with Jacobs but goes on to suggest that there is still something to be said for open-mindedness as an intellectual virtue. It might just take some work to uncover "the essential or defining character of this virtue."[222] I agree. We still need open-mindedness as an intellectual virtue. My aim in this chapter is to try to capture what is salvageable about this virtue, and then to go on to describe, defend, and apply what I believe is a preferred ideal of "committed openness."

DEFINITIONS

Philosophical definitions of open-mindedness tend to be rather complex.[223] Here is my bare-bones definition: **Open-mindedness** involves a willingness to listen to opposing viewpoints and a willingness to change one's mind in the light of new evidence and argument. **Closed-mindedness** involves an unwillingness to do the same. A related intellectual vice is **dogmatism**, which involves an arrogant and unbending assertion of opinions or beliefs that arises from a disposition of closed-mindedness.

Here it is important to take special note of the word "willingness" in the above definitions. Open-mindedness does not mean that one is constantly listening to opposing viewpoints or changing one's mind. Rather, it means that one is *willing* to do so when there is good reason to do so. It involves a willingness to consider counter-evidence to one's present beliefs.

When there are conflicting opinions, a person with an open mind will listen to both sides of the issue. An open-minded person is able "to transcend familiar or default ways of thinking" about an issue.[224] An open-minded person is willing to "think again," to use the title of Adam Grant's insightful recent analysis of the importance of "the power of knowing what you don't know," and hence the ongoing need to "rethink" the convictions we hold.[225] An open-minded person doesn't jump to conclusions but considers alternative beliefs carefully. An open-minded person is interested in learning new things and is willing to cast aside cherished beliefs if new and better beliefs are on offer. At the same time, an open-minded person doesn't discard a belief simply because it is part of a long-standing tradition. An open-minded person also does not discredit an opinion simply because the person expressing it has a bad reputation.[226]

Of course, there is a problem here. How does one determine when a person is indeed willing to change his or her mind? Just because an atheist refuses to change his mind when you present an argument for the existence of God does not mean that this person is closed-minded. He may think your argument is weak, or he may have other countervailing evidence that over-rides the argument that you gave. It is difficult to measure someone else's *willingness* to change his or her mind. This is really a subjective and personal matter which, in most cases, only the person involved can assess. Of course, when an atheist does actually become a believer, then an outside person is in a position to say that this person really is open-minded and willing to change his or her mind. But generally, caution is in order when assessing the open-mindedness of another person.

Another complicating factor is that the beliefs that we hold vary in their importance. There are some beliefs which I can quite easily give up. For example, my claim that I still have about one hundred dollars in my wallet is easy to give up when my wife asks about this and finds that there is only one twenty dollar bill in my wallet. However, my belief in God is more important to me, so I am more hesitant to call it into question. I will have more to say about how the importance of beliefs affects our willingness to change our minds later in this chapter.

THE WAY AHEAD

We have seen that there are a number of popular misconceptions about open-mindedness. A common thread running through these misconceptions is that open-mindedness tends to be taken to an extreme. It is assumed that we can be completely open-minded or that we must be constantly critically evaluating our beliefs. But as I have already argued, this is quite unrealistic. We need somehow to allow for stable convictions and commitments.

Here we must be careful not to dismiss the ideal of open-mindedness entirely, as some writers have suggested. There is still much to be said for keeping open-mindedness as an intellectual virtue. It just can't stand alone. There is an incompleteness about the ideal of open-mindedness when it comes to describing a healthy mind. A focus on open-mindedness alone fails to do justice to the need for all people to be committed to certain beliefs. So rather than focusing only on open-mindedness, I want to suggest that we need a concept that tries to capture a needed balance between being committed and being open-minded.

I am, therefore, proposing the concept of "committed openness" as an intellectual virtue that balances the need for both commitment and critical openness.[227] I realize that "committed openness" sounds like an oxymoron, a contradiction in terms, but I don't think it is. I believe it captures the nature of a healthy mind. We need to be both committed to certain beliefs and at the same time open to reevaluating these same beliefs.

There are a few writers who have tried to capture this needed balance between commitment and openness. For example, Nathan King, in a recent treatment of intellectual virtues, recognizes that there are problems with treating open-mindedness on its own. He gives the following title to a chapter devoted to this subject—"Open-Mindedness and Firmness:

Transcend and Maintain Your Perspective."[228] In this chapter he proposes the notion of "open-minded firmness" to get at the balance needed between having convictions and yet being open to reevaluating them.[229] Other writers have suggested concepts closely related to the notion of "committed openness"—"proper confidence," "humble confidence," or "confident humility."[230] All of these concepts are trying to address our need to find a balance between firmness or confidence in our beliefs and open-mindedness. We need to be able to maintain a perspective and at the same time be willing to transcend it.

Definition: Committed openness is a disposition that maintains a proper balance between being committed to certain beliefs while at the same time being open to critically evaluating them. It balances our need to have firm convictions with a willingness to change our minds in the light of new evidence and argument. This intellectual virtue can also be described in terms of maintaining a middle position in a continuum between the two extremes of intellectual flabbiness and intellectual rigidity.

TWO EXTREMES

I will have more to say about the first part of the above definition later after I have laid some necessary groundwork. Here I would like to focus on the latter part of the above definition, which draws on Aristotle's classic description of virtues as a mean between extremes. I am describing the intellectual virtue of committed openness as a mean between the extremes of intellectual flabbiness and intellectual rigidity.[231] We can be too committed to our beliefs. We can also be too open-minded. Healthy minds avoid both over-confidence and under-confidence in our beliefs. I now want to look at each of these extremes in turn.

I referred earlier to Chesterton's description of H. G. Wells as a person who never seemed able to reach firm or settled conclusions of his own. This is an example of intellectual flabbiness. In George Eliot's novel *Middlemarch*, Mr. Brooke is described as a man of "miscellaneous opinions," "uncertain vote," and having a "rambling habit of mind." In this "glutinously indefinite mind," the "Puritan energy was clearly in abeyance."[232] James describes the doubter (better translated "the hesitant person") as one who is "like a wave of the sea, blown and tossed by the wind" (Jas 1:6). Paul describes someone who has "an unhealthy interest in controversies and arguments" and who is thus "robbed of the truth"

(1 Tim 6:4–5). Interestingly, this kind of person is also described as "conceited," so there would seem to be a link between intellectual flabbiness and intellectual pride.

Jay Newman, in his study of fanaticism and hypocrisy, concedes that healthy commitment is very necessary for human existence, not only for individuals but also for society as a whole. And yet, there are deep suspicions about commitment. We suffer from under-commitment in our society, according to Newman.[233] Another writer makes the same point even more strongly: "Hell is a forever without commitment."[234] And there are many people living in that hell today.

Let me give just one example of this—a student of mine, many years ago, who was a middle-aged, successful businessman. We had many intense discussions, as he reveled in attacking Christianity in class, and I warm up to such attacks! But in a discussion during class breaks and in his class journal he confessed to a deep insecurity that he felt about life. What were the roots of his insecurity? He listed them in a class journal—lack of firm beliefs, insecurity of existence, not being connected, deep suspicion that the economy was going to collapse, and an inability to deal with and live with uncertainty.

After the final exam, we had a long conversation, and he shared with me his spiritual pilgrimage, giving me a colorful account of frantically switching from one church to another. He was born a Roman Catholic but became disenchanted with the church. He was mentored by a Mennonite for a while, joined an Evangelical church and then a Baptist church. He went on to explore New Age thinking for a few years and then dabbled with Indian spirituality. I called him eclectic, and he didn't know what the word meant! But deep down inside, he knew what his problem was. He wasn't committed and he was suffering because of it. He was living in the hell of non-commitment and intellectual flabbiness.

At the other extreme of this continuum is intellectual rigidity. Whereas a person can be too pliable intellectually, rigidity is being too inflexible, too confident in one's beliefs. It involves a refusal to adjust beliefs in light of experiences and evidence. A good example of this is found in the initial reactions to Galileo's claim that there were craters on the moon and spots on the sun, which he had discovered with his telescope. Cesare Cremonini, professor of Aristotelian philosophy at the University of Padua and a colleague of Galileo, denounced Galileo's claims but refused to check things out for himself by looking through a telescope. Cremonini was later quoted as saying, "I do not wish to approve of claims about which I do not have any knowledge, and about things which I have not seen . . . and then to observe through those glasses gives me a headache. Enough! I do not want to hear anything more about this." Galileo replied to these rejections in a letter to fellow scientist Johannes Kepler:

> My dear Kepler, I wish that we might laugh at the remarkable stupidity of the common herd. What do you have to say about the principal philosophers of this academy who are filled with the stubbornness of an ass and do not want to look at either the planets, the moon or the telescope, even though I have freely and deliberately offered them the opportunity a thousand times? Truly, just as the ass stops its ears, so do these philosophers shut their eyes to the light of truth.[235]

This is a paradigm case of the intellectual vice of rigidity or closed-mindedness. It illustrates overconfidence in one's beliefs, which makes one unwilling to change his or her mind.

Another expression of intellectual rigidity is dogmatism. I have defined dogmatism as an arrogant and unbending assertion of opinions or beliefs that arises from a disposition of closed-mindedness.[236] A statement of John Adams, the second president of the United States, might indicate a tendency towards dogmatism: "Thanks to God that he gave me stubbornness when I know I am right."[237] Here it should be noted that one can be dogmatic about beliefs that are in fact true. For example, there is abundant scientific evidence that the mRNA vaccines for COVID-19 and its variants have proven to be safe and effective. This is a true statement. But a person making this statement can do so in a dogmatic fashion that is arrogant and won't tolerate any questioning of the claim. Dogmatism can become a habitual way of making claims, and then it is nearly indistinguishable from intellectual rigidity or closed-mindedness. Sadly, there are all too many examples of this kind of closed-mindedness today.

BIBLICAL JUSTIFICATION FOR COMMITTED OPENNESS

We are now in a position to examine what the Bible has to say about committed openness and its justification as an intellectual virtue. Here we need to return again to the creation story, where we find Adam and Eve created by God as finite human beings. As such, their knowledge was limited. So, they needed to trust in God. They needed to listen to God. They needed to start with faith. They needed to start with commitment to God and to his revelation. At the same time, they needed to be open to discovering new things about the world they lived in. They also needed to be open to discovering new truths in their walk with God.

They, and we, are part of a story, God's story, and as such we encounter surprises.[238] But we have confidence in the biblical narrative which tells the story of the cosmos and the human race in terms of the activity of its Author and Governor. As Christians we are committed to God as revealed in the Bible and in Jesus Christ. And we are open to a growing understanding of God. The Genesis story highlights the epistemological insight that all knowing starts with a faith commitment and moves on to openness and growth. This approach is so well captured in Augustine's phrase, "Faith [or commitment] seeking understanding."[239]

The Great Commandment gives us a summary statement of what commitment means. We are to love God with heart, soul, strength, and mind (Deut 6:4–5; Mark 12:29–30). We are to love God with our whole being. Commitment is surely at the heart of this commandment. God wants complete, wholehearted commitment to him, with everything we have. Commitment doesn't only involve feelings of love and devotion to God. It doesn't only involve believing with our minds that God exists and directs the course of the cosmos and the human story. It doesn't only involve serving God in action. Commitment involves all of these combined.

There is necessarily a risk involved in this commitment. We cannot be entirely sure that we have got it right. But we stake our lives on this commitment. With Paul, we say, "I know whom I have believed, and I am sure that he is able to guard until that Day what has been entrusted to me" (2 Tim 1:12 RSV). Yes, there is confidence here, but it is a humble confidence, not based on our own ability to understand but in the faithfulness and reliability of the One who has called us to follow him. The phrase "until that Day" suggests that we are on the way that leads to fullness of truth. But in the here and now, we need to be open to better understandings of the truth. We are confident that the One in whom we have put our trust, the one to whom we are committed, is able to bring us to the full grasp of what we now only partly understand.[240]

The first part of the Genesis story justifies both commitment and openness. Our finiteness requires that we put our faith or commitment in God, while at the same time we should be open to learning new things about God and the world he created. Such openness to learning obviously includes a willingness to change one's mind from an inadequate to a new and fuller understanding of truth. But there is another dimension of human nature that makes critical openness so essential. The Genesis story also reminds us that we are fallen creatures. We have sinned, and sin has a way of blinding us to the truth. Indeed, the problem of closed-mindedness is a major theme in the Scriptures.

Isaiah repeatedly makes mention of ears that do not hear and eyes that do not see.[241] Jesus, in explaining the parable of the sower to his disciples, draws on Isaiah to provide a penetrating analysis of a closed mind.

> You will be ever hearing, but never understanding; you will be ever seeing, but never perceiving. For this people's heart has become calloused; they hardly hear with their ears, and they have closed their eyes. Otherwise they might see with their eyes, hear with their ears, understand with their hearts and turn, and I would heal them.[242]

Jesus, like the prophet Isaiah, was speaking to the people of Israel and was bemoaning their inability to really hear God's message. And at the root of such closed-mindedness were hearts that did not allow ears and eyes and minds to function properly. Interestingly, Jesus ends this parable with the words, "He who has ears, let him hear" (Matt 13:9).

Paul similarly draws on Old Testament writers to describe eyes that do not see and ears that do not hear.[243] He speaks of the godless and wicked as suppressing the truth about what can be known about God in nature (Rom 1:18). "The god of this age has blinded the minds of unbelievers so that they cannot see the light of the gospel of the glory of Christ" (2 Cor 4:4). Clearly, this is not what God had in mind for us as human beings. So we need help in overcoming this blindness and closed-mindedness. We need somehow to have our hearts and minds open to God and his truth. More on this later.

Another dominant theme in the Old Testament is that the people of God are always in danger of regressing and falling away from the truth. In other words, there is a concern about failures of continuing commitment, trust, and obedience in God. The people of God are frequently described as "rebellious," "not loyal," and "not faithful."[244] There are warnings that God's people will "stumble," "turn from the way," and "wander" like lost sheep.[245] Before Moses dies, God gives him the pessimistic prognosis that his people "will forsake me and break the covenant I made with them," and this betrayal includes an intellectual component—"I know what they are disposed to," or "I know which way their thoughts incline already" (Deut 31:21 NEB). Then there is the prophet Amos, who describes a people who have strayed so far from God that they are "searching for the word of the LORD, but they will not find it." Hence the young men and women who "faint because of thirst" (Amos 8:11–13).

This same dire prognosis is found in the New Testament. Jesus foresees a time when "many will turn away from the faith" (Matt 24:10–13). Paul talks about a time "when men will not put up with sound doctrine" and "will turn their ears away from the truth and turn aside to myths" (2 Tim 4:3–4; cf. 1 Tim 6:20–21). So again, we face the question of how to overcome our tendency to stray from the truth.

THE REDEMPTION OF COMMITMENT AND OPENNESS IN THE BIBLE

Thankfully, the biblical narrative includes a story of redemption, and this includes redemption of our minds. God has provided a way to restore the ideal balance between commitment and openness found in the Garden of Eden before the fall. Thus, there are frequent calls in Scripture for the renewal of our minds. Paul talks about putting off the old self, which is "being corrupted by its deceitful desires," and putting on the new self, which includes "being made new in the attitude of our minds" (Eph 4:22–24).[246] Such renewal will include a restored commitment and stability of beliefs so that we are not "tossed back and forth by the waves, and blown here and there by every wind of teaching and by the cunning and craftiness of men in their deceitful scheming" (Eph 4:14). At the same time, redemption of the mind will include openness to learning and "being renewed in knowledge in the image of its Creator" (Col 3:10).

I believe a careful study of Scripture will reveal an equal emphasis on commitment and openness. I begin with the Old Testament and its repeated calls for and examples of commitment. God's instructions to Joshua include an implicit affirmation of confidence in the Book of the Law. "Do not let this Book of the Law depart from your mouth; meditate on it day and night, so that you may be careful to do everything written in it" (Josh 1:8). Job, in the midst of his troubles and in the face of accusations from his miserable comforters, gives this resounding declaration, "I know that my Redeemer lives, and that in the end he will stand upon the earth" (Job 19:25). There are repeated expressions of trust in God in the Psalms, trust which surely includes a component of confidence in the belief that God is faithful. "For you have been my hope, O Sovereign LORD, my confidence since my youth" (Ps 71:5). "The LORD is my rock, my fortress, and my deliverer; my God is a rock, in whom I take refuge" (Ps 18:2).[247] Similar references to God as a rock of refuge are found in the prophets.[248]

Jesus couples his warning about many turning from the faith with this affirmation: "But he who stands firm to the end will be saved" (Matt 24:13). In his prayer for the disciples, Jesus recounts the words he gave them and describes them as knowing "with certainty" that he came from God (John 17:5). Luke explains his purpose in writing his gospel account of Jesus—"that you may know the certainty of the things you have been taught" (Luke 1:4). There are repeated exhortations in the Epistles to stand firm in the faith. "So then, brothers and sisters, stand firm and hold to the teachings we passed on to you, whether by word of mouth or by letter" (2 Thess 2:15).[249] Paul sounds pretty committed when he writes to Timothy, telling him that he is not ashamed of the gospel: "Because I know whom I have believed, and am convinced that he is able to guard what I have entrusted to him for that day" (2 Tim 1:12).[250] And the author of Hebrews urges us to "pay more careful attention . . . to what we have heard so that we do not drift away" (Heb 2:1). And then later, the admonition, "Do not throw away your confidence" (Heb 10:35).[251]

I turn now to the second component of the balance I am arguing for in the ideal of committed openness. In addition to frequent examples and exhortations to be confident and committed to the beliefs of the gospel and to not stray from the truth, there are also frequent calls for openness. We have seen that Isaiah gives a penetrating analysis of closed minds, but then, by way of contrast, he goes on to describe a kingdom of righteousness where kings rule with justice, individuals feel safe, and people have open minds:

> Then the eyes of those who see will no longer be closed, and the ears of those who hear will listen. The mind of the rash will know and understand, and the stammering tongue will be fluent and clear. No longer will the fool be called noble nor the scoundrel be highly respected. (Isa 32:1–5)

Jesus picks up this same prophetic theme and laments the closed-mindedness that comes from blind conformity to tradition (Matt 15:1–20). Jesus draws on Isaiah's depiction of closed minds and hearts, but he goes on to express the desire to "heal them" (Matt 13:15). He then pronounces a blessing on his disciples. "But blessed are your eyes because they see, and your ears because they hear" (Matt 13:16). Then there is the last book in the Bible, where we have John writing letters to the seven churches in the province of Asia, each letter concluding with a plea: "He who has an ear, let him hear what the Spirit says to the churches."[252]

There are also scriptural exhortations to test and critically evaluate claims to truth. In the Old Testament there are repeated exhortations to watch out for false prophets.[253] Jesus echoes these warnings when he tells us to be on the lookout for false prophets who will deceive many (Matt 24:4–5). After encouraging us not to treat prophecies with contempt, Paul encourages us to "test everything" (1 Thess 5:21). John tells us not to believe every spirit, and he then goes on to exhort us to "test the spirits" (1 John 4:1). The author of Acts praises Paul's audience in Berea who, while they "received the message with great eagerness," nonetheless critically evaluated what was said, and "examined the Scriptures every day to see if what Paul said was true" (Acts 17:11).

The delightful story of Jesus' encounter with the Emmaus disciples after his resurrection provides an example of minds that were committed and even closed but are eventually opened (Luke 24:13–35). Jesus chastises the two men for being rather "foolish" and "slow of heart to believe all that the prophets have spoken" (v. 25). These two Jewish men simply couldn't fathom a Messiah who was crucified on the cross. It seems they also had trouble believing that men could rise from the dead. Jesus gives them a long lecture, reviewing how the Scriptures point to his death and resurrection. But the two still do not get it until Jesus breaks bread and gives thanks. Then, finally, "their eyes were opened" (v. 31). And only then did the two realize that their "hearts were burning within us" while Jesus was explaining the Scriptures to them (v. 32). Changing long-held beliefs is not easy. We are torn in two directions, but clearly these disciples were willing to change their beliefs. They were committed and yet open-minded.[254]

The Bible speaks about commitment and openness mainly in terms of listening to God and to God's word as delivered by the prophets and ultimately revealed in Jesus. But we must not think this concern for balance between commitment and openness is limited to "religious truth." Indeed, a sharp distinction between "religious truth" and "secular truth" is foreign to the Bible. All truth is God's truth. And there are hints in the Bible of a broader application of these concepts to all areas of knowledge and truth. For example, the problem of closed-mindedness is colorfully described in terms of men and women creating intellectual silos, gathering "around them a great number of teachers to say what their itching ears want to hear" (2 Tim 4:3). Of course, there is the other extreme of minds that are too open. Paul describes the Athenians who "spent their time doing nothing but talking about and listening to the latest ideas" (Acts 17:21). The problem of closed minds and minds that are too open extends well beyond how we respond to God's special revelation. All of us must cultivate commitment and open-mindedness in all areas of knowledge and truth.

HUMAN NATURE, BELIEF, AND COMMITMENT

In order to get a better grasp of the nature of committed openness, I want to step back a bit and address some additional questions about human nature, beliefs, and the nature of belief systems. First, what does it mean to believe something? We use a variety of metaphors to describe believing.[255] We talk about giving our assent to certain beliefs. We hold our beliefs. We embrace them. We even talk about having a tight grip on our beliefs. Assenting to a belief is a mental act whereby we welcome some claim into our intellectual framework. One could also talk about having a dispositional attitude of hospitality towards a belief.

In reflecting on our beliefs, all of us will recognize that we hold our beliefs with varying degrees of confidence. John Locke, in his groundbreaking book entitled *An Inquiry in Human Understanding* (1690), talks of "degrees of assent from full assurance and confidence, quite down to conjecture, doubt, and distrust."[256] Here one might object that Locke goes too far when he includes doubt and distrust as a kind of assent. Surely, distrust involves a lack of assent. But I agree that it is possible to give assent to a belief and yet entertain some doubts about this belief, or at least be open to critically evaluating this belief. However, at some point doubt becomes distrust and unbelief, and therefore rules out the level of confidence required to believe something. This is the error of Bertrand Russell considered earlier.

Locke's reference to confidence with respect to our beliefs is helpful. There is clearly a continuum of confidence in the beliefs that we hold. Some of my beliefs are held with "full assurance and confidence," for example, that I have six grandchildren. I am less sure about some of my beliefs, for example, that pacifism is an ideal. I still believe Christ taught us to love our enemies, but I am not entirely sure that Christ's teachings entail a full-blown pacifism. So, confidence is a matter of degrees.

We talk about giving our assent to a belief when a certain "threshold" of confidence is reached.[257] As evidence increases, so does my confidence in this belief. The higher the level of our confidence in a belief, the stronger our hold or assent to a belief. Similarly, once my confidence in a belief goes down, I may reach a certain threshold where I can no longer say that I believe or give my assent to this belief.

Lesslie Newbigin reminds us that confidence in a belief is directly related to our acting on our beliefs.[258] Believing and acting on our beliefs go together. If some pompous male head of state (I won't mention any names) says he believes in the dignity and equality of women but is regularly found treating them as chattel, then he doesn't really believe in the dignity and equality of women. Disbelief, too, is expressed in action. The atheist who swears at God when something bad happens to him isn't a very strong atheist. But even here, we have to be careful. For example, I believe it is wrong to tell lies. But you will occasionally find that I do tell a lie. Does this mean that I don't really believe that telling lies is wrong? No, it is just that because of my sinful nature, I don't always live up to what I believe about what is right and wrong.

There is another dimension of human nature that needs to be considered with regard to the way in which we hold our beliefs. We are naturally attached to the beliefs we hold. We don't give up a belief at the first appearance of seeming contrary evidence. For example, I believe that my wife loves me. I don't give up this belief the moment she scowls at me, especially if I have done something stupid. What is interesting here is that this tenacity in holding our beliefs begins to look like closed-mindedness. But we must be careful not to label our natural conservatism with regard to the beliefs we hold as being closed-minded or a vice. A degree of tenacity is a good thing. It makes for stability in our mental make-up. Of course, tenacity in holding on to our beliefs can be taken to an extreme. Confirmation bias is a real problem. Therefore, we need also to be open-minded, always willing to reevaluate our beliefs, as discussed earlier in this chapter.[259]

There is another aspect of human nature that acts as a balance to our tendency to hang on to the beliefs we already have. We naturally also want to know the truth, at least in part, as we have seen in chapter 2. We are curious. We are always investigating, checking, studying, looking, listening, and conversing with others.[260] These practices have the effect of opening us up to new knowledge, which sometimes challenges the beliefs we already hold. Thus, we are by nature also open to reviewing our conservatively held beliefs, at least to some degree. So there is a balance found in healthy minds. We tend to be conservatively attached to our beliefs and yet also open to reevaluating them in our pursuit of the truth. Sadly, this balance can be broken and thus we get the vices of intellectual rigidity or flabbiness. Hence the need for the cultivation of the intellectual virtue of committed openness.

BELIEF SYSTEMS

The balance between commitment and openness varies with the kinds of beliefs we hold. Here I want to expand on a point I hinted at earlier when I talked about different levels of importance in our beliefs. Harvard philosopher Willard Van Quine provides some useful descriptions and analogies of the structure of a belief system that is part of each person's mental make-up. Quine suggests we look at what we believe in terms of a system of interlocking beliefs which we use in trying to explain experience. Individual beliefs are always part of a whole belief system.[261] For Quine, the evaluation of our individual beliefs can never be isolated from evaluating a whole belief system. Quine also suggests that there are varying degrees of importance in the beliefs of each person's belief system. Beliefs in the interior of our belief system are more central and basic than empirical claims at the periphery of our belief system. Given the interconnectedness of our beliefs, an adjustment of one of our beliefs will always entail some further adjustments in our belief system. Quine stresses that there is much latitude in making adjustments to our beliefs as we attempt to account for experience. Even our central beliefs can be revised, although our "natural tendency" is not to do so.[262]

The following diagram is inspired by Quine's analysis of a belief system, taking some liberties in interpreting the levels of beliefs and their varying degrees of importance.

Belief Systems

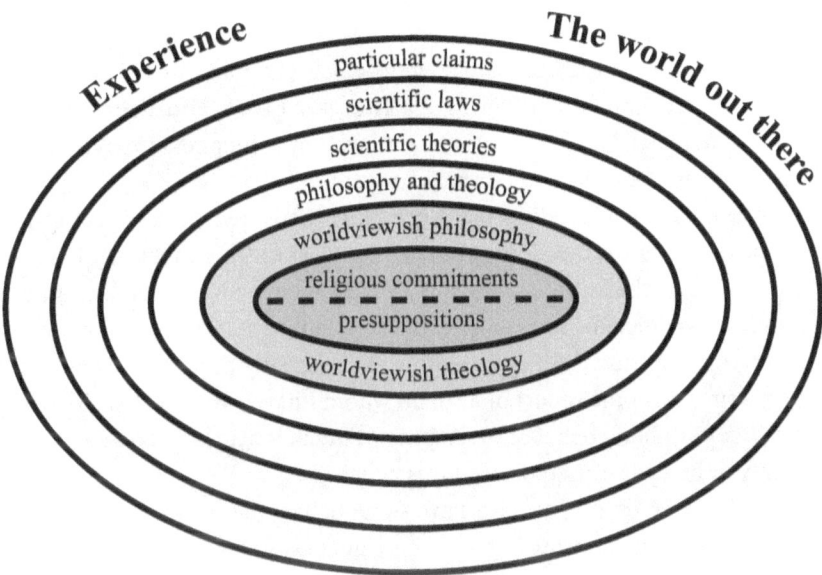

Figure 3: Belief Systems

There are several features of this diagram that deserve further comment. The beliefs at the center of our belief system (presuppositions and worldview perspectives—the grey area) shape all the rest of our beliefs, though this influence becomes less evident with beliefs at the outer edge of our belief system. The influence of presuppositions and worldviews can be compared to the diminishing ripples caused by a stone cast into a pond. Presuppositions and worldview perspectives also play a determining role in how we interpret reality. Compare, for example, the implications of a belief in God versus a materialistic worldview. Belief in God leads a person to interpret life as having meaning and purpose. A materialistic worldview leads to an emphasis on fate or chance.

This diagram also illustrates that there is a hierarchy of beliefs. Some of our beliefs are more important than others. Our basic beliefs or load-bearing beliefs (presuppositions and worldviews) are the most important beliefs that we have, even though many people may not even be aware of them. They are simply taken for granted. Beliefs on the periphery of our belief system are less important. Belief in God is more important than my belief that the sun is shining at this time.

What is of particular significance here is that we are especially conservative in the way we hold onto beliefs at the center of our belief system. Beliefs on the periphery of our belief system are more easily discarded.[263] A full account of the confidence with which we hold our beliefs must therefore recognize the differing levels of our beliefs and their importance. We must also allow for different levels of willingness to revise our beliefs given their place in our belief system.

There are some beliefs that I can quite easily give up. For example, suppose the sun was shining on my way to work this morning. I may continue to believe the sun is still shining after being cooped up in a windowless office for several hours. Now suppose someone tells me that it is raining outside. I am quite willing to change my mind on this matter based simply on the report of a friend whom I have come to trust. This is a rather peripheral belief of mine and not much is at stake here. So I find it easy to be open-minded about this belief.

However, each of us also have some beliefs that we consider to be more important and which are therefore not easy to give up. For example, my belief in God as revealed in Jesus Christ is an essential part of my personal identity, so I am very hesitant to call it into question. Here it might seem that I am being closed-minded. But the question can and should still be raised, am I *willing* to change my mind about the existence of God as revealed in Jesus Christ? This is harder to assess. In fact, I can identify a set of circumstances in which I would be willing to give up my belief. With Paul, I say that if Christ has not been raised, then my faith is indeed futile (1 Cor 15:12–19). Of course, determining whether Christ was indeed raised from the dead is itself complicated by the fact that this is an historical event. Some readers might therefore say that this doesn't really help in determining whether I am willing to give up my belief in God and whether I am open-minded. But it does surely show that my belief is open to refutation. It is just difficult to do so.

HOW TO ACHIEVE AND MAINTAIN COMMITTED OPENNESS

There are some important practical questions that need to be considered about how to achieve and maintain committed openness.[264] When do persons who have the virtue of committed openness critically evaluate their beliefs? And which of their beliefs are they morally required to evaluate? I offer a suggestion and two analogies to help us answer these questions.

It is not easy for a person to determine when to remain firm and to decide which of his/her beliefs need to be reconsidered. Indeed, taking this task too seriously could send one to an early grave. On the other hand, it is all too easy to be complacent about these matters. We should after all have a love for knowledge and truth, and this requires a balance between commitment and openness. What is needed here is practical wisdom.

Austrian philosopher Otto Neurath (1882–1945) provides a useful analogy to illustrate the wisdom needed in reevaluating our beliefs.[265] He compares the evaluation and revision of beliefs to rebuilding or doing repairs on a ship while at sea. It would obviously be disastrous to take the ship apart entirely while at sea in order to rebuild or do a repair on it. Instead, we keep the ship afloat, repairing it part by part. Similarly, a person's belief system can and should only be critically assessed part by part. You have to go on living with the beliefs you have as you do this gradual rebuilding and repairing. Too much of an emphasis on openness, deconstruction, criticism, and doubt leads to the sinking of our epistemological ships. This analogy further underscores the fact that critical openness always takes place within a certain tradition. We simply cannot start from scratch.

Finally, a comment on reevaluating our basic beliefs and worldviews. Although we should be willing to do so—and from time to time we should actually do so—we must be careful not to be too demanding here, an error made by some writers.[266] It is simply impossible to thrive in a state where we are constantly reevaluating our basic beliefs and worldview. This would be comparable to having a gardener dig up a flowering plant every morning to see how it is doing.[267] We hold on to our basic convictions rather firmly, and there is nothing wrong in doing so. At the same time, we should from time to time ask ourselves if we would be willing to give up our basic beliefs if counter-evidence should arise.

PROPER CERTAINTY AND PROPER CRITICISM

I now want to apply the notion of committed openness to two areas that I believe need special attention in our day. There is much confusion about certainty and critical evaluation in the church today. Sometimes

Christians are too certain about the claims they make. And sometimes any expression of certainty is viewed as a sin. Sometimes Christians shy away from any kind of critical reflection. And sometimes openness and critical evaluation becomes distorted into a kind of hyper-criticism. What is needed is proper certainty and proper criticism. Here I am drawing on Lesslie Newbigin's concept of proper confidence, which can be seen as a synonym of the "committed openness" we have been considering in this chapter.[268]

First a bit of historical background. To understand contemporary attitudes towards certainty and doubt, we need to go back to French mathematician and philosopher René Descartes (1596–1650), who is generally considered to be the father of modern philosophy. It has been well said that "the tendrils of Descartes's influence are long and all-embracing, and reach through the centuries into our own age with smothering effect."[269] To understand Descartes we need to keep in mind that he lived through a tumultuous time in Europe. There was considerable political and social unrest combined with turmoil in the realm of ideas, with skeptics undermining the very possibility of knowledge. Hence, Descartes's desperate search for certainty.[270]

He begins his famous *Meditations* (1641) by acknowledging that, from his earliest years, he has accepted many false opinions as true. This prompts him to resolve:

> If I wished to have any firm and constant knowledge in the sciences, I would have to undertake, once and for all, to set aside all the opinions which I had previously accepted among my beliefs and start again from the very beginning.... I will therefore make a serious and unimpeded effort to destroy generally all my former opinions.[271]

After systematically doubting all his beliefs, Descartes discovers one truth that he considers to be absolutely certain, his famous, "I think, therefore I am."

Unfortunately for Descartes, his one certain truth is not quite as certain as he thought it was. And if this one supposed certainty is dubious, Descartes is left drowning in a sea of uncertainty, a possibility he himself describes in the second meditation. Indeed, there are problems with the goal of absolute certainty that drove Descartes's methodological doubt. Absolute certainty is not possible for finite and fallible human beings. It is also impossible to question or doubt everything. You simply can't start from scratch. As Michael Polanyi has argued, every expression of doubt is at one and the same time a statement of faith in something else.[272] Wittgenstein also reminded us that we can only doubt something if we have first been given something to doubt.[273] Indeed, as already noted, thinking and reasoning is always faith seeking understanding.

Sadly, Descartes is still too much with us today, also in the church. Although I believe the label "fundamentalism" is much abused in our day, there is still a core meaning that deserves our attention, and this has to do with the prevalence of dogmatic certainty in the church. Expressions of absolute certainty range from assuming an inerrant Bible to presuming that one can be absolutely certain about one's interpretation of the Bible.[274] Here we must be careful to avoid the error of thinking that dogmatic certainty applies only to conservative expressions of the Christian faith. There is also such a thing as liberal fundamentalism, found especially in the position taken by those with a liberal progressive theological orientation in their treatments of race and gender theory as well as their dogmatic critical approach to Scripture. There is desperate need for more humility on the part of those who take great pride in being liberal and progressive. I have attended both conservative and liberal churches and have found the intellectual atmosphere in both to be quite stifling at times. What is needed is a proper kind of certainty that is honest about the convictions held and at the same time open to having these convictions subjected to critical scrutiny.

While fundamentalism as I have defined it involves excessive certainty, there is another error of ruling out any certainty with regard to our Christian convictions. This error comes to the fore in a book written by Peter Enns with the bold title *The Sin of Certainty*.[275] In part Enns is concerned with exposing the problem of excessive certainty in the church today, and I have no quarrel with this. But I believe he goes too far in condemning any expressions of certainty. Nowhere in the Bible is certainty described as sin. Indeed, such a description is contrary to what the Bible teaches in many places, as I have already shown earlier in this chapter. Job sounds pretty confident when in the midst of his troubles he nevertheless declares, "I know that my Redeemer lives" (Job 19:25). And the writer of Hebrews describes faith as "being sure of what we hope for and certain of what we do not see" (Heb 11:1). Again, there is such a thing as a proper confidence, which expresses a degree of certainty while at the same time avoiding "the sin of excessive certainty," which would have been a better title for Peter Enns's book.

Peter Enns also illustrates how Descartes's preoccupation with doubt has influenced the church today. Enns spends a good deal of space in *The Sin of Certainty* and in his earlier book, *The Bible Tells Me So*, raising questions and doubts about the stories of the Bible.[276] Now as I have already argued, there is a legitimate place for criticism and critical openness with regard to our beliefs. But an emphasis on criticism must be balanced with an emphasis on commitment. Without this balance, criticism can be carried to an extreme, and we are left with the intellectual vice of hyper-criticism.

German philosopher Friedrich Nietzsche (1844–1900) followed Descartes in giving expression to the modern preoccupation with criticism and doubt. "One should not let oneself be misled: great intellects are skeptics. Zarathustra is a sceptic. The vigour of a mind, its *freedom* through strength and superior strength, is *proved* by scepticism. . . . Convictions are prisons."[277]

We need to stop here and take note of what is really being said by Descartes and Nietzsche. Convictions are prisons. Really? This is an expression of the same kind of hyper-criticism exemplified by Chesterton's friend who was "a permanent reactionary." We need convictions just to get by one day of ordinary living. Great intellects are skeptics. Really? This is not only practically impossible to live by, but it smacks of intellectual arrogance. Nietzsche drew with inescapable clarity the necessary conclusion of Descartes's method of doubt. All we are left with is the individual will to power. Proper confidence acknowledges the importance of convictions while at the same time allowing for the humble admission that we might be wrong, and therefore need to be open to reevaluating our convictions to see if they are in accordance with the truth.

Where do we find this vice of hyper-criticism today? We seem to revel in criticism. A fundamental aim of K–12 education is to teach students to be critical thinkers. Introductory logic courses at colleges and universities, often mandatory for various programs, specialize in critical thinking. In theology you have various critical approaches—feminist criticism, biblical criticism, historical criticism, form criticism, source criticism, and the list could go on. Why this preoccupation with the word "criticism"? It seems to be a badge of honor. There has also been a growing emphasis on "deconstruction" and questioning in our churches today. "Question-shaped faith" is the title of a provocative piece in a Canadian religious periodical.[278] Troy Watson, the author, is pastor of a church tellingly named "Quest Christian Community." "Questioning one's beliefs is also at the heart" of an innovative church which meets at a downtown hotel in Kitchener, Ontario, says Brad Watson, pastor of the Nexus Centre.[279] A video series used in some adult Sunday School classes in churches is suggestively entitled "Living the Questions."[280] There is even a hymn entitled "Ask the Complicated Questions" in the new Mennonite hymnal, *Voices Together*.[281] While there is something to be said for honestly facing questions, it is simply impossible to live by questioning only.

Lest I be misunderstood, let me say once more that I am not at all opposed to the raising of honest questions or an honest wrestling with doubts that Christians might be facing. Jesus himself was most sensitive to doubters like John the Baptist and "doubting Thomas" (Matt 11:1–19; John 20:24–31). What I am objecting to is an obsession with doubts and questions that is all too prevalent in our churches today. I am objecting to questioning for the sake of questioning. I am objecting to deconstruction without reconstruction. I am objecting to approaching the Bible with a hermeneutics of suspicion rather than a hermeneutics of humility and trust.[282] I am objecting to the sin of hyper-criticism. Here again what is needed is a proper kind of criticism that is an essential part of the virtue of proper confidence.

Let me conclude this section by giving one delightful expression of proper confidence and committed openness that I ran across recently in an insightful book by J. Todd Billings, *The End of the Christian Life: How Embracing Our Mortality Frees Us to Truly Live*. After a moving account of being diagnosed with an incurable cancer when he was thirty-nine years old, Billings describes the objective of his book as one of showing how life is lived among the dying. He then describes the Christian perspective from which he is writing:

> While I write as a committed Christian, like many others I feel the cross-pressures of identity as I approach death. With the church, I trust God's promise that death will not have the final word. But I do so with an awareness that we could be wrong. I also realize that many others follow different paths. In facing death, mortals face a mystery we cannot master. My approach to the cross-pressures and this humbling mystery is not to set my Christian convictions on the shelf but to live into them, trusting that truth is possessed first and foremost by God.[283]

Here you have a beautiful example of proper certainty and proper doubt. Billings clearly identifies the Christian convictions that he holds and from which he is writing. But then he adds a rather surprising note, "We could be wrong." This is what intellectual humility and proper confidence looks like for the Christian. Commitment is combined with openness. Personal testimony is combined with the acknowledgment that "others follow different paths." And so we continue to search for truth, "trusting that truth is possessed first and foremost by God."

I conclude with some summary statements that try to capture the central thrust of this chapter. Too tight a grip on our beliefs and we suffer from closed-mindedness. Too loose a grip on our beliefs and we are left wandering in the wilderness of indecision. Conviction without open-mindedness leads to dangerous dogmatism and fanaticism. Open-mindedness without conviction leads to rootlessness and relativism. We need to have the intellectual virtue of committed openness. Sadly, "we all have some convictions that are unsettled when they ought to be settled, and others that are settled when they ought to be unsettled."[284]

5

Intellectual Forbearance, Fairmindedness, and Intellectual Courage

Remind the people . . . to slander no one, to be peaceable and considerate, and to show true humility toward all men.

(TITUS 3:1–2)

But the wisdom that comes from heaven is first of all pure; then peace loving, considerate, submissive, full of mercy and good fruit, impartial and sincere.

(JAMES 3:17)

Before you complete the questionnaire that follows, give yourself a rating (0–10) on the virtues of intellectual forbearance (or tolerance), fairmindedness, and intellectual courage.

QUESTIONNAIRE: A SELF-EVALUATION

For each of the following statements, answer **yes**, **no**, or **unsure/maybe**.

1. I readily accept the fact that other people might disagree with me, even strongly, and I don't let this upset me.
2. I make it a practice to listen carefully to someone with whom I disagree, asking questions so that I can better understand that person, and I only respond after having carefully weighed what has been said.
3. I am dogged in the pursuit of truth, even in the face of established opinion in the church or in society at large.
4. I avoid making immediate comments to opinions and articles expressed on the internet, but wait a while before I write a response, in order to give myself time to reconsider and treat the position being expressed carefully and fairly.
5. I never disparage the intelligence of those I disagree with.
6. When disagreeing with someone, I always make it a point to distinguish between the person and the position being held, and I try to express my disagreement in such a way that the other person's dignity is upheld.
7. I am willing to speak truth to power, e.g., tell my boss that he or she is wrong about something.
8. I always go out of my way to construct the best version of someone else's views and arguments, even if they differ from my own.
9. When confronting a person about a contrary position, I am always careful to take into account this person's feelings, and therefore tread cautiously.
10. I am quite willing to hang on to my deeply held beliefs and convictions in the face of opposition and even ridicule, while at the same time being willing to reevaluate them if I hear good arguments against them.

> Now give a numerical value to each of your answers—**1 for yes; ½ for unsure/maybe; 0 for no**. Then total your numerical values. The total out of 10 gives the percentage grade for your having the virtues of intellectual forbearance (tolerance), fairmindedness, and intellectual courage.
>
> See the end of the questionnaire in chapter 2 for some additional comments about the validity of this exercise.

IN THE PREVIOUS CHAPTERS I have considered three intellectual virtues—the love of knowledge and truth, intellectual humility, and committed openness. These three virtues are often highlighted in the scholarly literature as the most important intellectual virtues. This is no doubt because they are more general in nature and thus more foundational than the intellectual virtues that I will consider in this chapter. I have also shown how the Bible has a lot to say about each of the intellectual virtues treated in the previous three chapters, again probably due to their general nature. For all these reasons I have devoted an entire chapter to each of them.

In this chapter I will consider three additional virtues—intellectual forbearance, fairmindedness, and intellectual courage. These three virtues are more specific in nature. The intellectual virtues treated in this chapter can also be seen as derivative from the more important and general virtues treated in the previous chapters. For example, the love of knowledge and truth needs intellectual courage to persevere in the face of social and political opposition to truth. Intellectual humility needs fairmindedness towards the views of other people to properly assess one's own view and perhaps discover that one might be wrong. Intellectual forbearance can be seen as one expression of committed openness. I need to put up with the beliefs of others despite my disagreement. Indeed, putting up with the beliefs of others and humbly trying to learn from them is a key to my growing in knowledge and truth.

Several other characteristics of the three virtues I am considering in this chapter should be noted. They all make explicit or implicit reference to other people and the beliefs held by other people. The virtues considered in the previous three chapters are more focused on the individual thinker. For example, the intellectually virtuous person is primarily concerned about reaching the truth or acquiring knowledge for himself or herself. The three virtues being considered in this chapter are more relational in nature. Intellectual forbearance makes reference to the beliefs of other people and requires that we somehow put up with them despite our disagreement. Fairmindedness involves being fair about the views held by another person. Intellectual courage is required when facing opposition to what one believes.

This distinction between intellectual virtues that are more focused on the individual thinker versus those that are more relational or "community-related" is somewhat arbitrary.[285] All the intellectual virtues can be treated as both individual and relational. For example, the love of knowledge and truth need not be thought of as referring only to the individual. Surely, a community as a whole can be described as having the virtue of loving knowledge and truth. The love of knowledge of individuals can also be seen as benefiting the community. I have treated open-mindedness or committed openness as characterizing an individual person. But it has a relational element to it as well in that we need to be open to the ideas of others. So perhaps it is better to think of all the intellectual virtues as having both a personal and communal dimension. Indeed, some writers have complained about intellectual virtue theory being too focused on the individual.[286] However, I still maintain that some intellectual virtues are more easily described as relational in nature.

There is even more to be said about the relational dimension of the three intellectual virtues being considered in this chapter. The relational component is oppositional in nature. These three intellectual virtues all have to do with how we relate to other persons who disagree with us. Intellectual forbearance requires that I somehow put up with the beliefs of another person even though I may strongly disagree with him or her. Fairmindedness requires that I treat my opponent's beliefs fairly. Intellectual courage is needed in the face of strong opposition to the ideas one holds and expresses. I have chosen to focus on these three relational/oppositional intellectual virtues because they are so necessary for our contemporary world and its growing polarizations, about which I will say more in the concluding chapter.

It should be obvious that I am not covering all the intellectual virtues and vices in this and the previous chapters. My purpose in this book is not to provide an exhaustive analysis of all the intellectual virtues and vices. Besides, there are any number of different lists of intellectual virtues and vices in the scholarly literature. So, there is some arbitrariness in choosing which virtues to deal with. It should also be noted that one often finds overlaps in lists of intellectual virtues. For example, intellectual fair-mindedness is sometimes distinguished from intellectual justice, but surely there is considerable overlap in these two virtues.[287] Intellectual perseverance is sometimes listed as a separate intellectual virtue, but my treatments of the love of knowledge and intellectual courage already touch on perseverance. My aim in this book is to limit myself to a study of those intellectual virtues and vices that I consider to be very important and especially relevant for our time.

INTELLECTUAL FORBEARANCE

Paul was in Athens, waiting for his companions Silas and Timothy to arrive. Never one to waste time, he explored the city and "was greatly distressed to see that the city was full of idols" (Acts 17:16). This prompted his passion for evangelism. "So he reasoned in the synagogue with the Jews and the God-fearing Greeks, as well as in the marketplace day by day with those who happened to be there" (v. 17). Some listeners argued with him while others wanted to hear more from him. This should not be surprising because the Athenians, we are told, "spent their time doing nothing but talking about and listening to the latest ideas" (v. 21). Paul, it would seem, enjoyed this intellectual environment and used it as a missionary opportunity.

How does Paul engage with the curious as well as those opposed to his reasoning? He practices intellectual forbearance. He reports on what he has observed about their religiosity, their many "objects of worship," including "an altar with this inscription: TO AN UNKNOWN GOD" (v. 23). And then this segue: "Now what you worship as something unknown I am going to proclaim to you" (v. 23). This is what intellectual forbearance looks like. Paul speaks respectfully about Athenian religiosity and even tries to link his message to their religion and to their poets (v. 28). Indeed, as he gives a summary of Christian beliefs, he describes God as practicing forbearance, having "overlooked" the ignorance of the past (v. 30). But this does not stop Paul from being very clear about God's demands, calling on people to escape judgment by repenting and believing in Jesus whom God raised from the dead (vv. 30–31).

The notion of forbearance is rather foreign to the modern ear. A related concept that we are more familiar with is that of tolerance. Both the concept of forbearance and the concept of tolerance have a broader meaning which I have dealt with elsewhere.[288] Here I am limiting myself to *intellectual* forbearance and *intellectual* tolerance. The focus is on tolerating foreign ideas. Intellectual forbearance is not usually included in the scholarly literature on intellectual virtues. Neither is the notion of intellectual tolerance. I think this is unfortunate because I believe intellectual tolerance is a very important virtue for our time. But I prefer the label "intellectual forbearance" for the virtue under consideration in this chapter.

Why my hesitancy in using the label "intellectual tolerance"? Because I believe the contemporary liberal notion of tolerance has been stretched beyond recognition. The traditional concept of tolerance meant only to endure, to put up with (from the Latin *tolerare*)—nothing more than that. It did not mean one had to like something. It meant putting up with something you dislike. Indeed, the need for tolerance arises precisely because one doesn't like the other person's attitudes, behavior, or ideas. Despite our dislike for another person's ideas, we tolerate them because there is some other priority that we consider more important. We believe respect for persons is more important than fighting over a disagreement about ideas. This does not mean that truth is not important. It has been well said that error has no rights, but people do. That is why we endure or put up with ideas that we do not like.

Today, however, this notion of putting up with what one dislikes is condescendingly spoken of as *mere tolerance,* and it is not seen as good enough. Today a further demand is made of the tolerant person, namely the requirement of fully accepting and even agreeing with what is different. Indeed, to disagree with someone is to be intolerant. The preferred substitute for tolerance today is mutual acceptance of each other's ideas as equally valid. In other words, tolerance is equated with relativism. All beliefs are seen to be equally valid, and therefore any criticism of someone's belief makes you intolerant.

There are several problems with this reduction of tolerance to a relativistic acceptance of all ideas. First, there are difficulties surrounding relativism itself. The basic problem with epistemological relativism is that it is inconsistent, and those adhering to this doctrine invariably contradict themselves. While claiming that there is no truth, they are themselves saying that they have the truth. Second, to equate tolerance with relativism is itself intolerant and makes genuine dialogue with people impossible.

Third, the reduction of tolerance to relativism undercuts the very need for tolerance. We no longer need to put up with beliefs with which we disagree because there is nothing we can disagree with. All beliefs are true. So, one of the leading moral ideals of liberalism is itself undermined.

I therefore suggest that what we need is the old-fashioned notion of tolerance understood as "forbearance"—putting up with beliefs with which we disagree. This does not preclude criticism of these beliefs. But such criticism must be done respectfully. Forbearance requires that you suppress your "gag reflex" when you encounter someone whose ideas you find repugnant.[289] Above all, *the people holding beliefs* with which we disagree must be treated with love and respect. So rather than using the notion of tolerance which is all too easily misconceived and misapplied, I am going to refer to intellectual forbearance as an intellectual virtue in this chapter. Although the term "forbearance" might sound somewhat antiquated, I am attracted to it because it helps to distinguish it from distortions of the notion of tolerance, and, as I will show shortly, there are also biblical reasons for using the term.

DEFINITION OF INTELLECTUAL FORBEARANCE

Intellectual forbearance is the disposition to treat persons holding beliefs differing from one's own with love and respect. It entails that we endure or put up with someone's holding and expressing beliefs we consider to be inferior to one's own.

There are several ingredients in this definition that need to be highlighted. First, it is important to note that the concept of intellectual forbearance assumes that there are people who have beliefs and convictions that differ from our own. Disagreement is taken seriously. This of course raises the question as to what one does with those who disagree with us. Do we destroy them, or do we put up with them? Do we allow them to express their "mistaken" ideas, or do we silence them? Intellectual forbearance requires that we allow others to express their ideas even though we think they are wrong.

Another key ingredient of intellectual forbearance is that it requires that we distinguish between beliefs and the believer. Intellectual forbearance requires that we respect persons even if we disagree with their beliefs. This allows us to evaluate the opinions and beliefs of another person in abstraction from the person holding them. Of course, this will require that the recipient of our criticisms of his or her beliefs will also need to be careful not to take criticisms personally. This will be made easier if the person making the critique pays attention to how he or she makes the criticisms. Criticisms must be made in such a way that the other person's dignity is not undermined. At the same time, intellectual forbearance requires that the other person has to put up with the critic's beliefs. Forbearance is a mutual affair.

This leads to another feature of intellectual forbearance. We must not only respect persons holding wrong beliefs, we must also treat the beliefs themselves with some respect. This does not preclude disagreeing with these beliefs. But our expression of disagreement must be done in such a way that is civil and courteous. We must avoid the use of insulting and abusive language when describing beliefs we disagree with. This will preclude inflammatory language, flippant name-calling, ridicule, hostile denigration, and the misrepresentation of the other's beliefs. The misrepresentation of beliefs held by other people is so important that it deserves treatment as a separate intellectual virtue—see the next section.

I give one negative and one positive example of this dimension of intellectual forbearance. Sadly, after the terrorist attacks on the World Trade Center in New York on September 11, 2001, some Christian evangelical leaders were at the forefront of using inflammatory language against the Islamic faith. For example, Franklin Graham is quoted as having said that Islam is "a very evil and wicked religion."[290] Not only is this an unfair generalization but it exemplifies intolerance and the lack of intellectual forbearance.

How very different from the story of the apostle Paul which we considered at the beginning of this section. Paul spoke respectfully and even tried to link his message to the religion of the Athenians (Acts 17:16–34). Paul's forbearance of other religions is confirmed again later in Ephesus after he and his associates are threatened by a mob, incited by tradesmen who saw their economic interests undermined by the proclamation of the Christian gospel. The city clerk, after quieting the crowd and tactfully acknowledging the importance of the temple of Artemis, reminds them that Paul and his associates "have neither robbed temples nor blasphemed our goddess" (Acts 19:37). That is quite a testimonial to the intellectual forbearance of Paul. Indeed, the city clerk goes on to challenge the citizens of Ephesus to practice intellectual forbearance, as there "is no reason" for creating a public disturbance over someone who, while preaching another religion, is nevertheless respectful of the prevailing religion (v. 40).

Again, I want to stress that what intellectual forbearance does not preclude is the careful, patient, and respectful labeling of another person's beliefs as false. Indeed, exposure of error can be an expression of care and concern for the other person. Criticism can be a way of honoring someone whose beliefs we think are wrong.[291] But such criticism must be expressed in such a way that the other person's dignity is upheld.

BIBLICAL JUSTIFICATION OF INTELLECTUAL FORBEARANCE

A biblical justification of intellectual forbearance must start with the character of God. James Davis highlights one aspect of the character of God in a recent book with the colorful and timely title *Disagreement: A Theological Ethics for a Disagreeable Church*. Davis reminds us of God's forbearance. God is frequently described as being longsuffering, a term that is close in meaning to forbearance. Whenever God is described as longsuffering in the Old Testament, it is almost always in association with his gracious and merciful character towards sinful and rebellious people.[292] The apostle Paul, too, describes God as longsuffering (*makrothymia*), which is rendered as "tolerant" or "forbearing" in some translations. God restrains his anger in the face of provocation because he is rich in kindness, forbearance, and patience (Rom 2:4; 3:25; 9:22).

In the Sermon on the Mount, Jesus calls us to reflect God's character in loving our enemies, and this would surely include loving our ideological enemies (Matt 5:43–48). Interestingly, in giving this challenge, Jesus reminds us that God "causes his sun to rise on the evil and the good, and sends rain on the righteous and the unrighteous" (v. 45). And then this challenge: "Be perfect, therefore, as your heavenly Father is perfect" (v. 48). Paul, too, challenges us to love our enemies and to do all that we can to "live at peace with everyone" (Rom 12:17–21). Intellectual forbearance is a disposition to love and bless those who disagree with us.

Jeffrey Bilbro draws attention to another justification of forbearance based on the sovereignty of God.[293] He tells the story of Blaise Pascal, a Christian philosopher and mathematician, who in the mid-seventeenth century wrote a letter to his brother-in-law. Pascal's brother-in-law had written him about a political controversy in which he was involved and asked for his advice. Pascal replied by outlining a view of Providence as guiding not only Christian efforts but also those of our opponents: "The same Providence that has inspired some with light, has refused it to others."[294] This would suggest that God not only allows Christians to have the "right" perspective on issues but also allows others to have the "wrong" perspective on these same issues. This leads Pascal to argue for a kind of equanimity with regard to opposition that we face about our convictions on political matters. This equanimity is rooted in two convictions: a confidence that God is in control and a humility about our own ability to discern the workings of Providence in political affairs. At the very least this should cause us to cultivate and practice the virtue of intellectual forbearance when we face people who disagree with us.

This conclusion is reinforced by looking at God's judgment on the Tower of Babel (Gen 11:1–9). The story begins with the claim that "the whole world had one language and a common speech" (v. 1). The people then resolve to build a city and a tower that reaches to the heavens and would make a name for themselves so that they would "not be scattered over the face of the whole earth" (v. 4). God intervenes and confuses their language "so they will not understand each other" and he also scatters them "over all the earth" (vv. 7–8). This was God's judgment on "the primeval climax of collective human pride and folly," an enforced unity of language and culture, and "a religious ideology of empire."[295] From now on understanding others will require effort, humility, careful listening to others, and intellectual forbearance.

The above reference to humility leads to another justification of forbearance based on a biblical understanding of human nature. We are finite beings with a limited understanding not only of God but of everything. We always see and understand reality from our particular vantage point. Given this limited perspective, we must therefore practice intellectual forbearance with regard to the perspectives of others.[296] Indeed, we might even have something to learn from them. Truth is best discovered in community, with each person sharing his or her perspective and learning from the perspectives of others. Truth is best discovered within the context of everyone cultivating intellectual forbearance.

The ideal of intellectual forbearance is of course also rooted in one of the foundational biblical guidelines for ethics, namely treating people with dignity. This is surely implicit in the Great Commandment found in both the Old and New Testaments.[297] What does it mean to love our neighbors as we love ourselves in the realm of ideas? And what about the Golden Rule (Matt 7:12)? If we want others to treat our ideas with respect, we had better do the same with regard to their ideas.

A study of Scripture will reveal many other implicit references to the importance of intellectual forbearance. In the book of Proverbs, patience is frequently advocated as having practical value in the avoidance of strife and the wise ordering of human affairs, particularly where provocation is involved.[298] Paul's description of the fruits of the Spirit include love, joy, peace, forbearance (patience), and kindness (Gal 5:22). Notice especially the close link between kindness, patience, and forbearance. In Colossians Paul explicitly advocates forbearance in our interactions outside of the church: "Let your conversation be always full of grace, seasoned with salt, so that you may know how to answer everyone" (Col 4:6; cf. Titus 3:2). Then there are repeated exhortations to be gentle or considerate in our exchanges with outsiders.[299] Gentleness is surely part of intellectual forbearance.

Jesus and the apostles exemplified the virtue of intellectual forbearance. They lived in a religiously pluralistic environment, a point that is all too often forgotten today.[300] And it is within this religiously pluralistic environment that they conversed with others, disagreed with others, but always "speaking the truth with love," a phrase that Paul uses within the context of the church but is surely also applicable to disagreement with those outside of the church (Eph 4:15). Peter, too, exhorts us to "show proper respect to everyone," an exhortation that is found in the middle of an epistle that encourages Christians to respond to hostility with love and gentleness when defending their faith (1 Pet 2:17; 3:15–16).

LIMITS OF INTELLECTUAL FORBEARANCE

Are there limits to tolerance and forbearance? Are there limits to intellectual forbearance? This is an important question that is all too often ignored in discussions of the liberal ideal of tolerance. Here it is important to keep in mind that there are several components to my earlier definition of intellectual forbearance. My definition refers to both *persons* holding beliefs differing from one's own and to the *beliefs* themselves. Intellectual forbearance also makes reference to both the holding and expressing of contrary beliefs.

It should be fairly obvious that there are no limits to treating persons with love and respect. And that includes persons who hold beliefs that differ from our own. Persons need to be treated with dignity regardless of their beliefs. Loving and respecting persons also entails that we listen to them, that we pay attention to their contrary ideas. But even here there will be limits to the amount of time a person wants to spend listening to ideas that go contrary to his or her own beliefs. We are finite and limited beings and only have a limited amount of time for listening and reading. And clearly a person will want to spend more time reading and listening to ideas that are in keeping with his or her own belief system. But in the normal exchanges of life, there will be opportunity and a requirement to listen to the ideas of other persons.

It should further be fairly obvious that we can't put up with just everything in terms of the behavior and beliefs of others. Some behavior and some beliefs are so abhorrent that we need to limit their expression. We don't put up with murder or child abuse or sexual exploitation, for example. But what about limits to putting up with abhorrent beliefs? For example, should we put up with hate speech? Answering this question is more difficult and has been fraught with controversy, as I have pointed out elsewhere.[301] I will make only a few further suggestions here by way of examining some related concepts and providing some illustrations of necessary and unnecessary limits to intellectual forbearance.

The concept of hospitality has sometimes been proposed as capturing what I have labeled as intellectual forbearance, though it gives this virtue a more positive spin. Hospitality is classically understood as welcoming the stranger and caring for their needs, a virtue that is frequently applauded in the Scriptures.[302] Cherie Harder takes this ordinary notion of hospitality and extends it to include the welcoming of new perspectives and new ideas.[303] There is clearly something right about extending the ordinary notion of hospitality to include intellectual hospitality. We ought to put up with and even welcome the ideas of intellectual strangers.

There are, however, a number of problems with the ideal of intellectual hospitality. For one, the notion of hospitality presupposes that there is a home to which I can welcome the stranger. A home is a place of permanence, a dwelling place, a storied place with memories, a safe resting place, and a place of affiliation and belonging.[304] And while a home can and should be open to strangers, there are surely some limits here. Strangers can only be welcomed into a home if in fact there is a secure and safe resting place for the family. If you let in too many strangers, you no longer have a home from which to practice the virtue of hospitality.

This has important implications for intellectual hospitality. I can only welcome the ideas of a stranger if in fact I have an intellectual home. If I welcome too many strangers into my intellectual home, it will no longer be a home for me and will therefore undermine my ability to be intellectually hospitable. There are, therefore, some necessary boundaries to intellectual hospitality. For example, if my intellectual home involves belief and trust in God as revealed in Jesus Christ, I really can't fully welcome the ideas of an atheist into my intellectual home. I can certainly entertain the intellectual stranger and have a friendly dialogue, but it would be asking too much to welcome the ideas of the atheist into my intellectual home. This is surely behind the advice that John gives about false teachers who do not acknowledge Jesus Christ as coming in the flesh: "If anyone comes to you and does not bring this teaching, do not take him into your house or welcome him" (2 John 10). John is here highlighting the limits to intellectual hospitality and forbearance. More on this later.

Another problem with the notion of intellectual hospitality as an ideal is that all too often it is understood as precluding disagreement, debate, and persuasion.[305] Here we are back to the problematic doctrine of epistemological relativism, where all ideas are treated as equally valid. I have already given my reasons for objecting to relativism, so I won't say more here. Given these difficulties with the ideal of intellectual hospitality, I prefer the language of intellectual forbearance, which can accommodate what is right about hospitality but allows for disagreement and criticism.

There is another way in which the central thrust of intellectual forbearance gets distorted in our day, namely by an emphasis on creating safe spaces for people to express their ideas. Again, there is certainly something right about the need to create an environment where people feel free to give expression to ideas that not all will agree with. But all too often, creating a safe space is understood to mean that one cannot express any disagreement with what is being said.

The author experienced a sad example of this in a church that he attended. A number of people in the church were very upset about a lengthy article that had been carried in a denominational paper articulating a conservative viewpoint with regard to homosexuality and gay marriage. The pastor arranged for a meeting for those who might have been wounded and/or upset by this article. The meeting was described as providing a time of sharing, venting, and contemplating. The announcement went on to say that this meeting was not an occasion for debate. Instead, it was a gathering for those who supported a welcoming and inclusive church and for those who wanted to listen. It was very clear from the notice of this meeting that there would be no room for disagreement and debate. Critics were silenced in the name of creating a safe space for those who held to the established view in this church. This is a failure in intellectual forbearance. Perhaps it would be well for all of us to develop a thicker skin so controversial issues can be discussed and debated. And let's not forget Jesus' encouragement to forgive those who hurt us.

This same problem exists in our college and university campuses. Greg Lukianoff and Jonathan Haidt, in *The Coddling of the American Mind*, describe the recent emergence and rapid spread on our campuses of what they call "safetyism." They use the word "safetyism" to label the tendency of students today to equate emotional discomfort with physical danger. Safetyism, they write, teaches students "to see words as violence and to interpret ideas and speakers as safe versus dangerous, rather than merely true versus false."[306] Confronted with words or ideas they dislike, a growing number of students claim they are in danger of suffering psychological or even bodily harm.

Another expression of safetyism is the growing practice of giving trigger warnings on articles and books that might upset students at colleges and universities. For example, early in 2023 Scottish papers reported that the University of Aberdeen had slapped a trigger warning on J. M. Barrie's *Peter Pan*, a classic children's novel about a place where nobody ever grows up.[307] The reason: the book's "odd perspectives on gender" may prove "emotionally challenging" to some adult undergraduates. Other books that came with an advisory at the University of Aberdeen include Robert Louis Stevenson's *Treasure Island*, Edith Nesbit's *The Railway Children*, and C. S. Lewis's *The Lion, the Witch and the Wardrobe*.

This rapidly growing trend is troubling for a number of reasons. For one, there are several studies showing that trigger warnings do not alleviate emotional distress. On the contrary, some research has found that trigger warnings actually increase the anxiety of individuals with severe PTSD, prompting them to "view trauma as more central to their life narrative."[308] Further, this practice undermines the purpose of literature, which is to help us understand both the heights and the depths of human nature. It also infantilizes students by treating them as fragile creatures, when universities should be helping them to mature. More significantly for my purposes, putting trigger warnings on books involves a failure in intellectual forbearance. Universities should be places where ideas can and should be freely explored. Sadly, today, trigger warnings at universities are only one example of the failure to put up with ideas that are not in keeping with current fads of political correctness and wokeness.

More generally, in society at large, we seem to be running into the limits of what we are willing to put up with more and more often, over an ever-widening range of issues. We have difficulties debating topics like abortion, LGBTQ+ issues, and racism because these issues are too controversial. And yet, these are surely issues that need to be discussed in the public square. As Alan Jacobs notes, "This matters because it's when our forbearance fails that the social fabric tears."[309] The growing polarizations in our societies are due to the lack of intellectual forbearance.

Here I would refer the reader to John Stuart Mill's classic defense of liberty of thought and expression.[310] He urges us to allow others to speak and then to listen to them for three main reasons. First, the other person's idea, however controversial it seems today, might turn out to be right. ("The opinion . . . may possibly be true.") Second, even if our opinion is largely correct, we will hold it more rationally and securely as a result of its being challenged. ("He who knows only his own side of the case, knows little of that.") Third, opposing views may each contain a portion of the truth, which need to be combined. ("Conflicting doctrines . . . share the truth between them.") More recently, John Inazu has argued for a "confident pluralism" which accepts the fact of pluralism while at the same time calling for the cultivation and practice of virtues of tolerance (forbearance), patience, and humility.[311] Inazu wisely maintains that it is possible to be confident in our own beliefs even as we engage in a world of deep differences.

Of course, once again, the hard question arises. Are there any limits to what we should put up with in the expression of ideas in the public realm? I believe there are some occasions—for example, when a society faces a health crisis. Here it might be justified in the short term to engage in silencing misinformation that can cause serious and extensive harm. But these restrictions of intellectual forbearance should be kept to a minimum. Of course, much more could be said on this, but this is far beyond the scope of this chapter.

Some final comments about the limits of intellectual forbearance in the church. A study of the New Testament will reveal that while there is a place for intellectual forbearance in the church, there are also limits to such forbearance because the church is a confessional community. In Ephesians Paul calls for patience and forbearance in maintaining unity in the church: "Be completely humble and gentle; be patient, bearing with one another in love" (Eph 4:2). But this admonition is immediately followed by a reminder that there is "one Lord, one faith, one baptism; one God and Father of all" (v. 5). It would seem that forbearance has doctrinal limits.

A similar juxtaposition is found in Colossians. After Paul has countered wrong teachings about Christ and the Christian life, he nonetheless reminds the church to practice forbearance by putting on the character of Christ. The call to "bear with each other" (*anecho*) is rooted in Christian virtues of compassion, kindness, humility, patience, and love (Col 3:12–14). But we must not forget that this call to forbearance is coupled with a very clear denunciation of false teaching in the church. "See to it that no one takes you captive through hollow and deceptive philosophy" (Col 2:8). Don't lose "connection with the Head" (2:19).

This is reinforced by Paul's instructions to young Titus regarding his work of appointing elders or overseers in churches. An overseer "must hold firmly to the trustworthy message as it has been taught, so that he can encourage others by sound doctrine and refute those who oppose it" (Titus 1:9). Titus is told to "encourage and rebuke with all authority" (2:15). And divisive persons who are obsessed with "foolish debates" are to be warned twice after which "have nothing to do with him" (3:10). There are many other passages of Scripture that give us similar instructions.[312]

It is again far beyond the scope of this chapter to sort out the question of limits to forbearance in the church. I believe that ultimately there have to be some doctrinal limits to forbearance in the church, at least for preachers and teachers in the church. But where these limits are to be drawn and how these limits are enforced are questions that I believe deserve much more attention in the church today. What is significant is that calls for maintaining orthodoxy and calls for intellectual forbearance in the church are often coupled with a reminder of the importance of Christian character. Be humble and patient and kind and compassionate, even as you counter false teachings. Perhaps Paul's words to the Philippians have something else to teach us about this dilemma. After a reminder that "all of us who are mature" should hold to a certain point of view, Paul goes on to say, "If on some point you think differently, that too God will make clear to you" (Phil 3:15). Perhaps trust in God is a key to forbearance in the church.

We have seen that intellectual forbearance is a complex virtue. While there is certainly a need for putting up with ideas that we disagree with, there are limits to forbearance. These limits vary with context. In some cases we might err on the side of too many limits, and in other cases we might err on the side of too few limits. What does not vary, however, is the need to respect the persons with whom we disagree. Even their ideas need to be treated with respect, though this does not rule out disagreement, debate, and persuasion.

FAIRMINDEDNESS

Alan Jacobs gives an illuminating, double-pronged example of the importance of fair-mindedness. Jacobs, himself a Christian in the Anglican tradition, introduces this example by commenting on how Anglicans have been "a combustibly angry tribe" for the past fifteen years or so, largely due to issues surrounding homosexuality. He describes an Anglican blog in which Rowan Williams, then Archbishop of Canterbury, was vilified. "The writer argued that not only was Williams largely to blame for the rise of pro-homosexual views within the Anglican world but also he took these unacceptably antibiblical positions on sexuality because he didn't believe in the Bible at all, held no orthodox theological positions, and may not even have believed in God."[313]

Upon first reading this blog, Jacobs considered these charges to be an outrageous violation of fairmindedness and began to write a response in which he defended Williams's orthodoxy even though he had some concerns about Williams's theology of sexuality. But in hammering out his response, Jacobs realized that he was constructing a terribly unfair characterization of the writer's bad logic and bad faith. In the midst of constructing his assault on his opponent's position and character, Jacobs paused. And then after pausing a little, he deleted his angry and unfair response to the unfair argument given by the critic of Rowan Williams. Jacobs concludes: "And I have not commented on an Anglican blog since."

I am limiting my discussion to a narrow definition of fairmindedness which is quite straightforward and about which I will therefore have less to say. **Definition: Fairmindedness** is a disposition to understand and represent positions different from one's own in a fair and even-handed way.[314] Again, we are dealing with an intellectual virtue that is relational in nature and arises in contexts where there are strongly opposing voices. Nathan King illustrates by referring to the internet jungle, where vicious attacks can come from the Right and the Left. Those defending liberal causes are labeled "snowflakes," "social justice warriors," "communists," "loons," or "hippies." And those who articulate and defend conservative causes are dubbed "wingnuts," "racists," "sexists," and "bigots."[315] These labels are not only unfair but also involve *ad hominem* attacks on persons.

The need for fairmindedness arises because we often find ourselves disagreeing with others. Indeed, with serious disagreements we are tempted to see others as our intellectual enemies. And when this happens we are tempted to misrepresent our enemies' viewpoints, often starting with some name-calling. We are also tempted to be unfair in the way in which we evaluate conflicting viewpoints—we apply a relatively lax set of criteria or standards to views that we agree with, but apply a different and more demanding set of standards to views that we strongly disagree with.[316] Of course, this isn't fair, and hence again the need for fairmindedness. And where someone has a personal stake in the views or explanations being considered, then one will also need the related intellectual virtues of impartiality, open-mindedness, and intellectual empathy.

Intellectual empathy involves "a willingness and ability to view things from the standpoint of the other person, to get inside another's head."[317] Here some contemporary exercises might help us to understand what is needed. During and after the Trump presidency, there have been many Americans who have had a lot of trouble being empathetic and trying to think inside the head of an evangelical supporter of Donald Trump. These people simply can't understand the Trump supporter, and this has led to personal attacks and misrepresentations of their opponents' viewpoints. Maybe, just maybe, evangelical supporters have some legitimate concerns about the liberal left establishment.

In Canada we had the infamous "Freedom Convoy" in the winter of 2022, which converged on Parliament Hill in our capital city of Ottawa. Although the presence of a large convoy of trucks with horns blaring loudly much of the time was a nuisance, and although there were some expressions of a lack of intellectual forbearance and fairmindedness on the part of the truckers who occupied the streets of Ottawa for three weeks, the protesters were remarkably restrained in what they said. What I found most disquieting was Prime Minister Trudeau's treatment of the truckers. Before the first anti-mandate protesters had even rolled into the capital, Trudeau was branding the protest as a "fringe" and "unacceptable" minority with whom he refused to meet. Following the convoy's arrival in Ottawa, Trudeau stayed the course, saying he was "disgusted" with the demonstrators, whom he charged with being in the thrall of "conspiracy theories."³¹⁸ There were in fact some legitimate grievances of the truckers, and they also raised some legitimate concerns about vaccine mandates. It is simply unfair to ignore these or misrepresent them. And to make the generalization that all the protestors adhere to conspiracy theories is terribly unfair. And of course, this does not display forbearance and does nothing to foster understanding and the search for truth.

BIBLICAL JUSTIFICATION FOR FAIRMINDEDNESS

There are a number of biblical principles that can be extrapolated to apply to the intellectual virtue of fairmindedness. For example, the Golden Rule: "In everything do to others what you would have them do to you, for this sums up the Law and the Prophets" (Matt 7:12). In other words, treat the ideas of your opponents as you would like your own ideas treated. We want others to treat our own ideas fairly and so we should do the same with ideas that we disagree with. Then there is the principle of justice that runs throughout the Scriptures. For example, Micah summarizes what God requires of us: "To act justly and to love mercy and to walk humbly with your God" (Mic 6:8). Epistemologically, this means that we treat the ideas of others justly, that we extend generosity to those we disagree with, and that we exercise intellectual humility as we interact with people who have opposing viewpoints.

FAILURES IN FAIRMINDEDNESS AND HOW TO OVERCOME THEM

There are a number of ways in which we can fail to be fair-minded. As already suggested, we can ignore or misrepresent the real concerns of people we disagree with. We can make hasty generalizations which are unfair. How often, for example, have I heard that believing in the ideal of truth leads to narrow dogmatism, conflicts, and even open warfare. Prove! And then there are the generalizations about the risks inherent in evangelistic activities—"the risk of promoting social disunity, hatred, bitterness and conditions of barbarism."³¹⁹ Prove! Christians can also be selective in their reading of the Bible in order to support a position they hold. Then there are unfair reviews of articles and books. I have had one review of my own work where I wondered whether the reviewer had even read what I had written, given that he completely misinterpreted the overall aim of my book.

Alan Jacobs coins the expression "in-other-wordsing" to describe another example of not being fair-minded.[320] It happens every day, says Jacobs. Someone points to a blog post or an op-ed column and then someone else replies, "In other words, you're saying . . ." And often, when the argument is put in these other words it is revealed to be quite unsound and even silly. Of course, it is quite possible to restate someone's argument fairly, and this is what we should do. But all too often the other words people use to summarize an opponent's argument grossly distort what was said and are therefore easy to attack. This violates fairmindedness.

Closely related is the straw man fallacy. Here one sets up an argument that no one really holds but is easy to refute. Refuting an obviously silly straw man argument is easier than refuting the argument that is actually held by the opposing side. The result is that the argument of straw goes up in flames, but the real argument remains intact. Again, this is not fair. It involves treating your opponent unjustly, and God is not pleased.

I have already provided two examples of the straw man fallacy in my earlier description of Alan Jacobs's response to a blog attacking Rowan Williams, who was then archbishop of Canterbury. I draw special attention here to Jacobs's pausing in the midst of constructing his assault on his opponent's position and character. The pause was significant, in that it highlights one of a number of suggestions Jacobs makes about ways in which to achieve fairmindedness.

When we find ourselves upset and even angry about the position held and defended by someone, we need to follow what Jacobs calls a "give it five minutes" rule.[321] It is all too easy to move immediately into "Refutation Mode" without trying to understand our opponent's viewpoint and argument. Indeed, all too often we are not even listening to what is being said but are already formulating our rebuttal.[322] And when we don't pay close attention to what is being said, we are very likely to misrepresent the position and the argument being put forth by our opponent. The result is an injustice. It is also a violation of the Golden Rule that Jesus taught us, because we certainly don't like to have our own viewpoints distorted.

The "give it five minutes" rule needs to be applied, especially on the internet. Sadly, given the impersonality of the internet, the temptation is to write a quick response to something we disagree with. And all too often these comments are rather nasty. How much better to wait a few minutes to let our visceral reaction cool down a bit before we type a response.

Better still, to follow Jacobs's own example when, after pausing a little, he deleted his angry response to the straw man created by the critic of Rowan Williams and then vowed not to comment on Anglican blogs again.

Jacobs makes a second suggestion to help us achieve fairmindedness. He describes a unique approach to formal debates which has been adopted by some debating societies.[323] Before a debater can present a counter-argument to his opponent's argument, he must first summarize his opponent's argument, and only if his opponent agrees that he has given a fair summary of the argument is he allowed to proceed. I would like to see this approach extended beyond the debating context. When we strongly disagree with someone, it might be well for us to first summarize our opponent's argument and then ask our opponent whether we are treating his or her argument fairly. And only when our opponent agrees with our summary should we proceed.

Finally, I propose a "neighbor rule" to help us to be fair-minded. We need to see those we disagree with as neighbors rather than enemies. The Great Commandment of Jesus tells us to love our neighbors as ourselves (Matt 22:38). Jesus extends this principle to include loving our enemies (Matt 5:43). This would surely entail that we also love our ideological enemies. Paul calls on the Lord's servants to correct opponents with gentleness (2 Tim 2:25). So, love, gentleness, and fairmindedness belong together. Rules are not enough. We need to move beyond rules to moral and intellectual virtues. We need to cultivate the disposition of fairmindedness.

INTELLECTUAL COURAGE

One cannot help but feel a little sorry for Jeremiah, appointed by the Sovereign LORD, even before he was born, to be a prophet to the nations (Jer 1:4–5). Jeremiah tries to escape this appointment by giving excuses, but to no avail. Instead, the Lord responds with a direct challenge to be courageous. "You must go to everyone I send you to and say whatever I command you. Do not be afraid of them, for I am with you and will rescue you" (Jer 1:7–8). After a brief overview of the message of judgment that Jeremiah is to proclaim, the challenge to be intellectually courageous becomes even more specific.

> "Get yourself ready! Stand up and say to them whatever I command you. Do not be terrified by them, or I will terrify you before them. Today I have made you a fortified city, an iron pillar and a bronze wall to stand against the whole land—against the

kings of Judah, its officials, its priests and the people of the land. They will fight against you but will not overcome you, for I am with you and will rescue you," declares the LORD. (Jer 1:17–19)

Jeremiah is faithful to this demanding commission, though at one point he bemoans his birth and the fact that he has become "a man with whom the whole land strives and contends" (Jer 15:10). He goes on to complain about the reproach he is suffering and the isolation he feels because of the message he has been given to deliver to the people (Jer 15:15, 17). And once again God challenges him to be "my spokesman" and then encourages him with words similar to those given to him at his commission (Jer 15:19–21). Jeremiah faces opposition not only from the people, but also from false prophets (chapter 23) and from kings themselves, one of whom has the audacity to burn the scroll on which Jeremiah had written a summary of the LORD's message of judgment on Israel, Judah, and the nations (chapter 36). Jeremiah is thrown into cisterns and prisons and there are threats on his life, and yet he continues to courageously speak the words that the Lord God had given him.

Defining intellectual courage is again rather straightforward because we are quite familiar with the more general notion of courage. Indeed, most of us will be able to cite examples of moral courage, examples of people who did the right thing even in the face of dangers and threats to their lives. Think of Nelson Mandela's courageous stance against apartheid in South Africa, or Martin Luther King's courageous resistance to racism in America. Only after her death did we learn about Mother Theresa's courage in the face of her dark night of the soul. Then there are the many ordinary acts of courage of individuals facing adversities in their day to day lives.

There are any number of biblical exhortations to be courageous. Joshua, for example, was frequently exhorted to "be strong and courageous."[324] Paul, too, is told by the Lord to "take courage" after he was put into barracks because of an uproar caused by his testimony before the Sanhedrin (Acts 23:11). New Testament scholar N. T. Wright has pointed out that the most frequent command in the Bible is, "Do not be afraid."[325] Indeed, this phrase and its correlate, "Don't be afraid," come up over one hundred times in the Bible. There is much to fear in life; therefore, God's people often need to be encouraged to be courageous.

It might seem somewhat arbitrary to distinguish ordinary moral courage from the virtue of intellectual courage. After all, situations that call for courage invariably also include the mind. But there is still some merit in focusing specifically on intellectual courage. So, what do I mean by intellectual courage? **Intellectual courage** is the disposition to perform intellectual tasks like seeking knowledge and truth, holding on to the truth, or communicating what you believe to be true, even in the face of apparent or real dangers and threats to oneself.[326]

Any number of historical examples of intellectual courage come to mind. For example, Copernicus, Galileo, Brahe, Kepler, and Newton, all key figures in the scientific revolution of the sixteenth and seventeenth centuries, exemplified intellectual courage in the face of resistance to their scientific discoveries.[327] More recently, there were the suffragists of the nineteenth and twentieth centuries, who showed tremendous intellectual and moral courage in challenging a long-standing tradition of male dominance, and who did so in the face of overwhelming opposition.[328] Even more recently, there are the brave dissidents around the world who challenge authoritarian regimes, expose corruption, and argue for human rights.[329]

The above definition identifies three different types of intellectual tasks that call for intellectual courage.[330] Let me illustrate each of these. First there is the courage required in the pursuit of knowledge and truth.[331] It takes intellectual courage to face unpleasant truths about oneself. For example, it takes courage to face up to the fact that one has a tendency to be arrogant. It takes intellectual courage for a student with orthodox Christian beliefs to take a philosophy major at a secular university and in a department where it is common knowledge that many of the professors are avowed atheists. It takes intellectual courage to choose a dissertation topic in a PhD program that runs counter to established opinion. It takes intellectual courage for a journalist to doggedly research an issue that will create a public furor when eventually published.[332]

Sometimes intellectual courage is required simply to adopt or to hold on to a position that one regards as intellectually credible but that is rejected by the public at large or by one's peers. It takes intellectual courage to maintain an orthodox evangelical stance in a liberal progressive church where one encounters frequent slurs against narrow-minded fundamentalists. It takes intellectual courage to be identified as a Christian at a secular university. It takes courage to believe that abortion is wrong in the face of fierce pro-choice advocacy of radical feminists.[333] I fear that

Christians today tend to think of persecution only in terms of physical persecution. There is such a thing as intellectual persecution, and it takes a lot of intellectual courage to hold on to Christian beliefs in the face of a constant barrage of insults from the liberal progressive chattering classes which tend to be very anti-Christian.

Finally, there is the intellectual courage required in communicating knowledge and truth. It takes courage to speak truth to power. One might lose one's job for exposing some corruption within an organization or in the leader of a corporation. All too many women have had to be very courageous in telling the truth about unwanted sexual advances and sexual abuse from men in power, even within the church. It takes intellectual courage to counter the cancel culture that prevails at far too many universities today and sadly even exists within the church. As I am writing these lines, I have to think of the tremendous courage displayed by Russian citizens and journalists who dare to use the label "war" to talk about the invasion of Ukraine in the spring of 2022.

What should be immediately apparent is that intellectual courage is very much context dependent, and here I turn to the final component of my definition—the dangers and threats that sometimes surround the seeking, holding, and communication of truth. Courage is required because there are oppositional forces at work which make it difficult to seek or to speak the truth. As with the other virtues treated in this chapter, intellectual courage is relational in nature. Other people are involved, and these people are in some way opposed to the open pursuit and free expression of knowledge and truth. Hence the need for intellectual courage.

Of course, opposition can vary in degrees. The greater the danger or threat, the more intellectual courage is required. For example, there is little or no intellectual courage required when preaching a biblically based sermon in an evangelical church. But it would take some courage for a pastor to preach a blunt sermon on the sin of greed in a congregation where many of the parishioners are very wealthy. The prophet Amos comes to mind when I think of blunt and courageous preaching. "Hear this word, you cows of Bashan on Mount Samaria, you women who oppress the poor and crush the needy and say to your husbands, 'Bring us some drinks!'" (Amos 4:1). How many pastors today display this kind of intellectual courage?

No courage is needed when defending orthodox Muslim ideas in a majority Muslim country. But it would take some courage to critique the Muslim idea of jihad in a Muslim country. Salman Rushdie comes to mind as someone who has displayed considerable courage in writing novels that call into question some Muslim ideas. There are many recent examples of professors at our colleges and universities who have lost their jobs because they have dared to challenge the dominant liberal orthodoxy that exists at these institutions. They paid the cost of being intellectually courageous. Sadly, all too many professors practice self-censorship in order to avoid the onslaught of political correctness on our campuses. This is the vice of intellectual cowardice.

One other feature about the dangers and threats surrounding intellectual courage should be noted. Dangers and threats create anxiety and fear in most cases. There is, therefore, a psychological dimension to intellectual courage.[334] What does one do with such anxiety and fear? Obviously, our fears, whether real or apparent, need to be acknowledged and faced. But the courageous person will somehow transcend these fears, search for truth, and speak the truth despite the fear that he or she is experiencing.

CAN INTELLECTUAL COURAGE BE TAKEN TO AN EXTREME?

Here an interesting question arises as to whether one can be too courageous in searching for and speaking the truth. Some writers follow Aristotle in treating intellectual courage as a mean between two extremes—cowardice and recklessness.[335] Clearly there is such a thing as having too little intellectual courage, which we typically label as cowardice. But should recklessness be understood as having too much courage? I believe there is something odd about the notion of having too much courage. Surely we don't want to say that the martyrs who refused to give up their Christian faith, even in the face of torture or burning at the stake, were too courageous. Nor would we call them reckless. Intellectual courage is a virtue, period. Perhaps the more appropriate question we should be asking ourselves is whether we are courageous enough today to be martyred for our faith.

So what do we do with the notion of recklessness? I expect most of us will acknowledge that there is something wrong with being rash or reckless. I agree. But I don't believe that recklessness should be interpreted as having too much intellectual courage. Instead, recklessness is better understood as the opposite of being careful and cautious.[336] I quite agree that there is a need for care and caution when communicating with others. We don't want to hurt people unnecessarily. This also applies to contexts where we face opposition to speaking the truth. Here, too, there is a need for wisdom and sensitivity. There is sometimes a place for caution when being intellectually courageous. One can be reckless in courageously speaking the truth in the face of strong opposition. But this has to do with *how* we express our courage in communicating the truth. Being reckless in expressing truth has to do with a failure to be wise or sensitive in speaking the truth even in the face of resistance. But it is not the opposite of courage. And it is simply wrong to think that we can be too courageous in speaking truth to power.

There were times when Jesus chose caution rather than confrontation. But as will be argued later, there are many times when Jesus showed remarkable courage in challenging the religious establishment of his day. Indeed, even when he was being cautious, he was still being courageous, because he realized that the current moment might not be the proper time to confront the religious establishment of the day. As suggested by Aristotle, the brave person is one who faces and fears the right things and from the right motive, in the right way and at the right time, and who also feels confident in the right way and the right time.[337]

There are two further points about intellectual courage that I want to touch on very briefly. The first has to do with identifying or recognizing intellectual courage in ourselves and other people. Some people might not seem to be intellectually courageous because they do not display the usual marker of fear in the face of opposition to the ideas they hold or promulgate. The reason for this seeming fearlessness might be that they have exercised intellectual courage for a long time. They have repeatedly faced down the fear that "normal" people typically feel when encountering strong resistance to searching for or speaking the truth.[338] They have made it a habit to be courageous and so it seems to be natural for them to speak truth to power. But these people should still be credited with being intellectually courageous. Indeed, they have cultivated the *disposition* to be intellectually courageous. Recall that virtues are deeply ingrained dispositions to do the right thing.

A second point. It is all too easy for intellectual courage to slide into the vice of intellectual arrogance. Intellectual courage needs to be combined with intellectual humility. Matthew draws on Isaiah to describe Jesus as God's servant who, in proclaiming justice to the nations, "will not quarrel or cry out; no one will hear his voice in the streets" (Matt 12:19). This description comes after Matthew has given an account of a confrontation of Jesus with the Pharisees, after which Jesus withdraws and warns his many followers not to tell others who he is (v. 16). Paul, too, describes "the Lord's servant" as one who does not quarrel and who "gently" instructs those who oppose him (2 Tim 2:24–25). The willingness to become a martyr for giving gentle witness to the truth is a reliable indicator of a proper blend of intellectual courage and intellectual humility.[339]

BIBLICAL JUSTIFICATION AND EXAMPLES OF INTELLECTUAL COURAGE

There are any number of biblical examples of intellectual courage that could be reviewed. Moses might seem an unlikely example of intellectual courage. When God speaks to Moses in the burning bush and calls him to lead the Israelites out of Egypt, Moses gives one excuse after another. "Who am I" that I should confront Pharaoh? "What if they do not believe me or listen to me" or challenge my claim to be called of God? "I have never been eloquent." "O Lord, please send someone else to do it" (Exod 4). But in the end, "Moses and Aaron [do] just as the Lord commanded them," and they keep confronting Pharaoh and his best and brightest wizards, challenging their worldview, proclaiming the God of Israel as the only God, and demanding that Pharaoh submit to God Almighty and release the Israelites (Exod 7:6). What a transformation of Moses, from a person who is fearful of the task before him to being an intellectually courageous spokesperson for God, who dares to confront Pharaoh and a worldview which viewed the king as a descendant of creator god Amun-Re.[340]

The prophets Isaiah and Jeremiah are exemplars of intellectual courage. Isaiah is commissioned after having a vision of the holy LORD Almighty (Isa 6). After accepting his commission, he is told that his message of judgment will not be accepted by the people of Judah and Israel because their hearts are calloused, their ears are dull, and their eyes can't really see (Isa 6:9–10). Not surprisingly, Isaiah asks how long he is to continue to preach God's word to a people who oppose his unpopular message. The LORD's answer is that he is to keep preaching until judgment has been fulfilled (Isa 6:11–13). This assignment called for intellectual courage, which the prophet Isaiah displayed in abundance.

There are many examples of intellectual courage in the New Testament, but I will limit myself to just two. The first is John the Baptist's courageous confrontation with Herod. Luke informs us that John rebuked Herod about stealing his brother's wife, Herodias, "and all the other evil things he had done" (Luke 3:19). It takes a lot of courage to confront a king, and it takes a lot of intellectual courage to name certain actions as evil when the king obviously has a different view of right and wrong, including the idea that might makes right. Luke goes on to say that Herod added to his many evil actions by locking John up in prison. In the end, John was beheaded for his courageous stand against evil (Matt 14:1–12).

I can only provide a cursory account of how Jesus boldly proclaimed the truth in the face of opposition and threats on his life. Luke opens his account of the work of Jesus in Galilee with a summary description which highlights his activity as a controversial and courageous teacher (Luke 4:16–30). Jesus is in Nazareth, his hometown, and, as was his custom, Jesus goes to the synagogue on the Sabbath. In leading the service, Jesus chooses to read a passage from Isaiah 61:1–2. He then dares to suggest that this Scripture is being fulfilled "today" in his own person. When the people express surprise about "the gracious words" that were coming from a carpenter's son and wonder why Jesus isn't doing the miracles he has already done elsewhere, Jesus reminds them that "no prophet is accepted in his hometown." Jesus then refers to two Old Testament stories where God reaches out beyond Israel, at which point the people are outraged and want to murder him. Jesus knew this would upset them, but he said it anyway and then fled from the scene.

Luke highlights a number of controversial exchanges of Jesus with the Pharisees. At a dinner where the host was surprised to find Jesus not following the ceremonial rules of washing before a meal, Jesus gives him a lecture on the need for inner cleansing. He then goes on to pronounce a series of woes on the scribes and Pharisees, which leads them to "oppose him fiercely and to besiege him with questions, waiting to catch him in something he might say" (Luke 11:37–54). In Luke 16 Jesus speaks to the issue of wealth in the presence of Pharisees "who loved money," we are told (v. 14). Upon hearing Jesus, the Pharisees "were sneering at Jesus," but Jesus goes right on to give another parable to expose the dangers inherent in being wealthy.

A little later, the chief priests and the teachers of the law ask Jesus by what authority he was doing and saying these things (Luke 20:1–8). Jesus counters by giving them a question about John the Baptist's authority which they would have difficulty answering, and then tells the parable of the tenants of a vineyard. "The teachers of the law and the chief priests looked for a way to arrest him immediately, because they knew he had spoken this parable against them. But they were afraid of the people" (v. 19). What a contrast between the intellectual cowardice of the religious leaders and the intellectual courage of Jesus.

Luke goes right on to give us another story which is in fact found in all three Synoptic Gospels and which provides a summary account of the virtues Jesus displayed in his approach to teaching.[341] The Pharisees sent some "spies" to test Jesus and to trap him in his words. These spies had no doubt been prompted in what to say. First they acknowledge him as a "Teacher," a common ascription to traveling teachers of the day. And then a back-handed compliment: "We know you are a man of integrity and that you teach the way of God in accordance with the truth. You aren't swayed by men, because you pay no attention to who they are" (Matt 22:16). Then follows a question about paying taxes to Caesar which was meant to trap Jesus. What I find significant in this exchange is the recognition, even by the enemies of Jesus, that he was a man of integrity and that he spoke the truth without regard for what others might think. In other words, Jesus displayed the virtue of intellectual courage.

This summary account of the intellectual virtues of Jesus is also a fitting segue to the conclusion of this chapter. It might seem that the intellectual courage that Jesus displayed does not mesh with intellectual forbearance. Here we need to keep in mind that all the intellectual virtues need to be kept in balance with one another. There is a right time and a right place for both intellectual forbearance and intellectual courage. There are also limits to intellectual forbearance. Sometimes error needs to be confronted head-on. At other times we need to put up with error, and I believe a careful study of Jesus will reveal that there are times when he displayed remarkable intellectual forbearance. It is significant, for example, that he was often invited to the homes of Pharisees, which would suggest that he treated them in such a way that they respected him despite their opposition to him. The ascription of intellectual integrity to Jesus would also suggest that he was fair-minded in his disputes with those he disagreed with.

As noted in the beginning of this chapter, the three intellectual virtues treated in this chapter are inter-personal in nature. They are needed in contexts where there is disagreement and even hostility to what one believes or what one is trying to communicate. As such, these three virtues are not easy to put into practice. And they are difficult to cultivate. I will have more to say about the cultivation of intellectual virtues in the final chapter.

6

Conclusion

Make every effort to live in peace with all men and to be holy.

(Hebrews 12:14)

Lord, make me an instrument of your peace.
Where there is hatred, let me sow love.

(Prayer of St. Francis)

Jesus has been going through towns and villages preaching the good news of the kingdom and healing the sick. He comments on the need for workers to bring in the plentiful harvest and then sends out the twelve disciples to begin to fill this need. Among his careful instructions are these words: **"I am sending you out like sheep among wolves. Therefore, be as shrewd as snakes and as innocent as doves"** *(Matt 10:16).*[342]

The disciples are being sent on a suicide mission. Being compared to sheep in the midst of wolves doesn't sound particularly safe. Sheep are rather helpless creatures. Sheep are especially vulnerable to predators like wolves. They are very dependent on shepherds for protection and provision. Wolves are rather ferocious and cunning. They often operate in packs. Jesus is telling the disciples that they are facing a very hostile environment.

What is interesting is that Jesus does not instruct his disciples to adopt a "wolfish" mentality or behavior in order to survive or succeed. Instead, he instructs them to be as wise as snakes and as innocent as doves. Two qualities are required to work in a dangerous and hostile environment. Being shrewd or wise (phronismos) involves discernment in assessing a situation and then figuring out how best to respond. Then there is a moral requirement. Doves are associated with purity and harmlessness, traits that are diametrically opposite to that of wolves.

Wisdom and virtue. Is this what we need in today's polarized environment, where calcified ideologies are tearing us apart? Are we listening to Jesus?

WE ARE FACING A crisis today, a crisis in how we relate to each other in the realm of ideas. We disagree about many things, and our disagreements only seem to be deepening and widening. Not only do we disagree with each other, we can't seem to resolve our disagreements. We find ourselves talking past each other. We have difficulty finding any common ground from which to sort out our differences. Indeed, we often find that we can hardly understand each other.

Family members are at loggerheads with each other over politics, religion, and even scientific claims. The differences are so deep that members of a family simply avoid any topics that might blow up in their faces. Churches are struggling to maintain unity in the face of any number of doctrinal and practical issues—eschatology, biblical authority, critical race theory, LGBTQ+ issues, and vaccine passports. Pastors are suffering from burn-out and resigning because they find it impossible to calm church conflicts. Public citizens are dividing into polarized camps with tempers all too often flaring into open conflict.

"Culture wars" is a name often used to describe our current communication crisis.[343] This was the label that James Davison Hunter introduced over thirty years ago in one of the most important and controversial books about modern American politics: *Culture Wars: The Struggle to Define America*. Hunter, a sociologist, used the term "culture wars" to label a phenomenon that needed naming: the conflicts over gay rights, abortion, and other cultural issues that have dominated the United States since the closing decades of the twentieth century. While acknowledging that culture wars weren't new in the United States, what was new, Hunter argued, were the lines of battle.

> Cultural politics once split along denominational lines, Protestants clashed with Catholics and Jews. But these boundaries

began dissolving in the middle of the twentieth century, giving way to a new divide that was ideological rather than religious. Hunter discerned two competing impulses in American politics: the progressive and the orthodox.[344]

Orthodox Americans appeal to an authority outside of themselves—for example, God as revealed in the Bible—while progressives maintain that the so-called timeless truths of the Bible need to be changed and adapted to the modern world.

Hunter believed this divide was unbridgeable. Progressive and conservative Americans simply had different views of reality. The "culture wars" weren't only about policy but about the power to define reality. Each side was trying to redefine America to suit their own vision. Despite critiques of his analysis, Hunter's book has shown remarkable staying power, no doubt because the notion of culture wars was sufficiently vague to accommodate new centers of conflict like class wars and disputes over critical race theory. Indeed, a veritable cottage industry has grown around the notion of culture wars.[345]

Less than a year after Hunter's book appeared, conservative commentator Pat Buchanan took the stage at the Republican National Convention to declare: "There is a religious war going on in this country. It is a cultural war, as critical to the kind of nation we shall be as was the Cold War itself, for this war is for the soul of America."[346] This cultural war persists to this day, though the centers of conflict change. Listen to Jim Banks, a Republican representative from Indiana, who gave this advice to his fellow Republicans in a memo written in June of 2021: "Lean into it. Lean into the culture war."[347] Banks was urging his colleagues to "lean into" conflicts over critical race theory and other cultural issues as part of the GOP's effort to retake Congress in the 2022 elections. Clearly, the culture wars are not ending any time soon.[348] Indeed, they seem to be escalating.

Surveys show that 93 percent of Americans are troubled by the incivility in our public discourse, and over two-thirds think it is a major problem.[349] Incivility is not just a matter of how we talk to each other; it also keeps us from talking to each other at all. Nearly two-thirds of Americans say the social and political climate these days prevents them from saying things they believe because others might find them offensive. Why such self-censorship? Among other reasons, almost one-third of Americans are worried that they will lose employment or advancement opportunities if their political opinions become known. This percentage increases to 44 percent of those with post-graduate degrees. Then there are the results of a recent Pew Research Center survey which found that partisan hostility in the USA is growing. Republicans and Democrats are much more likely to view their political opponents as closed-minded, immoral, unintelligent, dishonest, and lazy than they were just four years ago.[350] It is data such as this that leads David French to suggest in a recent book that America is on the brink of a civil war.[351]

Cherie Harder, president of The Trinity Forum and former special assistant to the president and policy advisor to the senate majority leader, sums up our problems:

> Each hour seems to bring new confirmation of our angry, addled, and alienated state. We are so focused on the darkness in others we can no longer see clearly. The irony is that while partisans are busy asserting that their opponents are evil and stupid, the very act of doing so—widely replicated as it is, and provoking a corresponding vitriol from the other side—renders our public discourse and character as a whole ever more callous, clueless, and cruel. We are becoming what we denounce.[352]

Harder then asks the critical question: How can we disrupt this vicious cycle?

I want to suggest some solutions in this chapter. As might be expected, I will argue that a recovery of intellectual virtues is the key to overcoming our current communication crisis. I then want to focus specifically on the ideal of truth as another answer to solving our current problems of polarization and demonization. And to sum up, I will appeal to the Christian virtue of love. I will conclude with some suggestions on how to cultivate intellectual virtues and then a final prayer.

ETHICS OF THE MIND[353]

In the spring of 2022, my wife and I returned to Stratford (Canada) for the first time after the pandemic to enjoy a performance of Shakespeare's Richard III. *During the intermission, we couldn't help overhearing a conversation behind us, comparing Donald Trump to Richard III. Though somewhat sympathetic with this comparison, I was dismayed about what I heard next: "The supporters of Trump must all have very low intelligence." Fortunately, the performance of the play resumed and the conversation had to end.*

Sadly, this kind of denigration of those we disagree with is all too common today.[354] There is an arrogance here which is worrisome. We are the intelligent ones, and anyone who supports Trump just doesn't measure up to our superior intelligence. This kind of comment also commits the *ad-hominem* fallacy. It involves attacking people rather than the views they hold. And where is the evidence for this claim? I'm sure the range of intelligence of Trump supporters is roughly the same as that of the population at large. I happen to know that some of Trump's supporters have PhDs!

This is not at all to say there isn't some justification for comparing Trump to Shakespeare's portrayal of Richard III. Both are the epitome of wicked, ruthless, narcissistic, manipulative, and power-hungry leaders. And I can't understand the level of support Trump still enjoys among evangelical voters. But I believe it is a serious mistake to claim that Trump supporters have low intelligence.

It is also a mistake to assume that the growing polarizations of our day can be resolved by making people more intelligent, for example, by helping them to become more informed or giving them a better education. Educated people have strong disagreements too. Indeed, the educated chattering classes are often more polarized and more prone to vilify their opponents than the uneducated.[355] And giving people more information just doesn't seem to help in getting those who disagree with us to change their minds. We are not as rational as we think we are.[356] To think we can reason our way to truth and agreement is a "rationalist delusion," according to Jonathan Haidt.[357]

So, we need to discard the rationalistic assumptions that often underlie liberal attempts to resolve the polarizations we are facing today. We need less emphasis on knowledge and more emphasis on *how* we come to know. We need less argument and debate, and more focus on the character of the arguers and debaters. In other words, we need to focus more on the development of the virtues of the mind. At the same time, we need to become more aware of the vices of the mind. Instead of focusing specifically on the intelligence of people we disagree with, we need to look at ways in which intelligence can be twisted and corrupted by sin.

Here it is most important to note that this problem of warped thinking applies to all of us. Both the supporters and the critics of Trump suffer from minds that twist the data. Both have a tendency to be biased in looking at the facts. Both are in danger of being closed-minded. Both are prone to intellectual arrogance. Both are guilty of a lack of intellectual forbearance and fairmindedness. Both are guilty of intellectual vices.

So what is the solution to disagreements and culture wars which are of course much broader than divided opinions about Donald Trump? We need to repent of our intellectual sins. We need to repent and turn away from dogmatism and closed-mindedness and intellectual arrogance. And we need to cultivate the virtues of the mind. We need to become people who genuinely love the truth, who are open-minded, and who approach the other with an attitude of intellectual generosity. We need to become people who always demonstrate intellectual humility about the convictions that we hold. We need to cultivate deeply ingrained habits of intellectual forbearance and fair-mindedness.

Here it might be objected that the solution I am suggesting is no longer relevant for our troubled times. Christian critics have argued that the intellectual virtues I have described in this book are simply not suitable for today's deeply divided cultural climate. Intellectual humility and gentleness and intellectual generosity are just too soft, too nice. Intellectual forbearance might be all right for a civil society, but not in the context of deep disagreements and the toxic culture wars of our time. Here we need a more robust kind of response to our opponents, some Christian critics maintain. Desperate times call for desperate measures. Intellectual virtues might be suitable for a "neutral world," but times have changed and we now live in a "negative world" which requires a more confrontational approach.[358] We simply can't assume that morals and virtues remain the same for all time and for all contexts. This approach suggests a kind of moral relativism about the intellectual virtues I have been defending in this book.[359]

The basic problem here is that the Bible doesn't give us this relativistic option. Indeed, the moral standards of the Bible are universal and apply for all times.[360] The intellectual virtues discussed in this book are not optional for us as Christians. Even in times when there is a lot of hostility to Christian beliefs and values, we need to cultivate intellectual humility, intellectual forbearance, and fairmindedness. Even within the context of strong disagreements, Christians are called to love and gentleness and peace. This does not mean that we cower in the face of opposition. As Paul says to Timothy, "God did not give us a spirit of timidity, but a spirit of power, of love and of self-discipline" (2 Tim 1:7). But note here that the spirit of power is coupled with love. Even so, intellectual courage must always be combined with the fruits of the Spirit, which include love, peace, patience, and kindness (Gal 4:25–26).

In the preceding chapters I have tried to show that each of the central intellectual virtues as well as the virtues that are more relational in nature are mandated in Scripture. Jesus exemplified these virtues, and he did so in the midst of an extremely polarized society. The apostles encouraged the cultivation of these intellectual virtues. Paul called Christians to exhibit the fruits of the Spirit even when they were being nailed to the cross or clawed by lions. Peter called on Christians to defend the faith with "gentleness and reverence" even in the midst of hostility that would lead to suffering (1 Pet 3:15–16). James advocates divine wisdom, which is peaceable, gentle, and open to reason (Jas 3:13–18). So, we can't dismiss the intellectual virtues for pragmatic reasons or argue that they are no longer relevant for our troubled times. We cannot allow ourselves to think that "outrageous times call for outraged responses."[361] It is precisely in these outrageous times where most discourse is colored by rage that we as Christians need to remember that the Bible calls us to love even our intellectual enemies. The intellectual virtues described in the Bible are meant precisely for times like we are living in.

Indeed, the only way we can combat the growing polarizations of our times is for each of us to cultivate the intellectual virtues described in this book and mandated in our Scriptures. Oh what a difference it would make if in the midst of disagreement over COVID vaccines, we could join hands with those we disagree with and then together engage in a careful search for the truth. Imagine if all the shrill and strident expressions of convictions on the part of Democrats and Republicans, or Liberals and Conservatives, were replaced with humble affirmations of current convictions and a genuine willingness to admit that we might be wrong. Think of what might be accomplished by way of compromise if ardent supporters of the pro-life and pro-choice campaigns on abortion would really listen to each other and have the humility to admit that there might be some validity in each of these positions. What would happen if instead of attempts to silence and shame the opposing sides on critical race theory, there was instead an honest attempt to understand each other and acknowledge that there might be some truth and some error on both sides? There is a better way to fight culture wars.[362]

DEALING WITH DEEP DIFFERENCES

It it not easy to be a philosopher. Philosophers like to think. They spend a lot of time evaluating arguments and try very hard always to construct good arguments. I often find myself cringing when I run across a particularly bad argument. How could a person who is reasonably intelligent give such an implausible argument for the claim that he or she is making? I won't bore you with examples. But I have come to one conclusion after spending a lifetime listening to many very bad arguments. When arguments are very bad, there is always something deeper at stake in the position being held. Hence this section on "dealing with deep differences."

All too often our current disagreements and culture wars are dealt with at a surface level. We find ourselves covering the same ground over and over again. One person recounts the facts that he believes support his position, and the other person does the same for her position. But this doesn't end the debate or lead to a resolution. Or, two Christians stack up Bible verses that support each of their respective positions, but, not surprisingly, this doesn't lead to agreement. Or each person presents arguments for their position, but they are arguing past each other. Continuing any kind of argument at this surface level is really a waste of time.

I once made the above observations to a prominent church leader concerning the differences between a conservative and a liberal approach to gay marriage. I was following up on an earlier conversation in which we were trying to understand the growing sharp divide in Mennonite churches on the issue of gay marriage. In my subsequent email I was trying to help my brother by suggesting that we would only really understand these differences if we moved to a deeper level of discussion. Sadly, I received a very caustic response, which misrepresented what I was saying and was sarcastic and demeaning. I responded carefully and tried to clarify what I had said, but to no avail. Sadly, this put a stop to any further communication on this issue. Conversations about deep differences require respect from each party as well as the presence of intellectual virtues. Sometimes the most appropriate response to deep differences is silence, as exemplified in Jesus' response to Pilate (Matt 27:14).

Thankfully, many of our disagreements can be resolved more easily. If two people disagree about a specific empirical claim, it is generally easy to resolve this difference. For example, if two people disagree about a claim that their friend has been unfaithful to his wife, a little bit of investigation will probably resolve the disagreement, as long as each party is open-minded and sincere about finding the truth. However, if the disagreement goes further, and one person says that unfaithfulness in marriage is not a big deal while the other maintains that this is a sin, it may be harder to resolve this dispute. Here progress will only be made if we move the argument to a deeper level. We will need to try to understand the deeper assumptions that ground the opposing positions.

The difference between these two levels of disagreement is sometimes characterized as a difference between fact and value. While there is something to be said for this characterization, I believe this needs some nuancing which can be facilitated by raising a question about the nature of "facts." Let me illustrate this problem by referring to the infamous expression often used by Donald Trump in his campaigns and during his presidency. Trump has repeatedly appealed to the notion of "alternative facts." But this is a very odd expression. There can be no alternative facts. Facts just are what they are. But while there cannot be alternative facts, there can be alternative interpretations of facts. And here things become more complicated. Indeed, this is a problem that philosophers have been wrestling with for quite some time.[363] We really don't have direct access to "brute facts." We always come at facts from a particular interpretive vantage point. All human experience is already colored by a particular perspective. And it is here in the realm of perspectives and interpretations that we begin to encounter our deeper differences. Now we are forced to take into account foundational assumptions and differing worldviews that underlie competing interpretations.

Of course, sometimes our differences are specifically about our religious commitments and worldviews. These are clearly deep differences, and, as we all know, these differences are difficult to resolve. Indeed, the question can be raised as to whether it is even possible to evaluate and debate the foundational assumptions and worldviews that underlie our interpretations of facts. There are some thinkers who suggest that here we are simply stuck with incommensurable interpretations, so further discussion is futile if not impossible.[364] But this is being too skeptical. As Christians, we believe that all people are created in the image of God and that all of us live in the same reality created by God. So we can understand each other to some extent, and we can communicate with each other to some degree despite our deep differences.[365]

But evaluating alternate interpretations and worldviews is not as simple as is often assumed, and I believe most people, including philosophers, have not paid sufficient attention to this epistemological problem.

Here it is important to keep in mind that we are now dealing with entire belief systems. The reader is encouraged to review my treatment of "belief systems" and my argument that individual beliefs are always connected to a belief system (see chapter 4, pp. 100–102). All too often we think we can evaluate a single statement in isolation from the rest of a person's belief system. This is a simplistic approach to viewing our differences and leads to surface level arguments.

So how do we evaluate a whole belief system? How do we evaluate competing interpretations and worldviews? The central question that we need to ask here is which interpretative framework is better able to account for all of our experiences. We also need to look at the coherence of belief systems. Simplicity, elegance, and explanatory power are additional criteria.[366] Applying these criteria is not neat and tidy and will seldom lead to clear resolution of our differences. But we can't give up. We need to keep trying to find the best interpretation or the best worldview.

Here again intellectual virtues are essential. Indeed, I believe intellectual virtues are even more important when it comes to dealing with deep differences and culture wars. We need to start with forbearance, acknowledging that people think differently and start with different presuppositions and worldviews. When dealing with deep differences, we need to listen to the other person carefully and honestly try to understand where the other person is coming from. We need to be fair in articulating the other person's argument. Both parties need to be genuine in their search for truth about facts and the best way to interpret all the facts. We must also try to find the truth about competing worldviews. Again, humility is required, and the willingness to admit that one might be in error in one's interpretation of the facts.

Humility is especially important in light of the fact that our thinking is affected by sin. The effects of sin become particularly apparent when dealing with deep differences where ideologies and idols twist our thinking.[367] Ideologies have a way of closing our minds and demanding complete commitment, i.e., worship. We need to heed John's warning, "Dear children, keep yourselves from idols" (1 John 5:21). We need to pray that God will protect us from "zeal . . . not based on knowledge" (Rom 10:2).

Deep differences and worldviews are invariably linked to our identities. We seldom believe alone. We need "plausibility structures" to support our interpretive frameworks.[368] We try to find other people who share our beliefs. Of course, these deeper beliefs are often held with religious intensity. So not only do these beliefs give people a sense of enduring purpose but they also play a key role in forming enduring bonds of friendship and community. Now the problem of persuading someone to change their deeply held beliefs becomes even more complicated. As David French has reminded us, you can't just ask a person to give up their community and then leave them homeless.[369] If you want to change someone's basic beliefs, you will have to provide an alternative community. Indeed, it is probably a mistake to start with argument. What is needed instead is acceptance and love, which will make it possible for people to begin to reevaluate their strongly held positions. More on love later.

TRUTH

It happened in the spring of 2022. I was approached by a retired Anglican priest (a friend of a friend) at the end of an inspiring worship service in a Baptist church in Regina, Saskatchewan. He knew I was a philosopher and so he rather boldly asked me a challenging question. What did I think was the central philosophical question facing contemporary society? I didn't hesitate in giving my answer. "The key philosophical issue for our day," I suggested, "is our hesitancy to affirm the notion of truth." Of course, this isn't entirely a new problem. Pilate asked Jesus this penetrating question during his trial, "What is truth?" (John 18:37). And centuries earlier, the prophets of old bemoaned the loss of truth in their societies.[370]

The notion of truth is particularly under assault in today's postmodern climate. This assault has been captured so well in the title of an influential book written by J. Richard Middleton and Brian J. Walsh, *Truth Is Stranger Than It Used to Be*. They borrow Walter Anderson's delightful analogy to help us understand what has happened to truth in our postmodern world. They contrast the differing views of reality and truth in modernism and postmodernism by telling the story of three umpires having a beer after a baseball game. One says, "There's balls and there's strikes, and I call 'em the way they are." This is the Enlightenment view of knowledge and truth, which assumes there is a real world out there and we have direct access to it and can objectively interpret it. This position is sometimes called naïve realism. Another umpire responds, "There's balls and there's strikes, and they ain't nothin' until I call 'em." This position represents the postmodern denial of truth. Here reality is socially constructed by our language. Human beings are thought to have the power to define reality. The third umpire says, "There's balls and there's strikes, and I call 'em the way I see 'em." This is the critical realist view of truth and reality, which holds on to objective reality while at the same time acknowledging that our interpretations of reality might need to be critically evaluated.[371]

The postmodern denial of truth can be expressed in various ways. The second umpire gives expression to epistemological relativism, where truth is conceived as an arbitrary individual construction. Friedrich Nietzsche described truth as an illusion and a worn-out metaphor.[372] French postmodernist Michel Foucault gives expression to social constructivism, highlighting the collective dimension in the link between truth and power.[373] For Foucault, truth is merely a power construct. More recently, Steve Fuller captures the heart of Foucault's project in his book *Post Truth: Knowledge as a Power Game*.

There are of course problems with each of these reductionistic analyses of truth. The question can always still be asked: Do those with power to determine the truth, whether individual or corporate, really have the truth? All of us recognize that a power construct can be wrong. Truth is not determined by power. We can't simply create truth. The last word does not belong to any human construction of the truth.[374]

I believe we need to recapture the ideal of truth and recommit ourselves to an honest and humble search for truth if we want to overcome the disagreements and culture wars of today. Here the reader is encouraged to review my discussion of truth and the search for truth, including the diagram "The Ladder of Truth" on page 39 of chapter 2. In this diagram Truth is pictured as an ideal at the very apex of the ladder of truth. But there is a barrier separating Truth as an ideal and the human search for truth. Truth is therefore independent of any human power struggles to define truth. Truth is there to be discovered. We as human beings don't create truth. Instead, we are all on the ladder, searching for truth. This distinction between Truth as an ideal and human attempts to find or define truth serves to keep human beings properly humble—one of the intellectual virtues we have already considered.

This diagram also illustrates how an ideal of truth can help to overcome the polarizations and culture wars that we face today. Contrary to popular belief, the notion of truth as an ideal can bring us together. We now have a common goal. Each of us is (or should be) trying to find the truth about whatever we are quarreling about. An honest search for truth will bring us out of our intellectual silos and will help us to join hands and minds with others in searching for the truth. Here there is no need for power tactics to manipulate people to accept our version of the truth. Instead, we can cooperate in trying to find the truth. No need for a dogmatic assertion of my truth. Instead, there will be a humble pointing to what we think is the truth and an invitation to others to discover the truth for themselves, while admitting that we ourselves might be in need of having our understanding of truth corrected.[375]

Believing in truth is in fact freeing. People who believe in truth aren't afraid. They follow Plato, who said, "But we must go wherever the wind of the argument carries us."[376] People who believe in truth are also free to practice forbearance and tolerance. As S. D. Gaede observes,

> Intolerance of differences comes from those whose confidence in truth is shaky, who think truth depends on them. Thus, it is not the genuine truth lover we ought to fear, but those whose love of truth is not genuine. And that includes the hypocrite and the cynic as well as the relativist.[377]

Those who genuinely believe in truth will be the least likely to come to blows over it, since they know truth will stand regardless of their ability to defend it. Intolerance arises when truth is *used* rather than genuinely believed in, according to Gaede. The genuine believer in truth is able to conduct his or her life "in the gentle confidence that [what he or she believes] is true," while at the same time admitting that he or she is fallible and might have it wrong.[378]

There is another dimension of truth that is freeing for Christians. We believe that God is the ultimate source of all truth, and therefore we can trust that the God of truth will ultimately triumph. As we face those who we feel are in error, we can therefore relax, knowing that the battle for the truth is not just up to us. And yes, it is appropriate to talk about "the battle for truth." Paul uses war imagery to describe the spiritual battle we are engaged in (Eph 6:10–18).

> Put on the full armor of God so that you can take your stand against the devil's schemes. For our struggle is not against flesh and blood, but against the rulers, against the authorities, against the powers of this dark world and against the spiritual forces of evil in the heavenly realms. (vv. 11–12)

The battle for truth is ultimately a spiritual battle. As we have seen repeatedly in the previous chapters, human beings have a tendency to hide from the truth, stifle the truth, and twist the truth because of sin. Thus, we find ourselves engaged in a spiritual battle in acknowledging the ideal of truth, submitting to the truth, and worshiping the God of all truth.

Two things should be noted about this battle for truth. First, Paul reminds us that the weapons we use to fight our "enemies" are a "belt of truth," a "breastplate of righteousness," and a "gospel of peace" (Eph 6:10–17). The battle for truth needs to be fought with truthfulness, justice, and a desire for peace. Unusual weapons to be sure. But they point towards the importance of intellectual virtues in our battle for truth.

Richard Middleton highlights another important dimension of this spiritual battle. Paul also reminds us that our struggle is not really against flesh and blood. In other words, it isn't people who are the problem. There are "powers of this dark world" and "spiritual forces of evil" at work in our world (Eph 6:12). We as Christians are really helpless in the face of such powerful spiritual forces. But here is the good news. This isn't a battle that we actually need to fight. Middleton reminds us that in Ephesians 6:10–14, Paul tells us that instead of directly fighting the enemy, our characteristic action in this battle is to stand firm. It is God in Jesus Christ who fights for us. "Standing firm in Truth, in a reality that I did not construct, allows for non-anxious hospitality towards others, even those with whom I radically disagree. I don't need to be defensive about God's Truth. After all, who needs to defend a Lion?"[379] This doesn't mean that we don't have a part to play in articulating and defending our understanding of truth. But this needs to be done with humility and gentleness, leaving the final result up to God.

It should come as no surprise that, without the ideal of Truth and without a belief in a God of truth, we are left with nothing but human battles for the right to define truth. Opponents to vaccine mandates are forced to resort to tactics like a truck convoy storming the capital of Canada in 2022, occupying Parliament Hill, banging pots and pans, tooting their horns, and demanding that their truth be heard. Without the notion of truth, church debates on anti-racism and critical race theory will be resolved by those who speak the loudest and longest. Or they will be settled by a majority vote, with little or without any honest discussion or humble searching of Scripture. Without the ideal of truth, we are left helpless in the face of the manipulations of cancel or woke culture. The Psalmist seems to speak to situations like this. "When the foundations are being destroyed, what can the righteous do?" (Ps 11:3). Without the foundation of Truth as an ideal, it seems there is nothing we can do to resolve our disagreements. The only way to help us out of this epistemological quagmire is to reaffirm the notion of truth.

Of course, even with the ideal of Truth, things can still get a little bit messy. We will still have disagreements, but there is now a way to move beyond our disagreements. Here it should be noted that in my philosophical diagram the ladder narrows as we get closer to the truth. Humbly working together in the search for truth should gradually bring about a growing consensus. Of course, even a consensus is no guarantee that we have found the truth. Remember, there is a barrier separating Truth as an ideal and the human search for truth. The barrier represents our finiteness and our sinfulness, which makes it impossible for us to ever claim with certainty that we have arrived at Truth with a capital *T*. So even when we arrive at a consensus, we can't be absolutely sure that we have arrived at the truth. Sadly, consensus is all too often arrived at through a power play; therefore, consensus is not a guarantee of having arrived at the truth.

But reaching a consensus can still be a useful marker for coming closer to the truth under certain conditions. What is being assumed here is an intellectual environment where each individual or group is free to search for the truth on their own and to declare what they view to be the truth. Also assumed is that all are genuinely listening to other claims to have come closer to the truth. And all claims to truth will be made tentatively. Intellectual humility will lead all to say that we can at most arrive at temporary truths. We can never claim complete certainty. We only see through a glass darkly, as Paul reminded us (1 Cor 13:9, 12). Thus, there is something to be said for relativism. The human search for truth is relative. But there is still an ideal of Truth "towards which we imagine that all of our temporary truths will one day converge," as pragmatist William James put it.[380] The apostle Paul would seem to agree when he foresees a future time when we "shall know fully" (1 Cor 13:12).

So we continue to search for truth in hope that we will eventually find it. In the meantime, this hope, together with the ideal of truth that inspires this hope, will enable us to overcome the problems of disagreement, diatribe, disinformation, divisiveness, and power struggles, problems that are tearing our societies apart.

I realize that there might be readers who will view this rehabilitation of Truth with a capital *T* with a good deal of skepticism. Doesn't the notion of absolute truth lead to dogmatism and fundamentalism? Hasn't the notion of absolute truth led to all kinds of abuses of power? Am I not resurrecting the ghosts of colonialism? Is not a return to the concepts that were so dear to the so-called Enlightenment a backward step from which we have long been thankfully liberated?

The problem with these objections is that they are based on the fallacy of questionable cause. Can we prove that it is the notion of absolute truth that is the real cause of dogmatism and fundamentalism? Can we prove that abuses of power are directly linked to the holding of the ideal of truth? Can we prove that believing in the ideal of truth led to the evils of colonialism? I don't believe that any of these questions can be answered with an unequivocal yes. Causal connections of complex phenomena are hard to prove.

We also need to be reminded that many good things can become twisted and bad if used in excess or misused. Salt is good, but too much salt can be harmful to one's health. God's good laws can become twisted into a Pharisaic kind of legalism. Tolerance is good, but we can become too tolerant. So yes, holding onto an ideal of truth can lead to dogmatism and the abuse of power, but it need not do so. Again, I would remind the reader that we need to distinguish between an ideal of truth, which is intrinsically good, and the human search for truth, which can become misshaped in various ways.

So what is the real cause of these distortions of the ideal of truth and the human search for truth? It is the perversity of human nature, as has already been noted many times in this and previous chapters. The Bible declares that all of us are sinful by nature. Sin also affects our minds. Thus, Jesus talks about eyes that do not see and hearts that don't understand (John 12:40). Paul talks about thinking becoming futile, hearts being darkened, and wickedness causing us to suppress the truth about God (Rom 1:21, 18).

What I am calling for is a retention of the medieval and Enlightenment ideal of truth while at the same time acknowledging the insights of postmodernism and its reminder that we as human beings cannot escape viewing truth from a particular standpoint, which therefore calls for humility in the claims that we make. But we need truth as an ideal, and it is only if we retain this ideal of Truth with a capital *T* and combine this with a love of the truth and other intellectual virtues that we will be able to overcome the current polarizations and culture wars.

LOVE

It was in the middle of the pandemic when I heard a powerful sermon given by a good friend of mine, David Dyck. Like many Christians, my wife and I were listening to church services online, and occasionally we listened to services in other churches. This sermon boldly addressed a problem that was emerging in many churches—growing polarization over COVID vaccines and COVID mandates. So David, a seasoned pastor, addressed this problem by preaching a sermon based on Paul's letter to the Colossian church.

The Colossian church was also facing its fair share of controversy over doctrine and practice. In the sermon, David drew attention to the fact that Paul didn't say that in the midst of polarization we need to find out who is right and who is wrong. Instead, the Colossian Christians are reminded of their identity. You are "God's chosen people, holy and dearly loved" (Col 3:12). Paul urges the members of the Colossian church to clothe themselves with the virtues of "compassion, kindness, humility, gentleness and patience" (v. 12). They are also told to "bear with each other" (v. 13). In other words, cultivate the virtue of intellectual forbearance. "Let the peace of Christ rule in your hearts, since as members of one body you were called to peace" (v. 15). And then the final admonition: "And over all these virtues put on love, which binds them all together in perfect unity" (v. 14).

Love. That is the ultimate answer to divisions, disagreements, and culture wars. Even intellectual virtues are not enough. We need love, which in fact binds all these virtues together in a perfect unity. That is why I have already made frequent reference to love in this and previous chapters. It is hard to separate intellectual virtues from love. Intellectual virtues are finally grounded in love. I find it most significant that in Paul's famous exposition of love in 1 Cor 13, there are frequent references to knowledge. "If I have the gift of prophecy and can fathom all mysteries and all knowledge, . . . but have not love, I am nothing" (v. 2). "For we know in part and we prophesy in part, but when perfection comes, the imperfect disappears" (vv. 9–10). "Now we see but a poor reflection; then we shall see face to face. Now I know in part; then I shall know fully, even as I am fully known" (v. 12). And then the grand conclusion: "And now these three remain: faith, hope and love. But the greatest of these is love" (v. 13).

What a fitting conclusion. And what a fascinating interplay between knowledge and love. We must not separate the two, and one way to see their connection is to focus on the cultivation of intellectual virtues. Yes, knowledge is important and the search for knowledge is important, but these need to be combined with love. We only know in part—hence the need for intellectual humility. We need faith to believe that harmony and unity can be achieved. We will only know fully at some future time—hence the importance of hope. And then there is love, the greatest of these virtues, which binds all these themes into a unified whole.[381]

But that is not all that Paul has to say about love in his epistles. He also gives us this series of exhortations: "Do not repay anyone evil for evil. . . . If it is possible, as far as it depends on you, live at peace with everyone. Do not take revenge. . . . . If your enemy is hungry feed him; if he is thirsty, give him something to drink. . . . Do not be overcome by evil, but overcome evil with good" (Rom 12:17–21). Of course, Paul is here reflecting Jesus' own admonition: "Love your enemies and pray for those who persecute you" (Matt 5:44). Loving our enemies surely also involves loving our ideological enemies.

Here it might be objected that labeling someone an "enemy" is already problematic. But this is quibbling over words. It represents a failure to really face the problem of deep disagreements and culture wars. When there is strong disagreement, the other is invariably viewed as an enemy. Culture wars by their very nature involve a war between enemies. So let's not sugarcoat the problem. But the question still remains, how do we treat our enemies? And here Jesus and Paul advocate love.

What does loving our intellectual enemies entail? It means that we learn to disagree without being disagreeable.[382] We don't repay an unfair criticism of our position with a personal attack of our opponent. Instead, we respond with love, trying to find something of value in what our opponent has said, and humbly admitting that we might have it wrong. Christians should be known for responding to caustic remarks with gentleness and graciousness, trying as much as possible to live at peace with our enemies. Reading the literature of our ideological enemies means that we will approach their words and ideas with the "gift of constant and loving attention."[383] Critiquing an "enemy's" work must also be done with love and fairness. A loving argument will be patient, always seeking gently to move the enemy and ourselves closer to the ideal of truth. We can afford to be patient because we can leave the outcome in God's hands.[384] As

Thomas Merton has reminded us, "The victory of truth is inevitable."[385] And so we live in hope and faith and love.

> Love is patient, love is kind. It does not envy, it does not boast, it is not proud. It is not rude, it is not self-seeking, it is not easily angered, it keeps no record of wrongs. Love does not delight in evil but rejoices with the truth. It always protects, always trusts, always hopes, always perseveres. (1 Cor 13:4–7)

Oh, that we would follow this advice also in the realm of competing ideas and ideologies and our culture wars.

CULTIVATING INTELLECTUAL VIRTUES

I conclude this book with some practical suggestions on how each of us can cultivate intellectual virtues. Much could and should be said about cultivating intellectual virtues in our schools, colleges, universities, and seminaries.[386] But I want to focus on the development of intellectual virtues in ourselves. We are all tempted to begin by pointing out the flaws and intellectual vices of other people. But Jesus cautioned about finding a speck of sawdust in the eye of another when there is a plank in your own. "You hypocrite, first take the plank out of your own eye," Jesus says (Matt 7:4–5). So we need to examine ourselves first, then work constructively at cultivating intellectual virtues in ourselves.

Where to begin? Reading this book is a good start, I would hope. Even better would be to study this book as a group in a book club or a Sunday School class. But a better understanding of intellectual virtues and vices is not enough. Here we need to remember that intellectual virtues are character traits or dispositions to think in healthy ways. Unfortunately, we are prone to think in unhealthy ways. Our thinking has a tendency to get corrupted by sin.

That is why I have included questionnaires at the beginning of each of the central chapters. Hopefully completing these questionnaires will expose areas that you need to work on. Here again, combining self-examination with some form of accountability to others would be helpful. Ask others to evaluate you in terms of each of the intellectual virtues. Give your friends the freedom to criticize you when they find that you are being too dogmatic or closed-minded.

But self-examination is not enough. Where we discover the presence of intellectual vices, we need to repent. We may even need conversions of the heart, which will lead to conversions of the mind. It is only such conversions that will allow us to begin to genuinely desire the cultivation of the intellectual virtues which are so necessary in a climate of growing polarizations. There are repeated reminders in the book of Proverbs that wisdom and knowledge and understanding are more precious than silver and gold, that we should therefore desire these intellectual virtues above all else (Prov 3:13–16; 8:10–11). So, we need to ask God for help in the transformation of our desires so that we will make the cultivation of intellectual virtues a high priority in our lives.

We also need models to emulate. So, we need to let the story of Jesus inspire us. Pay particular attention to friends who exemplify intellectual virtues. Read biographies of people who have excelled in having healthy minds. Seek out mentors.[387] Take special note of essays that display intellectual humility, open-mindedness, and fairmindedness. Richard Hughes Gibson cites a notable example in an essay entitled "In Search of Charitable Writing." He refers to an editorial by *Christianity Today*'s then-president and CEO Timothy Dalrymple, "Why Evangelicals Disagree on the President." Contrary to some claims made in the media, evangelicals were and are strongly divided in their evaluations of former President Trump. "Unable to see reason in the opposing view, each side asserts the other has succumbed to unreason, to prejudice, or to the lust for power or approval."[388]

Although not himself a supporter of Trump, Dalrymple carefully explains why many of his fellow believers are. He gives equal space to both sides of this dispute. He argues that "charitable disagreement requires that we represent our brothers and sisters at their best." He doesn't try to explain away the differences between the two positions. He is firm in his own convictions, and he takes a risk in stating them so directly given that the readership of *Christianity Today* presumably includes many who voted for Trump. The essay clearly shows that Christian love cannot be sacrificed in the process of making arguments. "Our love, Dalrymple would remind us, should keep the channel open to our fellow believers when we disagree because our love knows a higher loyalty than national politics."[389] Love, he memorably concludes, is "the last radical act in a radically polarized age."[390] We need examples like this to help us cultivate intellectual virtues.

Finally, we need to work on the actual cultivation of intellectual virtues. And this takes practice. Here we need to be realistic. If we are by nature prone to being dogmatic and closed-minded, we can't change this overnight. Change requires constant vigilance, growing awareness of when we fail, and repeated practice in being open-minded or developing intellectual humility. Here it might be well to work at the development of one intellectual virtue at a time. If you are prone to uncritically accepting what is said in the media as true, you need to work at cultivating critical thinking and having the virtue of committed openness. Watch for generalizations that are not backed by evidence. Do some fact checking. Make it a practice to look at other news channels. Draw on resources that can help you to be more discerning in the way in which you get your information. Ask your friends to challenge you in your thinking. You might even need to cultivate new friends who will be more ready to do this for you.

Once you see some progress in avoiding this vice of uncritical thinking, you might want to select another vice and work at the development of the corresponding virtue. Cultivating intellectual virtues takes time. Rebecca Konyndyk DeYoung offers this advice: "There is no quick and easy substitute for daily repetition over the long haul. First, we have to pull the sled out of the old rut, and then gradually build up a new track."[391] We also need to heed Eugene Peterson's advice in his treatment of discipleship as found in his book with the inspiring title *A Long Obedience in the Same Direction*. And let's not forget the importance of prayer. Remember the fight against intellectual vices is finally a spiritual battle. We need God's help in cultivating intellectual virtues.

Ideally, of course, the cultivation of intellectual virtues should take place in community. We really can't do this alone. Churches should be communities of love and sanctuaries in fragmented and polarized societies. And this will require that churches take up the challenge of cultivating intellectual virtues in all who belong to the church.[392] As noted earlier, Paul reminds us of the importance of our identity "as God's chosen people" (Col 3:12). It is within the context of the church that we can help each other cultivate such virtues as humility, gentleness, and patience (v. 12). Paul goes on: "Let the word of Christ dwell in you richly as you teach and admonish one another with all wisdom" (v. 16). We need churches committed to teaching intellectual virtues. We need churches where members admonish one another when they detect intellectual vices.

And how will we know that we have achieved the development of a virtuous mind? We will know we have arrived once the habit has become "natural" to us. Konyndyk DeYoung observes that philosophers have described the perfect achievement of virtue as yielding internal harmony and integrity.[393] This is the ultimate aim in the cultivation of intellectual virtues. We want them to become "second nature" to us, and the result will be a sense of internal peace and harmony and human excellence.

PRAYER[394]

O Lord, Creator of all that exists and the fountain of all goodness,
> beauty, and truth;
>> You have called us to love you with our whole being,
>>> including our minds.

Merciful God, we confess that we have not always been faithful
> in the use of our intellects.
>> We are sometimes intellectually lazy, sometimes too sure
>>> of ourselves, and often too arrogant about giving voice
>>> to what we believe to be true.
>> When we disagree with others, we sometimes do not listen
>>> carefully to what they say, or we distort what they say.
>>> And sometimes we treat dialogue and even argument
>>> as a battle that has to be won at all costs.
>> We also confess that sometimes we do not have the courage
>>> of our convictions and we keep silent when we should speak up.
>>> And sometimes we speak when it would be better to keep silent.

For all these intellectual vices, we are truly sorry and humbly repent
> of our sins.
>> Forgive us, our Lord and Savior, and restore us so that we might
>>> serve you in newness of life, to the glory of your precious name.

Lord Jesus Christ, we pray for grace to love the truth and to be
> diligent in the search for truth.
>> Give us wisdom, a keenness of perception, a sharpness
>>> of understanding, and the ability to grasp ideas correctly.
>> Help us to avoid error and to be careful in detecting error.
>> Help us also to be gracious in helping others to love the truth.
>>> In doing so, give us the ability to express ourselves with clarity,
>>> charity, and charm.

We pray that our convictions will always be held and shared

with intellectual humility.
Help us to acknowledge that we only see through a glass darkly,
> that we only know the truth in part.
Give us the humility to admit that we might be wrong.
Remind us to look joyfully to a future time when you will appear
> in all your glory, when we will know fully, even as we are known,
> and when truth will triumph. In the meantime, help us to live
> in the present and to be teachable.

We pray for minds that are genuinely open to the delights of new
> discoveries as we study your revelation in Scripture and in nature.
> Help us also to be open-minded as we entertain the ideas
> > of other people who are created in the image of God,
> > and who therefore might have discovered truths that
> > we have so far missed.
> Help us to display a proper confidence in our convictions,
> > not too sure of ourselves, and yet not too timid either,
> > believing that you the Source of all truth have graciously
> > let rays of your brilliance penetrate the darkness
> > of our own puny understanding.

We pray that we will possess those intellectual virtues that are so
> necessary in a deeply divided world with many languages
> and worldviews and claims to truth.
> Help us to practice the virtue of forbearance, recognizing that while
> > error has no rights, people do, and so they need to be given
> > the time and space to declare their understanding of the truth.
> Help us also to be fair in representing the beliefs of those we
> > disagree with, expressing our disagreement with grace
> > and in such a way that peace will always prevail.
> And give us courage, too, in the face of established belief,
> > whether in the church or in society at large, to give expression
> > of our contrary understanding of the truth. But again,
> > help us to do so with humility and love.

We pray all this in the name of the Father, the Son, and the Holy Spirit,
Amen.

Endnotes

PREFACE

1. The final book in question was published in 2018. See Thiessen, *Scandal of Evangelism*.
2. See Thiessen, *Stumbling Heavenward*.
3. For documentation on today's toxic university environment, see Lukianoff, *Unlearning Liberty*.
4. At Wilfrid Laurier University, where I began my teaching career and where I have done some teaching since my retirement, a major controversy concerning free speech emerged in 2017 after Lindsay Shepherd, a graduate student, used a Jordan Peterson video clip to illustrate a position on gender-neutral language in a tutorial for a communications class. See Hutchens, "What Really Happened."
5. Jacobs, *How to Think*, 11.
6. Jacobs, *How to Think*, 11–12.
7. Jacobs, *How to Think*, 17.
8. Jacobs, *How to Think*, 150, 29.
9. Jacobs, *How to Think*, 150.
10. Jason Baehr speaks to a double need for a book like this. He confesses that concern about intellectual virtues "has yet to trickle down to a non-academic audience." He has also called for a treatment of intellectual virtues that "issues from a richly and distinctively Christian standpoint" ("Foreword" to Dow, *Virtuous Minds*, 16).
11. See Thiessen, "In Pursuit of Intellectual Virtue."

1: THE NATURE AND STUDY OF INTELLECTUAL VIRTUES

12. For example, the reaction to the 2022 landmark decision of the US Supreme Court to overturn Roe v. Wade revealed how so many liberal progressives found it impossible to appreciate that there might be good arguments on the pro-life side of the abortion debate. The lack of virtues of intellectual forbearance and open-mindedness was astounding as I read the reactions of "the chattering class" to the decision. One would have thought the sky was falling.

13. The book in question was written by a philosopher friend of mine, Darrin W. Snyder Belousek, *Marriage, Scripture, and the Church*.

14. Aristotle, *Nicomachean Ethics* 2.6.

15. Nathan King makes much of Aristotle's golden mean in his analysis of intellectual virtues and vices, though he is forced to admit that not all intellectual virtues fit into this framework (*Excellent Mind*, 24–25).

16. There has been some debate as to whether intellectual virtues should be understood as a subset of moral virtues, or whether these two virtues should be understood as independent and distinct from one another. Roberts and Wood argue that there is no strict dividing line between moral and intellectual virtue (*Intellectual Virtues*, 180). Baehr argues for a middle position in this debate (*Inquiring Mind*, appendix, 206–22).

17. This list and my treatment of epistemic faculties draws on Roberts and Wood, *Intellectual Virtues*, 86.

18. Roberts and Wood define intellectual virtues as "acquired bases of excellent intellectual functioning" (*Intellectual Virtues*, 60). Baehr gives the following definition: "An intellectual virtue is a character trait that contributes to its possessor's personal intellectual worth on account of its involving a positive psychological orientation towards epistemic goods" (*Inquiring Mind*, 102). I find Baehr's definition too focused on psychology.

19. My general description of intellectual virtues takes a middle position on a hotly debated topic among virtue epistemologists. Virtue reliabilists conceive of intellectual virtues as stable dispositions (or faculties) that produce good epistemic outcomes, i.e., that produce true beliefs. Virtue responsibilists conceive of intellectual virtues as acquired character traits for which we are to some degree responsible. I prefer to see these approaches as inter-related. We are in part responsible for developing our natural knowledge-producing faculties. For a good summary of this debate, see Heather Battaly, "Introduction," in Battaly, *Routledge Handbook of Virtue Epistemology*, 1–11. Battaly also takes a blended approach to this debate, as does Linda Zagzebski, *Virtues of the Mind*.

20. See Mao, *Ethics and the Moral Life*.

21. Roberts and Wood, *Intellectual Virtues*, 5.

22. For some examples of this despair about epistemology, see Roberts and Wood, *Intellectual Virtues*, 6.

23. Code, *Epistemic Responsibility*, ix.

24. Code, *Epistemic Responsibility*, 8.

25. Code, *Epistemic Responsibility*, 44.

26. The term "intellectual virtue" was first introduced in contemporary epistemological literature by Ernest Sosa in 1980. For a brief history of virtue epistemology, see Baehr, *Inquiring Mind*, 6–8.
27. I see virtue epistemology as supplementing traditional approaches to epistemology, rather than replacing it.
28. Roberts and Wood, *Intellectual Virtues*, 6.
29. Earlier endnotes have already referred to some of this philosophical literature. Of special significance are the following: Linda Zagzebski's influential book *Virtues of the Mind* (1996), and two books written by Christian philosophers—Roberts and Wood, *Intellectual Virtues* (2007) and Baehr, *Inquiring Mind* (2011). Another important resource is Heather Battaly's *Routledge Handbook of Virtue Epistemology*.
30. For a short review of the recent literature on specific intellectual virtues and vices, see Heather Battaly, "Introduction," in Battaly, *Routledge Handbook on Virtue Epistemology*, 4–5. Battaly's anthology also carries a good number of essays that review the literature on individual virtues and vices. I have drawn on four helpful books that provide more extensive treatments of individual intellectual virtues: Roberts and Wood, *Intellectual Virtues* (2007); King, *Excellent Mind* (2021); Dow, *Virtuous Minds* (2013). Baehr, *Inquiring Mind* (2011), devotes a chapter each to open-mindedness and intellectual courage.
31. Nathan King has used this phrase in the subtitle of his book *Excellent Mind: Intellectual Virtues for Everyday Life*. However, many of King's examples are academic and even exotic in nature. On the other hand, the book does a good job of simplifying philosophical ideas. Another more readable book on intellectual virtues and vices is written by Dow, *Virtuous Minds*. However, this book is written specifically for Christian teachers and to my mind suffers from some conceptual confusions.
32. Jason Baehr speaks to this need in his Foreword to Dow, *Virtuous Minds*, 16.
33. See, for example, Anselm's "Proslogium," 93; Hart, *Faith Thinking*, 21, 60.
34. See chapters 3–8 in Aquinas, *On the Truth of the Catholic Faith*.
35. Rawls, "Idea of an Overlapping Consensus."
36. I have borrowed this diagram from a presentation Trevor Cooling made at the International Seminar on Religious Education and Values, held at Banff, Alberta, in 1992. All diagrams have been designed by Gregory Thiessen.
37. For some passages in the Bible on politics, see 1 Sam 8 and Rom 13:1–7; economics, Amos 2:6–8 and Matt 6:19–24; marriage, Gen 2:18–25 and Matt 19:1–12.
38. See Holmes, *All Truth Is God's Truth*.
39. Johnson, *Scripture's Knowing*, xiv. See also chapter 6 in Johnson, *Scripture's Knowing*, and chapter 6 in *Biblical Knowing*.
40. Johnson, *Scripture's Knowing*; *Biblical Knowing*; Smith, *Such a Mind as This*.
41. Hays, *Moral Vision of the New Testament*, 306.
42. For a useful summary of his approach, see Hays, *Moral Vision*, 209, 212–13, 309–10. I am re-wording and re-ordering Hays's four approaches, although the changes are minor. I am also adding an additional mode of ethical discourse, as a way of resolving an ambiguity in Hays where he sometimes refers to narrative texts (plural) while at other times he focuses on the story of the New Testament as a whole (295). Hence the addition of (d).

43. Hays isn't entirely clear about which mode of ethical discourse is primary. Sometimes this status is given to the paradigmatic mode (or narrative texts—my "stories") (*Moral Vision of the New Testament*, 295), sometimes the narrative of the New Testament as a whole (295), and sometimes the mode of symbolic world construction (my "worldview") (303).

44. Hays, *Moral Vision of the New Testament*, 294.

45. This is the error of biblical scholars (and lay Christians) who are oriented to the spirit of the Enlightenment and therefore insist on an uncommitted approach to Scripture which, in turn, produces a distancing effect.

46. This tends to be the error of those who like to take the Bible literally. For a short summary of these two extremes in biblical interpretation, see Michael Goheen, "Critical Examination of David Bosch's Missional Reading of Luke," in Bartholomew, *Reading Luke*, 229–64.

47. Hays describes the challenge in this way: "The use of the New Testament in normative ethics requires an integrative act of the imagination, a discernment about how our lives, despite their historical dissimilarity to the lives narrated in the New Testament, might fitly answer to that narration and participate in the truth that it tells" (Hays, *Moral Vision of the New Testament*, 298). See also Wells, *Improvisation*.

48. Plantinga, *Warranted Christian Belief*. See also Mavrodes, *Belief in God*; Wolterstorff, *Reason within the Bounds of Religion*; Alston, *Perceiving God*.

49. For a critique of Plantinga and Reformed epistemology, see Johnson, *Biblical Knowing*, 173–79.

50. See the following books by Esther Meek: *Longing to Know*; *Loving to Know*; *Little Manual for Knowing*. Meek's thinking has been influenced by Michael Polanyi's book *Personal Knowledge*.

51. Meek, *Little Manual for Knowing*, 13.

52. Meek, *Little Manual for Knowing*, 14.

53. Meek, *Little Manual for Knowing*, 15–16. See also Meek's *Loving to Know*; Smith, *Such a Mind as This*, 16–23.

54. Meek, *Little Manual for Knowing*, 17.

55. See Johnson, *Biblical Knowing*; *Scripture's Knowing*. Also Smith, *Such a Mind as This*.

56. Johnson, *Scripture's Knowing*, 7–8.

57. Johnson, *Scripture's Knowing*, 15–16.

58. The parable of the sower reinforces this idea. Jesus uses the analogy of seed sown on good ground to refer to everyone who hears the word, accepts it, and produces a bountiful crop (Mark 4:1–20). See also Jas 1:22 and 3:13.

59. Johnson, *Scripture's Knowing*, 16.

60. Johnson, *Scripture's Knowing*, 14.

61. Johnson, *Scripture's Knowing*, 89. See also chapter 6 in Johnson, *Biblical Knowing*.

62. One exception to this is a reference to intellectual virtues in Smith, *Such a Mind as This*, 6. But I am not sure Smith has demonstrated how God exemplifies all the

intellectual virtues he lists.

63. For a classic statement on the importance of the mind in the Bible, see the booklet written by Stott, *Your Mind Matters*.
64. Prov 1:7; 9:10; Job 28:28; Ps 111:10; Isa 33:6.
65. See Thiessen, *Ethics of Evangelism*; *Scandal of Evangelism*.
66. Meek, *Little Manual for Knowing*, 13.
67. In this section I am drawing on the following writers for their treatments of the creation, fall, and redemption themes of a Christian worldview and their implications for epistemology: chapters 2–3 in Johnson, *Biblical Knowing*; chapters 1–3, 8 in Smith, *Such a Mind as This*; Wolters, *Creation Regained*.
68. See also Ps 104:24; Jer 10:12.
69. Hence the frequent contrast in Scripture between God's infinite knowledge and the limited nature of human knowledge. See, for example, Job 21:22; 36:26; Pss 92:5; 139:6; 147:5; Prov 3:5; Isa 40:14, 28; 55:9; Rom 11:33; 1 Cor 13:9, 12; Col 2:3.
70. The Psalmist seems to come to a similar conclusion: "My heart is not proud, O Lord, my eyes are not haughty; I do not concern myself with great matters or things too wonderful for me" (Ps 131:1).
71. Smith, *Such a Mind as This*, 23.
72. How a tree can communicate knowledge of any sort, and what exactly is meant by knowledge of good and evil, are questions that we can leave for theologians to sort out. What is clear is that knowledge will play a central role in the narrative that follows (Johnson, *Biblical Knowing*, 24).
73. Smith, *Such a Mind as This*, 9.
74. Wolterstorff, *Until Justice and Peace Embrace*, 70.
75. Vanhoozer, *Is There a Meaning?*, 299.
76. See chapter 8 in Smith, *Such a Mind as This*. My treatment of redemptive epistemology in the paragraphs that follow draws heavily from Smith.
77. Smith, *Such a Mind as This*, 196–201.
78. Smith, *Such a Mind as This*, 219. See Deut 5:16; 6:18; 8:1; 11:8–9; 16:20; 25:15; 30:6.
79. The covenantal disjunction of blessings and curses runs throughout the Bible. See Deut 11:26–32; 27:9—28:68; Josh 8:30–35; Isa 1:19–20; Matt 7:24–27; Gal 6:7–8.

2: LOVE OF KNOWLEDGE AND TRUTH

80. Roberts and Wood, for example, treat the love of knowledge as "basic to the whole of intellectual life" (*Intellectual Virtues*, 73). However, Roberts and Wood also classify the love of knowledge as one of the intellectual virtues in part 2 of their book. So, their position is not entirely clear. See also Dow, who treats "curiosity" (his term for the love of knowledge) as "the most foundational" of all the intellectual virtues and vices (*Virtuous Minds*, 56). Strangely, Dow also says that curiosity is not the most important of intellectual traits (56). Surely, if it is foundational it

should also be the most important. Jason Baehr identifies the love of truth as "the very heart" of virtuous intellectual character (Foreword to Dow, *Virtuous Minds*, 13).

81. Roberts and Wood, *Intellectual Virtues*, 310. See also Lani Watson, who treats "curiosity" (her term for the love of knowledge) as a "common motivation" of all the intellectual virtues and vices ("Curiosity and Inquisitiveness," in Battaly, *Routledge Handbook of Virtue Epistemology*, 158). Watson also lists a number of other philosophers who agree with her.

82. Jason Baehr, for example, gives us this definition of intellectual virtues generally: "An intellectual virtue is a character trait that contributes to its possessor's personal intellectual worth on account of its involving a positive psychological orientation towards epistemic goods" (*Inquiring Mind*, 102). Epistemic goods, for Baehr, include the love of knowledge, truth, understanding, and rationality (6, 111, 203). However, Baehr goes on to list inquisitiveness, attentiveness, carefulness, and thoroughness in inquiry as intellectual virtues (89). So, he isn't entirely clear as to whether the love of knowledge and truth is a separate intellectual virtue, or whether it defines the general nature of intellectual virtues.

83. Baehr talks about "the deep interrelatedness of the intellectual virtues," which makes it difficult if not impossible to classify them (*Inquiring Mind*, 18n1). King also talks about a heavy overlapping between the intellectual virtues (*Excellent Mind*, 173).

84. Plato, for example, describes the philosopher or virtuous "lover of wisdom" as one who "love[s] the sight of truth" (*Republic*, 475b–476b, in *Complete Works of Plato*; Baehr, *Inquiring Mind*, 101n23). Roberts and Wood give wisdom "a privileged place in the array of intellectual virtues, one that corresponds to the special place occupied by the love of knowledge" (*Intellectual Virtues*, 305). Each intellectual virtue "has its own department of practical wisdom," they maintain (311). Practical wisdom is needed to switch from one intellectual virtue to another as occasion requires, or for blending the virtues, or for adjudicating between the different appeals of virtues when they seem to conflict (311).

85. Aristotle, *Metaphysics* 1.1 980a1–2.

86. Smith, *Such a Mind as This*, 1. Smith provides a delightful speculative account of what it must have been like for Adam to wake up and learn about the world around him (24–27).

87. On this point, see Kapic, *You're Only Human*, 150.

88. Johnson, *Biblical Knowing*, 192.

89. Comenius, as quoted in Smith, *Such a Mind as This*, 23n7. Smith gives an excellent account of "Edenic Epistemology" in chapter 2 of his book. See also chapter 2 in Johnson, *Biblical Knowing*.

90. Smith, *Such a Mind as This*, 25.

91. Smith, *Such a Mind as This*, 25.

92. On this point, see Kapic, *You're Only Human*, 84.

93. Smith, *Such a Mind as This*, 61.

94. Lesslie Newbigin correctly points out that it is precisely here that the Christian tradition challenges the Enlightenment claim that human beings have a natural

desire to know the truth and that we can arrive at truth on our own by human reason (*Proper Confidence*, 68, 78, 104).

95. See also Prov 10:21; 14:7; 18:2; 24:7.
96. See also Isa 35:5; 42:20; 43:8.
97. Matt 13:14–15; Isa 6:9–10; cf. Mark 4:1–20; Luke 8:1–15; Acts 28:26–27.
98. 2 Tim 2:14, 23; 1 Tim 6:3; Titus 3:9.
99. Plantinga has described this divided nature in terms of proper and normal functioning of our cognitive faculties. God has designed us in such a way that when our cognitive faculties are functioning properly, we will acquire knowledge and truth. "A thing's design plan is the way the thing in question is 'supposed' to work" (Plantinga, *Warrant and Proper Function*, 21). Sadly, the fall has led to some flaws in the normal functioning of our cognitive faculties (199–211).
100. See chapter 2 in Hospers, *Introduction to Philosophical Analysis*.
101. See Gettier, "Is Justified True Belief Knowledge?," 121–23. Since then, epistemologists have uncovered other examples of justified true beliefs that fail to be knowledge. These examples have come to be known as the Gettier problem.
102. See chapter 1 in Johnson, *Scripture's Knowing*. Meek also objects to the "knowledge-as-information" paradigm in epistemology in *Little Manual for Knowing*, 2, 32, 48–49.
103. See chapter 6 in Johnson, *Scripture's Knowing* and *Biblical Knowing*.
104. Johnson, *Biblical Knowing*, 16. Johnson is also forced to use the language of "illumination" and knowing as an "event" (*Scripture's Knowing*, 2, 4). Similarly, Meek is forced to admit that knowing does have an end goal, a moment of "insight," and thus also includes an element of "knowledge-as-information" (*Little Manual for Knowing*, 88, 96, 98–99).
105. Here are just a few examples. The prophet Jeremiah is called to proclaim God's word to Israel that has forsaken God. And what does he find? "Everyone is senseless and without knowledge" (Jer 10:14; 51:17). To Daniel and his friends "God gave knowledge and understanding of all kinds of literature and learning" (Dan 1:17). The prophet Hosea says "my people are destroyed from lack of knowledge," indeed, they have rejected knowledge (Hos 4:6). In explaining the parable of the sower, Jesus tells the disciples that they have been given "the knowledge of the secrets of the kingdom of God" (Matt 13:14). Paul, in defending his authority as an apostle, at one point admits that while he might not be a trained speaker, "I do have knowledge" (2 Cor 11:6).
106. Roberts and Wood, *Intellectual Virtues*, 33.
107. See chapter 12 in Roberts and Wood, *Intellectual Virtues*.
108. See also Prov 1:1–7; 8:1–11; 9:10. The qualifications for craftsmen in the building of the tabernacle include wisdom, understanding, and knowledge combined with practical skill (Exod 31:1; 35:30; 36:1). For a discussion of the breadth of the Hebrew meaning of wisdom, see Johnson, *Biblical Knowing*, 136–41.
109. Bloom, *Closing of the American Mind*, 25.
110. Putting this into philosophical terminology, I am an ontological realist and an epistemological relativist with regard to truth. Trevor Hart makes a similar distinction in his excellent book, *Faith Thinking*, 62–69, 220–25.

111. This diagram was designed by Gregory Thiessen and also appears in three of my earlier books: *In Defence of Religious Schools and Colleges*, 214; *Ethics of Evangelism*, 69; *Stumbling Heavenward*, 353. An indication of how important I feel the distinction is between truth and the search for truth!

112. Russell, *Problems of Philosophy*, 160–61. William James refers to some idealists who "seem to say that they [ideas] are true whenever they are what God means that we ought to think about that subject" (*Essays in Pragmatism*, 160).

113. As William James puts it, all of us instinctively "dogmatize like infallible popes" (*Essays in Pragmatism*, 97). My apologies to Catholics who might find this reference objectionable.

114. James, *Essays in Pragmatism*, 170.

115. Johnson, *Scripture's Knowing*, 8.

116. Johnson, *Scripture's Knowing*, 10.

117. Johnson, *Scripture's Knowing*, 11–13.

118. Baehr, *Inquiring Mind*, 102.

119. John Locke describes the lover of truth in this way: "For he that loves it not, will not take much pains to get it, nor be much concerned when he misses it" (*Inquiry Concerning Human Understanding* 4.19).

120. My definition draws in part on Roberts and Wood, *Intellectual Virtues*, 73.

121. John Paul II followed up *Veritatis Splendor* with his 1998 encyclical *Fides et Ratio* (Faith and Reason). I am drawing here on an essay by Charles J. Chaput, "Believe That You May Understand: *Fides et Ratio* at Twenty."

122. Meek, *Little Manual for Knowing*, 14.

123. Meek, *Little Manual for Knowing*, 86.

124. See chapter 8 in Smith, *Such a Mind as This*.

125. Phil 1:9; Col 1:9, 2:2–3; Titus 1:1; 1 Tim 2:4; 2 Tim 2:25. Peter, too, develops this theme: "For this very reason, make every effort to add to your faith goodness; and to goodness knowledge. . . ." (2 Pet 1:5).

126. Smith, *Such a Mind as This*, 15; Isa 65:17.

127. See also Isa 2:3–4; 65:17–25; Ezek 36:33–36; 37:26–27; Rev 21:1–8.

128. See chapter 8 in Meek, *Little Manual for Knowing*.

129. Watson tries to make a rather fine distinction between curiosity and inquisitiveness. Curiosity is more positive in nature, while inquisitiveness is understood in terms of asking questions. See Watson, "Curiosity and Inquisitiveness," chapter 13 in Battaly, *Routledge Handbook of Virtue Epistemology*.

130. King treats carefulness as a separate virtue. See chapter 4 in King, *Excellent Mind*.

131. See, for example, chapter 4 in King, *Excellent Mind*.

132. Locke gives the following as "one unerring mark of" being a lover of truth: "The not entertaining any proposition with greater assurance, than the proofs it is built upon will warrant. Whoever goes beyond this measure of assent, it is plain, receives not truth in the love of it; loves not truth for truth's sake, but for some other by-end" (*Inquiry Concerning Human Understanding* 4.19).

133. Plantinga, *Warranted Christian Belief*.
134. See, for example, Saint Anselm's "Proslogium," 93.
135. Here I am drawing on Roberts and Wood, *Intellectual Virtues*, 155–64.
136. Some philosophers describe this qualification in terms of "worthiness" of knowledge. See Roberts and Wood, *Intellectual Virtues*, 157–60.
137. Roberts and Wood, *Intellectual Virtues*, 157. For an interesting list of questions and their relative importance, see King, *Excellent Mind*, 44.
138. See, for example, chapter 10 in Roberts and Wood, *Intellectual Virtues*; chapter 5 in King, *Excellent Mind*; Heidi Grasswick, "Epistemic Autonomy in a Social World of Knowing," chapter 16 in Battaly, *Routledge Handbook of Virtue Epistemology*. To their credit, all these writers, especially Grasswick, qualify autonomy by admitting that we are by nature dependent on others in our knowing.
139. See Thiessen, *Ethics of Evangelism*; *Scandal of Evangelism*.
140. King, *Excellent Mind*, 41. King in turn acknowledges his source of this anecdote in note 19 on the same page.
141. Roberts and Wood, *Intellectual Virtues*, 170.
142. Grant, *Think Again*, 257.
143. See, for example, articles by Gourlay, "Assessment of Bible Knowledge"; Mohler, "Scandal of Biblical Illiteracy"; Berding, "Crisis of Biblical Illiteracy."
144. King draws attention to this phenomenon in relation to philosophical skeptics of the ancient world who thought that suspension of judgment was always the reasonable attitude to take (*Excellent Mind*, 68).
145. Here I am drawing on "Intellectual Carefulness," chapter 2 in Dow, *Virtuous Minds*.
146. King, *Excellent Mind*, 67.
147. James, "Will to Believe," in *Essays in Pragmatism*, 100. Aristotle gives this wise advice: "It is the mark of the educated man and a proof of his culture that in every subject he looks for only so much precision as its nature permits" (*Nicomachean Ethics* 1.3).
148. Augustine, *Confessions*, 241. Augustine draws on 1 John 2:16, which refers to "the lust of his eyes." For a more recent treatment of idle curiosity, see Griffiths, *Vice of Curiosity*.
149. For a treatment of the seeming increase in people's appetite for mindless sensory stimulation and other kinds of contextless knowledge, see Kennedy, "Curiosity and the Integrated Self."
150. Bilbro argues that this "news-as-spectacle, whether a political scandal, a natural disaster, a terrorist attack, or almost any story as rendered by television, shapes those who consume it to be passive spectators" (*Reading the Times*, 28).

3: INTELLECTUAL HUMILITY

151. Collier, *Burning in My Bones*, 96.
152. Philip Dow, for example, thinks intellectual humility might very well be the most important virtue (*Virtuous Minds*, 70).
153. See, for example, Prov 26:12; Isa 5:21; 57:15; 66:2; Matt 5:5; Luke 14:11; 18:14; 1 Pet 5:5.
154. See also Deut 8:14; Prov 16:5; 21:4; Ezek 28:5.
155. Dru Johnson objects to interpreting the fall primarily in terms of a desire or search for autonomy apart from God. He puts the focus instead on who Adam and Eve are listening to (see chapter 3 in Johnson, *Biblical Knowing*). But choosing to listen to the serpent instead of God is still an exercise in autonomy. Johnson is also forced to concede that autonomy does play a role in the totality of actions of Adam and Eve (62). Richard Smith follows Johnson to some extent (see chapter 3 in Smith, *Such a Mind as This*), though he also interprets the fall in terms of Adam and Eve reimagining themselves "apart from their creational situatedness" and assuming "epistemological autonomy" (51, 53).
156. See also Prov 16:18; 21:4.
157. See also Matt 18:1–4; 19:13–14.
158. See chapter 2 in Gooch, *Partial Knowledge*.
159. 1 Cor 1:20. In fact Paul has quite a lot to say about pointless arguing in his other letters. See, for example, 1 Tim 6:4; 2 Tim 2:23; 3:7.
160. 1 Cor 1:27, 29, 31; cf. 1 Cor 3:21; 4:7; 9:16. The theme of boasting is also prominent in 2 Corinthians. Here it is significant that although Paul is often boasting, he is embarrassed about doing so. It is because of all the attacks against him that he is forced to engage in "foolish boasting" (see esp. 2 Cor 10–13). Paul is very much aware of the fact that ultimately he is answerable to God, and here there is little room for boasting (2 Cor 1:12; 4:2; 5:12).
161. I am indebted in the following paragraphs to the excellent introduction to the virtue of intellectual humility found in chapter 7 in Dow, *Virtuous Minds*.
162. Lewis, *Screwtape Letters*, 73.
163. Dow, *Virtuous Minds*, 70.
164. Chesterton, *Orthodoxy*, 32.
165. Nancy E. Snow, "Intellectual Humility," in Battaly, *Routledge Handbook of Virtue Epistemology*, 178–79.
166. Snow, "Intellectual Humility," in Battaly, *Routledge Handbook of Virtue Epistemology*, 178.
167. See chapter 9 in Roberts and Wood, *Intellectual Virtues*. It is significant, I believe, that Roberts and Wood title this chapter "Humility" when in fact their book is about intellectual virtues. This leads to an unfortunate tendency to talk about the moral virtue of humility rather than focus specifically on the virtue of intellectual humility.
168. Roberts and Wood, *Intellectual Virtues*, 236. In the end, when Roberts and Wood finally deal specifically with intellectual humility, they still define it negatively. For

example, intellectual humility is defined as having "an unusually low dispositional concern of self-importance" within the context of intellectual communities. Or, intellectual humility involves "a very low concern for intellectual domination" in terms of influencing others. Or intellectual humility is a disposition not to make unwarranted intellectual entitlement claims (250).

169. Meek, *Little Manual for Knowing*, 16–17.
170. Collier, *Burning in My Bones*, 96.
171. I am drawing here on an essay by John Dickson, "How Christian Humility Upended the World."
172. Aristotle, *Nicomachean Ethics* 4.3.
173. Kapic, *You're Only Human*, 100.
174. Schuurman, "You're Only Human."
175. Here I am drawing on Roberts and Wood, *Intellectual Virtues*, 250–55.
176. Schuurman, "You're Only Human."
177. See chapter 8 in Meek, *Little Manual for Knowing*.
178. See also Prov 9:10; Job 28:28; Ps 11:10; Isa 33:6.
179. See Plato's "Apology," in Plato, *Complete Works of Plato*, 17–36.
180. Snow, "Intellectual Humility," in Battaly, *Routledge Handbook of Virtue Epistemology*, 178, 187–89.
181. Vanhoozer, *Is There a Meaning?*, 562–63.
182. See my blog, Thiessen, "Bible and a Hermeneutic of Suspicion."
183. Oberholtzer Lee, "Critical Thinking or Just Critical?"
184. For a depressing account of Christian syncretism, see Burton, *Strange Rites*.
185. See 2 Cor 4:7; 11:29–30; 12:8–10. See also Gombis, *Power in Weakness*.
186. Nagel, *View from Nowhere*, 70.
187. Nagel, *Last Word*, 5. See also Hart, *Faith Thinking*, 62–69, 220–25.
188. Dow, *Virtuous Minds*, 71–72.
189. Roberts and Wood, *Intellectual Virtues*, 237.
190. Roberts and Wood, *Intellectual Virtues*, 238.
191. Quoted in Roberts and Wood, *Intellectual Virtues*, 237.
192. For two examples of philosophers who treat autonomy as an intellectual virtue, see chapter 5 in King, *Excellent Mind*; chapter 10 in Roberts and Wood, *Intellectual Virtues*.
193. See chapter 5 in Thiessen, *Teaching for Commitment*.
194. On the concept of "normal autonomy," see chapter 5 in Thiessen, *Teaching for Commitment*. On "relational autonomy," see Heidi Grasswick, "Epistemic Autonomy in a Social World of Knowing," in Battaly, *Routledge Handbook of Virtue Epistemology*, 200–202.
195. This is the subtitle of the chapter King devotes to the intellectual virtue of autonomy (chapter 5 in *Excellent Mind*).

196. Jacobs, *How to Think*, 37.

197. Both King and Roberts/Wood make these qualifications in their treatments of autonomy as an intellectual virtue. See chapter 5 in King, *Excellent Mind*; chapter 10 in Roberts and Wood, *Intellectual Virtues*.

198. The need for balance has been recognized in social epistemology, particularly feminist epistemology. For a good treatment of a balance between autonomy and interdependence, see Grasswick, "Epistemic Autonomy in a Social World of Knowing," chapter 16 in Battaly, *Routledge Handbook of Virtue Epistemology*.

199. 1 Cor 13:11. Paul urges us to "stop thinking like children" (1 Cor 14:20). The author of Hebrews encourages us to grow beyond "the elementary truths of God's word" ("milk") to solid food (Heb 5:11–14).

200. Caws and Jones, *Religious Upbringing and the Costs*.

201. For a book-length refutation of the charge of indoctrination against Christian nurture, see Thiessen, *Teaching for Commitment*.

202. Raymond D. Bradley, "From Fundamentalist to Freethinker (It All Began with Santa)," in Caws and Jones, *Religious Upbringing and the Costs*, 50.

203. Lewis defines chronological snobbery as "the uncritical acceptance of the intellectual climate common to our own age and the assumption that whatever has gone out of date is on that account discredited" (*Surprised by Joy*, 167).

204. For some examples and exhortations about falling away from the truth in the Old Testament, see Deut 11:28; 28:14; 31:16–17, 21, 29; Judg 2:16–23; Pss 78:8; 95:10; Jer 5:23; 11:10; 13:10, 18:15; Amos 8:11–13. For some New Testament references that do the same and also urge us to hold on to the faith, see Matt 24:10–13; 1 Cor 15:2; Eph 4:14; 6:14; 2 Tim 4:3–4; 2 Thess 2:15; Titus 1:9; 2 Pet 1:12; 1 John 4:1–6; Heb 2:2.

205. For some background on the origins of this unease about influence and persuasion, see Thiessen, *Ethics of Evangelism*, 55–59.

206. Johnstone, "Towards an Ethics of Rhetoric," 306.

207. On humble evangelism and apologetics, see Thiessen, *Scandal of Evangelism*, 66–68, 123–24, 168–69; Stackhouse, *Humble Apologetics*.

208. Quoted in Bofetti, "How Richard Rorty Found Religion," 29.

209. Peters, *Authority, Responsibility and Education*, 47, 54.

210. Roberts and Wood, *Intellectual Virtues*, 241–43.

211. Grant, *Think Again*, 54, 188, 250.

212. King, *Excellent Mind*, 108.

4. COMMITMENT AND OPENNESS

213. Baehr, *Inquiring Mind*, 140.

214. Jacobs, *How to Think*, 125.

215. Baehr, *Intellectual Virtues*, 140.

216. Chesterton, *Autobiography*, 223–24.
217. Newbigin, *Proper Confidence*, 47. Newbigin is here summarizing the thinking of Michael Polanyi, *Personal Knowledge*. See also MacIntyre, *Whose Justice? Which Rationality?*
218. Gardener, "Should We Teach Children?," 39. For a treatment of neutrality, see also King, *Excellent Mind*, 201–3.
219. See chapter 6 in Thiessen, *Teaching for Commitment*.
220. Quoted in Hare, *Open-Mindedness and Education*, 31.
221. Jacobs, *How to Think*, 125. Jonathan Haidt also questions the value of open-mindedness (*Righteous Mind*, 94–95, 105).
222. Baehr, *Intellectual Virtues*, 140–41.
223. See, for example, Jason Baehr's definition: "An open-minded person is characteristically (a) willing and (within limits) able (b) to transcend a default cognitive standpoint (c) in order to take up or take seriously the merits of (d) a distinct cognitive standpoint" (*Intellectual Virtues*, 152). My definition draws on William Hare's classic treatment of open-mindedness: "Open-mindedness involves a willingness to form and revise one's views as impartially and as objectively as possible in the light of available evidence and argument" (Hare, *In Defence of Open-Mindedness*, 3).
224. Baehr, *Intellectual Virtues*, 149, cf. 156.
225. Grant, *Think Again*.
226. Some of these descriptions of an open-minded person are borrowed from an essay by Wayne Riggs, "Open-Mindedness," in Battaly, *Routledge Handbook of Virtue Epistemology*, 141–54.
227. See Thiessen, "Teaching for Committed Openness," in Winsor, *Cultivating Inquiry across the Curriculum*, 159–85.
228. See chapter 10 in King, *Excellent Mind*.
229. King, *Excellent Mind*, 213. Roberts and Wood, in a chapter they have misleadingly entitled "Firmness," end up defending a notion close to my concept of "committed openness" when they talk about "the openness of firmness" (*Intellectual Virtues*, 213).
230. Newbigin, *Proper Confidence*. Paul Weston, in a recent study of Newbigin, interprets him as advocating a "humble confidence" (Weston, *Humble Confidence*). The concept of "confident humility" is a favorite of Grant, *Think Again*, 54, 188, 250.
231. Roberts and Wood, *Intellectual Virtues*, 184. Roberts and Wood introduce the notion of degrees of confidence which begins to hint at the notion of proper confidence or committed openness (207). They also use the term "flaccidity" to describe intellectual flabbiness (185–93). Other more familiar names for flaccidity could include "looseness" or "spinelessness" (King, *Excellent Mind*, 214).
232. Quoted in Roberts and Wood, *Intellectual Virtues*, 185.
233. Newman, *Fanatics and Hypocrites*, 131–33.
234. Smedes, *Caring and Commitment*, 153.
235. This account and quote from Galileo's letter are taken from Lightman, *Searching*

for the Stars, 38.

236. King and Roberts/Wood also treat dogmatism as an expression of closed-mindedness (King, *Excellent Mind*, 214; Roberts and Wood, *Intellectual Virtues*, 194–98).

237. Quoted in McCullough, *John Adams*, 228.

238. In this paragraph I am drawing on Newbigin, *Proper Confidence*, 54–55, 72–73.

239. The exact phrase "faith seeking understanding" was introduced by Anselm of Canterbury (1033–1109) in his book *Proslogium*. Before Anselm, Augustine of Hippo (AD 354–430) coined a similar phrase, "Unless you believe, you will not understand" (quoted in Hart, *Faith Thinking*, 90). For an extended and excellent treatment of faith seeking understanding, see Hart, *Faith Thinking*.

240. Newbigin, *Proper Confidence*, 66–67. This point becomes even clearer in Paul's eloquent description of love where he looks forward to a time when "I know in part" will be replaced with "I shall know fully" (1 Cor 13:12).

241. See Isa 6:9–10; 35:5; 42:20; 43:8; 44:18.

242. Matt 13:14–15; Isa 6:9–10; cf. Mark 4:1–20; Luke 8:1–15; Acts 28:26–27.

243. Rom 11:7–10; cf. Deut 29:4; Isa 29:10.

244. See, for example, Deut 31:27; Ps 78:8, 37; Jer 5:23.

245. See, for example, Deut 11:27; 28:14; 31:16–17; 29; Judg 2:16–23; Ps 95:10; Jer 11:10; 13:10; 14:10; 18:15; Hos 4:5.

246. See also Rom 12:2; Col 3:10; 1 Cor 15:34.

247. See also Pss 18:31; 19:14; 28:1; 31:2; 42:9; 62:6; 71:3; 78:35; 92:15.

248. See Isa 26:4; 30:29; Jer 16:19; 17:17; Joel 3:16; Nah 1:17; Hab 1:12; cf. 2 Sam 22:3.

249. See also 1 Cor 11:2; 15:1–2, 58; Eph 6:14; Col 2:5; 2 Tim 3:14; 2 Thess 2:15; Titus 1:9; 2 Pet 1:12; Heb 3:14; Rev 3:3.

250. See also 1 Thess 1:5; 2 Tim 1:8, 12; 3:14.

251. See also Heb 3:12, 14; 4:11; 13:6.

252. Rev 2:7; 11, 17, 29; 3:6, 13, 22.

253. Jer 23:9–40; Lam 2:14; Ezek 13.

254. For some modern examples of open-mindedness, see Heim, *How My Mind Has Changed*.

255. Roberts and Wood, *Intellectual Virtues*, 207.

256. Locke, *Inquiry Concerning Human Understanding* 2.4. See also another quotation from Locke in chapter 2 (n132).

257. Roberts and Wood, *Intellectual Virtues*, 207.

258. Newbigin, *Proper Confidence*, 66.

259. This need for a balance between tenacity and openness is also found in science. For example, Thomas Kuhn, in his ground-breaking work *Structure of Scientific Revolutions*, first published in 1962, argued that firmness is required of a good scientist. A scientist can give up a theory too soon. There are often anomalies, recalcitrant data, and unexpected results that seem to undermine a scientific theory. A good scientist needs to worry about these, but he or she can adopt a wait and

see attitude for a while. Of course, there is the danger that a scientist dismisses anomalies too easily and refuses to admit that the theory he presently holds might be wrong. Now we are dealing with closed-mindedness. But some firmness of belief is needed even in the sciences.

260. Roberts and Wood, *Intellectual Virtues*, 183.

261. "The beliefs face the tribunal of observation not singly but in a body," Quine maintains (Quine and Ullian, *Web of Belief*, 22). Quine reinforces this point with the use of several analogies in an oft-reprinted essay entitled "Two Dogmas of Empiricism." "The totality of our so-called knowledge or beliefs . . . is a man-made fabric which impinges on experience only along the edges. Or, to change the figure, total science is like a field of force whose boundary conditions are experience" (Quine, *From a Logical Point of View*, 42).

262. Quine, *From a Logical Point of View*, 43.

263. Roberts and Wood, *Intellectual Virtues*, 183–84, 209. Roberts and Wood draw attention to Alvin Plantinga's use of the term "depth of ingression" to refer to degrees of importance of our beliefs. Depth of ingression is the degree to which giving up the belief would cause reverberations in the subject's noetic structure (208).

264. Here I am drawing on Roberts and Wood, *Intellectual Virtues*, 199.

265. Neurath's shipbuilding analogy is referred to in Haworth, *Autonomy*, 4.

266. For example, David Foster Wallace has suggested that "you have to be willing to look honestly at yourself and at your motives for believing what you believe, and to do it more or less continually" (quoted in Jacobs, *How To Think*, 143).

267. I owe this analogy to Jacobs, *How To Think*, 147.

268. Newbigin, *Proper Confidence*.

269. Hart, *Faith Thinking*, 57.

270. For a penetrating analysis of the origins of Descartes's thought, see Toulmin, *Cosmopolis*.

271. Descartes, *Discourse on Method* and *Meditations*, 75.

272. As summarized in Hart, *Faith Thinking*, 57.

273. See chapter 6 in Thiessen, *Teaching for Commitment*. As Ludwig Wittgenstein puts it, "The child learns by believing the adult. Doubt comes after belief" (Wittgenstein, *On Certainty* §160).

274. Hart, *Faith Thinking*, 137.

275. For a review of this book, see my blog, Thiessen, "Sin of Certainty."

276. For a review of Enns's *The Bible Tells Me So*, see my blog, Thiessen, "Philosopher Examines Peter Enns."

277. Nietzsche, *Twilight of the Idols*, 172.

278. Watson, "Question-Shaped Faith."

279. Monteiro, "Different Kind of Sunday Service."

280. See my blog, Thiessen, "Question-Focused Christian Faith."

281. Kauffman, *Voices Together*, no. 440.

282. See my blog, Thiessen, "Bible and a Hermeneutic of Suspicion."
283. Billings, *End of the Christian Life*, 15.
284. Jacobs, *How to Think*, 126.

5: INTELLECTUAL FORBEARANCE, FAIRMINDEDNESS, AND INTELLECTUAL COURAGE

285. Nathan King uses the term "community-related" intellectual virtues to refer to open-mindedness, fair-mindedness, charity, and firmness (*Excellent Mind*, 195).
286. See, for example, Heidi Grasswick, "Epistemic Autonomy in a Social World of Knowing," in Battaly, *Routledge Handbook of Virtue Epistemology*, 200.
287. See Baehr, *Inquiring Mind*, 21.
288. See Thiessen, *Ethics of Evangelism*, 105–14.
289. Jacobs, *How to Think*, 145.
290. Buckley, "Onward, Christian Missionaries," 58. For some additional examples of evangelical intolerance and lack of forbearance, see Thiessen, *Ethics of Evangelism*, 112–13, 199.
291. I have expanded on this argument in relation to evangelism in Thiessen, *Ethics of Evangelism*, 146–47.
292. See, for example, Exod 34:6; Num 14:18; Ps 86:15.
293. Bilbro, *Reading the Times*, 36–43.
294. Quoted in Bilbro, *Reading the Times*, 36.
295. Smith, *Such a Mind as This*, 68.
296. For a good treatment of a perspectival approach to human knowing and its implications for our relationship with people who have different perspectives, see Hart, *Faith Thinking*, esp. 69, 179, 228.
297. See Lev 19:18; Deut 6:4–5; Mark 12:29–31; Gal 5:14.
298. See, for example, Prov 14:29; 15:18; 16:32; 19:11; 25:15. There are also frequent references to a gentle tongue as a key to overcoming dissension and opposition (Prov 15:1, 4; 25:15). At other times, holding our tongue is advocated for perhaps the same reason (Prov 10:19; 11:12; 13:3; 17:28).
299. See, for example, Phil 4:5; 2 Tim 2:24–25; Titus 3:2; 1 Pet 3:15–16.
300. Jesus, living in Palestine, will have been very much aware of Roman deities. Paul was evangelizing in very cosmopolitan cities, and at times he identifies other gods (e.g., Acts 17:23). See Jozef Tomko, "Missionary Challenges to the Theology of Salvation: A Roman Catholic Perspective," in Witte and Martin, *Sharing the Book*, 197.
301. For a brief treatment of this controversy, see Thiessen, *Ethics of Evangelism*, 199–200.
302. See, for example, Lev 19:34; 25:35; Deut 10:19; Matt 25:31–46; Heb 13:2.

303. Harder, "Reviving Intellectual Hospitality."
304. For a delightful analysis of "home," see Bouma-Prediger and Walsh, *Beyond Homelessness*, 56–66.
305. Harder is not entirely consistent in defending the notion of "intellectually hospitable disagreement" when she seems to agree with a few writers who claim that this notion "does not insist on persuasion" and is not focused on "dispute" ("Reviving Intellectual Hospitality," 56, 58, 53). She also muddies the waters when "dismiss" and "ridicule" are grouped together with "dispute." Intellectual hospitality allows for dispute but rules out ridicule and a dismissive attitude to new ideas.
306. Lukianoff and Haidt, *Coddling of the American Mind*, 158. Another expression of safetyism is the frequent use of the word "weaponize" to describe any speech that defends a position that someone disagrees with or finds offensive. While I agree that words can become weapons, there is surely something very distorting about interpreting all disagreement in terms of warfare. Disagreement and debate are simply not the same as firing artillery against the enemy.
307. Khalid, "Futility of Trigger Warnings."
308. Khalid, "Futility of Trigger Warnings."
309. Jacobs, *How to Think*, 145.
310. Mill, *On Liberty*, esp. chapter 2. I have summarized Mill's argument in Thiessen, *Ethics of Evangelism*, 134–35.
311. Inazu, *Confident Pluralism*; "Why I'm Still Confident."
312. Jesus' teaching about binding and loosing surely has some implications for the limits of intellectual forbearance in the church (Matt 16:17–20). Paul, in dealing with the question of food sacrificed to idols, calls for intellectual forbearance coupled with intellectual humility (1 Cor 8:1–13). Paul is upset with the churches in Corinth and Galatia for putting up with false teachers (2 Cor 11:4; Gal 2:4–5). Peter has some very harsh words for false teachers (2 Pet 2). In his letter to the churches in Asia, John frequently identifies some false teachers in the church, praising some churches for not tolerating them and condemning others for tolerating them. And after calling for repentance about being too tolerant, John warns that, if they do not repent, "I will soon come to you and will fight against them with the sword of my mouth" (Rev 2:16; 2:6, 20).
313. Jacobs, *How to Think*, 109.
314. There are a number of concepts that are closely related to fairmindedness. For example, much has been written recently about epistemic justice, which is a broader notion, but includes fairmindedness. See Laura Beeby, "Epistemic Justice: Three Models of Virtue," in Battaly, *Routledge Handbook of Virtue Epistemology*, 232–43. Another concept related to fairmindedness is intellectual generosity or charity (see chapter 11 in King, *Excellent Mind*).
315. King, *Excellent Mind*, 226.
316. Baehr, *Inquiring Mind*, 19.
317. Baehr, *Inquiring Mind*, 156.
318. Hopper, "This Could Cost Him His Job."
319. Jay Newman, as quoted in Thiessen, *Ethics of Evangelism*, 114.

320. Jacobs, *How to Think*, 106.

321. Jacobs, *How to Think*, 110, 18.

322. See chapter 3, pages 67–68, for a contemporary example of this failure.

323. Jacobs, *How to Think*, 108.

324. Deut 31:7, 23; Josh 1:6, 7, 9, 18; 10:25.

325. Wright, *Following Jesus*, 66.

326. This is close to the definitions given by Roberts and Wood, *Intellectual Virtues*, chapter 8, and Baehr, *Inquiring Mind*, chapter 9. Intellectual courage was also an important ideal of the Enlightenment of the seventeenth and eighteenth centuries. Immanuel Kant has this to say about intellectual courage and the closely related intellectual virtue of autonomy: "Have courage to make use of your *own* understanding! . . . is the motto of enlightenment" (quoted in King, *Excellent Mind*, 84).

327. For a review of the courage and autonomy displayed by these scientists, see King, *Excellent Mind*, 84–88.

328. King, *Excellent Mind*, 83, 89–90.

329. Stroehlein, "Other Navalnys."

330. Here I am following Baehr's analysis of a tripartite definition of intellectual courage (*Inquiring Mind*, 172–76).

331. This aspect of intellectual courage is closely related to intellectual perseverance, which is sometimes listed as a separate intellectual virtue. See chapter 8 in King, *Excellent Mind*; Ian James Kidd, "Epistemic Courage and the Harms of Epistemic Life," in Battaly, *Routledge Handbook of Virtue Epistemology*, 245.

332. Baehr gives the example of American journalist Edward R. Murrow, who put himself in harm's way for the sake of reaching the truth in his dogged pursuit of Senator Joseph McCarthy (*Inquiring Mind*, 165–66).

333. Baehr gives the example of Supreme Court Justice Sandra Day O'Connor, who in 1989 wrote a minority opinion that satisfied neither pro-choice or pro-life advocates of abortion (*Inquiring Mind*, 166–67).

334. Both Roberts and Wood (*Intellectual Virtues*, chapter 8) and Baehr (*Inquiring Mind*, chapter 9) get a bit carried away with the psychological dimension of courage. Baehr goes so far as to say that his "primary aim" is "to identify the characteristic psychology of intellectual courage" (163).

335. See chapter 8 in Roberts and Wood, *Intellectual Virtues*; King, *Excellent Mind*, 188–90.

336. I believe Roberts and Wood fail to see this because they associate courage with caution. Indeed, the chapter title is already misleading: "Courage and Caution" (chapter 8 in *Intellectual Virtues*).

337. Aristotle, *Nicomachean Ethics* 3.7.

338. See Roberts and Wood, *Intellectual Virtues*, 217–19; Ian James Kidd, "Epistemic Courage and the Harms of Epistemic Life," in Battaly, *Routledge Handbook of Virtue Epistemology*, 247.

339. See Huebner, *Suffering the Truth*.

340. To understand the contrasting worldviews of Moses and Pharaoh, see chapter 4 in Smith, *Such a Mind as This*.

341. Luke 20:20–26; Matt 22:15–22; Mark 12:13–17.

6: CONCLUSION

342. The following paragraphs draw on an insightful blog by Smith, "Christian Academic Commission."

343. I am drawing here on an excellent article by William Schultz, "Don't You Know There's a War On?" The article appeared in the regular column "Sightings," published by the University of Chicago Divinity School.

344. As summarized in Schultz, "Don't You Know There's a War On?" §5.

345. See Hartman, *War for the Soul of America*.

346. Quoted in Schultz, "Don't You Know There's a War On?" §12.

347. Quoted in Schultz, "Don't You Know There's a War On?" §1.

348. Hartman, in his *War for the Soul of America*, argues that culture wars are coming to an end. A second edition of this book was published in 2019 because the emergence of Donald Trump seemed to refute Hartman's optimistic outlook. Hartman maintains that Trump's success represents the last gasp of culture war politics. I'm not so sure! It would seem that Hartman's thesis is simply not open to falsification.

349. These data are drawn from the introduction of a recent issue of *Christian Scholar's Review*, which focuses on the theme "Conviction, Civility, and Christian Witness." The introduction is edited by Langer, Muehlhoff, and Woods.

350. Pew Research Center, "As Partisan Hostility Grows."

351. French, *Divided We Fall*. Here is his opening paragraph: "It's time for Americans to wake up to a fundamental reality: the continued unity of the United States of America cannot be guaranteed. At this moment in history, there is not a single important cultural, religious, political, or social force that is pulling Americans together more than it is pushing us apart. We cannot assume that a continent-sized, multi-ethnic, multi-faith democracy can remain united forever, and it will not remain united if our political class will not adapt to an increasingly diverse and divided American public."

352. Harder, "Reviving Intellectual Hospitality," 53.

353. For a good recent treatment of this topic, see King, "How Intellectual Virtues Can Help Us."

354. For example, Sam Harris in a recent interview suggested that anyone who opposes gay marriage on the basis of religious convictions "loses thirty IQ points" (Mounk, "Sam Harris on Whether Religion").

355. Yascha Mounk, quoted in Bilbro, *Reading the Times*, 136. Bilbro also cites some studies showing that the most factually informed people are often the most partisan (136n42).

356. Jonathan Haidt, a social psychologist and author of *The Righteous Mind: Why Good People are Divided by Politics and Religion*, compares our mind to a rider

on an elephant. The rider symbolizes the rational part of human nature, our controlled processes, our conscious verbal reasoning, including "reasoning-why." The elephant symbolizes the bulk of what is going on in your mind that you're not aware of, the automatic processes, including emotion, intuition, and all forms of "seeing-that." Haidt argues that most of us spend our time trying to persuade other people's "riders" by giving arguments, when the real way to persuade is to "talk to their elephants," and this speaking may look quite different from rational persuasion (*Righteous Mind*, 52–57).

357. Haidt, *Righteous Mind*, 34, 103–6.

358. A version of this argument has been articulated by John Wood, associate editor of *First Things* at the time, and once a fan of Tim Keller who has long advocated for a "winsome" approach to interacting with the cultured skeptics of our time (Wood, "How I Evolved on Tim Keller"). For other writers arguing for a winsome approach to handling disagreements, see Muehlhoff and Langer, *Winsome Persuasion*; *Winsome Conviction*.

359. I am drawing here from an article by Rick Langer, "Have We Become Moral Relativists?"

360. The Psalmist describes God's laws as eternal and enduring to this day, because God's word stands firm in the heavens, the same word that established the earth and that makes all things serve him for all time (Ps 119:89–91). A sign of degeneration is everyone doing what they see as fit (Judg 21:25; cf. Jer 8:6–7).

361. Langer, "Have We Become Moral Relativists?" §5.

362. Adam Grant provides a helpful list of skills to help us "rethink" issues and overcome polarizations. Many of his skills relate to intellectual virtues (Grant, *Think Again*, 251–57).

363. This problem has been highlighted by French postmodernist Jacques Derrida (1930–2004), one of the most well-known twentieth-century philosophers. For a readable summary of Derrida, see Smith, *Who's Afraid of Postmodernism?* I have written a lengthy critical review of this book (Thiessen, "Review of *Who's Afraid of Postmodernism*"). For a first-rate treatment of the distinction between facts and interpretations of facts, see Hart, *Faith Thinking*.

364. For discussions of incommensurability, see Kuhn, *Structure of Scientific Revolutions*; MacIntyre, *Whose Justice? Which Rationality?*

365. See Dorman, "Yes, We Can Understand Each Other."

366. See Kuhn, *Structure of Scientific Revolutions*, 152–59; Ratzsch, *Philosophy of Science*, 70–71; Hart, *Faith Thinking*, 66, 104, 221–23.

367. See "Myth, Ideology, and Idolatry," chapter 2 in Goudzwaard et al., *Hope In Troubled Times*.

368. Berger and Luckmann, *Social Construction of Reality*, 147–63.

369. See French, "Why Is It So Hard To Reach?"

370. Isaiah identifies the lack of truthfulness as one of many sins of Israel, and there is a hint that the problem also concerns the notion of truth itself. "Truth has stumbled in the streets, honesty cannot enter. Truth is nowhere to be found" (Isa 59:14–15). Jeremiah's description is even more poignant: "Truth has perished" (Jer 7:28). Or consider one of Daniel's visions about the abomination of Antiochus Epiphanes,

when "truth was thrown to the ground" (Dan 8:12).

371. Anderson, *Reality Isn't What It Used to Be*, 75.
372. Nietzsche, *Philosophy and Truth*, 84.
373. Rabinow, *Foucault Reader*. Commenting on Nietzsche, Foucault writes, "Truth is undoubtedly the sort of error that cannot be refuted because it was hardened into an unalterable form in the long baking process of history" (Rabinow, *Foucault Reader*, 79).
374. See Nagel, *Last Word*.
375. Trevor Hart provides some helpful descriptions of standing within a tradition and inviting others to try to understand our point of view, and doing all this in a humble manner (*Faith Thinking*, 101–3, 228, 230).
376. Plato, *Republic*, 394d, in Plato, *Complete Works of Plato*.
377. Gaede, *When Tolerance Is No Virtue*, 59.
378. Gaede, *When Tolerance Is No Virtue*, 118n5.
379. Middleton, "Our Postmodern Moment," 3.
380. James, *Essays in Pragmatism*, 97.
381. For a good example of the application of intellectual virtues like humility and forbearance and love to difficult conversations in the area of race relations, see Vazquez et al., *Healing Conversations*.
382. Grant, *Think Again*, 89; King, "How Intellectual Virtues Can Help Us," 316–17.
383. Quoted in Gibson, "In Search of Charitable Writing" §3. See also Gibson et al., *Charitable Writing*.
384. Paul can be an inspiration here. After expressing his philosophy of life, he goes on to say that "if on some point you think differently, that too God will make clear to you" (Phil 3:15).
385. Quoted in Bilbro, *Reading the Times*, 53.
386. For a treatment of the development of intellectual virtues in the home and in the classroom, see chapter 13 (and appendices) in Dow, *Virtuous Minds*. See also Baehr, *Deep in Thought*; *Intellectual Virtues and Education*. The focus could also be broader to include the cultivation of good character and virtue generally. For a more general treatment of the cultivation of virtues, see Brooks, *Road to Character*.
387. For a good treatment of the importance of mentors, see King, *Excellent Mind*, 263–67.
388. Dalrymple, "Why Evangelicals Disagree on the President" §4.
389. Gibson, "In Search of Charitable Writing" §17.
390. Dalrymple, "Why Evangelicals Disagree on the President" §26.
391. DeYoung, *Glittering Vices*, 15.
392. For a good historical survey of the place of virtue education in the church, see Oxenham, "Renaissance of Character and Virtue."
393. DeYoung, *Glittering Vices*, 16.
394. This prayer has been inspired by John Calvin's "Student Prayer" and Thomas Aquinas's "Prayer before Study."

Bibliography

Alston, William P. *Perceiving God.* Ithaca, NY: Cornell University Press, 1991.
Anderson, Walter. *Reality Isn't What It Used to Be: Theatrical Politics, Ready-to-Wear Religion, Global Myths, Primitive Chic, and Other Wonders of the Postmodern World.* San Francisco: Harper and Row, 1990.
Anselm. "Proslogium." In *Complete Philosophical and Theological Treatises*, edited by Jasper Hopkins and Herbert Richardson, 88–112. Minneapolis: Arthur J. Banning, 2000.
Aquinas, Thomas. *On the Truth of the Catholic Faith: Summa Contra Gentiles.* Translated by Anton C. Pegis. New York: Doubleday, 1955.
———. "Prayer Before Study." *Archdiocese of Saint Paul and Minneapolis Catholic Center.* 2012. Online. https://www.archspm.org/faith-and-discipleship/prayer/catholic-prayers/st-thomas-aquinas-prayer-before-study.
Aristotle. *Metaphysics.* Translated by W. D. Ross. In *Introduction to Aristotle*, edited by Richard McKeon, 237–96. New York: Modern Library, 1947.
———. *Nicomachean Ethics.* Translated by J. A. K. Thompson. London: Penguin, 1976.
Augustine. *Confessions.* Translated by R. S. Pine-Coffin. Harmondsworth, UK: Penguin, 1976.
Baehr, Jason. *Deep in Thought: A Practical Guide to Teaching Intellectual Virtues.* Cambridge, MA: Harvard Education Press, 2021.
———. *The Inquiring Mind: On Intellectual Virtues and Virtue Epistemology.* New York: Oxford University Press, 2011.
———, ed. *Intellectual Virtues and Education: Essays in Applied Virtue Epistemology.* London: Routledge, 2016.
Bartholomew, Craig G., ed. *Reading Luke: Interpretation, Reflection, Formation.* Milton Keynes, UK: Paternoster, 2005.
Battaly, Heather, ed. *The Routledge Handbook of Virtue Epistemology.* London: Routledge, 2019.
Belousek, Darrin W. Snyder. *Marriage, Scripture, and the Church: Theological Discernment on the Question of Same-Sex Union.* Grand Rapids: Baker Academic, 2021.

Berding, Kenneth. "The Crisis of Biblical Illiteracy." *Biola Magazine*, May 29, 2014. Online. https://www.biola.edu/blogs/biola-magazine/2014/the-crisis-of-biblical-illiteracy.

Berger, Peter L., and Thomas Luckmann. *The Social Construction of Reality: A Treatise in the Sociology of Knowledge*. New York: Anchor, 1967.

Bilbro, Jeffrey. *Reading the Times: A Literary and Theological Inquiry into the News*. Downers Grove, IL: IVP Academic, 2021.

Billings, J. Todd. *The End of the Christian Life: How Embracing Our Mortality Frees Us to Truly Live*. Grand Rapids: Brazos, 2020.

Bloom, Allan. *The Closing of the American Mind*. New York: Simon and Schuster, 1987.

Bofetti, Jason. "How Richard Rorty Found Religion." *First Things* 54 (2004) 24–30.

Bouma-Prediger, Steve, and Brian J. Walsh. *Beyond Homelessness: Christian Faith in a Culture of Displacement*. Grand Rapids: Eerdmans, 2008.

Brooks, David. *The Road to Character*. New York: Random House, 2015.

Buckley, William F. "Onward, Christian Missionaries." *National Review* 55 (June 30, 2003) 58.

Burton, Tara Isabella. *Strange Rites: New Religions for a Godless World*. Reprint ed. New York: Public Affairs, 2022.

Calvin, John. "Student Prayer." Online. http://grace-ed.org/blog/archives/291.

Caws, Peter, and Stefani Jones, eds. *Religious Upbringing and the Costs of Freedom: Personal and Philosophical Essays*. University Park: Pennsylvania State University Press, 2010.

Chaput, Charles J. "Believe That You May Understand: *Fides et Ratio* at Twenty." *First Things*, March 2018. Online. https://www.firstthings.com/article/2018/03/believe-that-you-may-understand.

Chesterton, G. K. *Autobiography*. London: Hutchinson, 1937.

———. *Orthodoxy*. New York: Doubleday, 1990.

Code, Lorraine. *Epistemic Responsibility*. Hanover, NH: University Press of New England, 1987.

Collier, Winn. *A Burning in My Bones: A Biography of Eugene Peterson*. Colorado Springs: Waterbrook, 2021.

Dalrymple, Timothy. "Why Evangelicals Disagree on the President." *Christianity Today*, November 2, 2020. Online. https://www.christianitytoday.com/ct/2020/november-web-only/trump-election-politics-church-kingdom.html.

Davis, James Calvin. *Forbearance: A Theological Ethic for a Disagreeable Church*. Grand Rapids: Eerdmans, 2017.

Descartes, René. *Discourse on Method* and *Meditations*. Translated by Laurence J. Lafleur. Indianapolis: Bobbs-Merrill, 1960.

DeYoung, Rebecca Konyndyk. *Glittering Vices*. Grand Rapids: Brazos, 2009.

Dickson, John. "How Christian Humility Upended the World." *ABC*, October 27, 2011. Online. https://www.abc.net.au/religion/how-christian-humility-upended-the-world/10101062.

Dorman, Daniel. "Yes, We Can Understand Each Other." *Convivium*, May 27, 2021. Online. https://www.convivium.ca/articles/yes-we-can-understand-each-other/.

Dow, Philip E. *Virtuous Minds: Intellectual Character Development*. Downers Grove, IL: IVP Academic, 2013.

Enns, Peter. *The Bible Tells Me So . . . : Why Defending Scripture Has Made Us Unable to Read It*. New York: HarperOne, 2014.

———. *The Sin of Certainty: Why God Desires Our Trust More Than Our "Correct" Beliefs*. New York: HarperOne, 2016.

French, David. *Divided We Fall: America's Secession Threat and How to Restore Our Nation*. New York: St Martins, 2020.

———. "Why Is It So Hard To Reach the Christian Conspiracy Theorist?" *Dispatch*, February 21, 2021. Online. https://thedispatch.com/newsletter/frenchpress/why-is-it-so-hard-to-reach-the-christian.

Fuller, Steve. *Post Truth: Knowledge as a Power Game*. New York: Anthem, 2018.

Gaede, S. D. *When Tolerance Is No Virtue*. Downers Grove, IL: InterVarsity, 1993.

Gardener, Peter. "Should We Teach Children to Be Open-Minded? Or Is the Pope Open-Minded about the Existence of God?" *Journal of Philosophy of Education* 27 (1993) 39–43.

Gettier, Edmund L. "Is Justified True Belief Knowledge?" *Analysis* 23 (1963) 121–23.

Gibson, Richard Hughes. "In Search of Charitable Writing." *Plough*, December 14, 2020. Online. https://www.plough.com/en/topics/justice/peacemaking/in-search-of-charitable-writing.

Gibson, Richard Hughes, et al. *Charitable Writing: Cultivating Virtue through Words*. Downers Grove, IL: IVP Academic, 2020.

Gombis, Timothy G. *Power in Weakness: Paul's Transformed Vision for Ministry*. Grand Rapids: Eerdmans, 2021.

Gooch, Paul W. *Partial Knowledge: Philosophical Studies in Paul*. Notre Dame, IN: University of Notre Dame Press, 1987.

Goudzwaard, Bob, et al. *Hope in Troubled Times: A New Vision for Confronting Global Crises*. Grand Rapids: Baker Academic, 2007.

Gourlay, Kenneth H. "An Assessment of Bible Knowledge among Adult Southern Baptist Sunday School Participants." *Christian Education Journal: Research on Educational Ministry* 10 (2013) 7–29.

Grant, Adam. *Think Again: The Power of Knowing What You Don't Know*. New York: Viking, 2021.

Griffiths, Paul J. *The Vice of Curiosity: An Essay on Intellectual Appetite*. Winnipeg, MB: Canadian Mennonite University Press, 2006.

Haidt, Jonathan. *The Righteous Mind: Why Good People Are Divided by Politics and Religion*. New York: Vintage, 2013.

Harder, Cherie. "Reviving Intellectual Hospitality." *Comment: Public Theology for the Common Good* 39 (2021) 53–58.

Hare, William. *In Defence of Open-Mindedness and Education*. Kingston: McGill-Queen's University Press, 1985.

———. *Open-Mindedness and Education*. Kingston: McGill-Queen's University Press, 1979.

Hart, Trevor. *Faith Thinking: The Dynamics of Christian Theology*. Downers Grove, IL: InterVarsity, 1995.

Hartman, Andrew. *A War for the Soul of America: A History of the Culture Wars*. Chicago: University of Chicago Press, 2015.

Haworth, Lawrence. *Autonomy: An Essay in Philosophical Psychology and Ethics*. New Haven, CT: Yale University Press, 1986.

Hays, Richard B. *The Moral Vision of the New Testament*. New York: HarperSanFrancisco, 1996.

Heim, David, ed. *How My Mind Has Changed: Essays from the Christian Century*. Eugene, OR: Cascade, 2012.

Holmes, Arthur F. *All Truth Is God's Truth.* Downers Grove, IL: InterVarsity, 1983.
Hopper, Tristan. "'This Could Cost Him His Job': A Blockaded Canada Turning on Trudeau, Poll Finds." *National Post*, February 12, 2022. Online. https://nationalpost.com/news/politics/this-could-cost-him-his-job-a-blockaded-canada-turning-on-trudeau-poll-finds.
Hospers, John. *An Introduction to Philosophical Analysis.* 4th ed. Upper Saddle River, NJ: Prentice Hall, 1997.
Huebner, Chris. *Suffering the Truth: Occasional Sermons and Reflections.* Winnipeg, MB: Canadian Mennonite University Press, 2020.
Hunter, James Davison. *Culture Wars: The Struggle to Define America.* New York: Basic, 1991.
Hutchens, Aaron. "What Really Happened at Wilfrid Laurier University." *Macleans*, December 11, 2017. Online. https://macleans.ca/lindsay-shepherd-wilfrid-laurier.
Inazu, John D. *Confident Pluralism: Surviving and Thriving through Deep Difference.* Chicago: University of Chicago Press, 2016.
———. "Why I'm Still Confident about 'Confident Pluralism.'" *Christianity Today*, August 13, 2018. Online. https://www.christianitytoday.com/ct/2018/august-web-only/john-inazu-why-im-still-confident-about-confident-pluralism.html.
Jacobs, Alan. *How to Think: A Survival Guide for a World at Odds.* New York: Currency, 2017.
James, William. *Essays in Pragmatism.* Edited by Alburey Castell. New York: Hafner, 1968.
Johnson, Dru. *Biblical Knowing: A Scriptural Epistemology of Error.* Eugene, OR: Cascade, 2013.
———. *Scripture's Knowing: A Companion to Biblical Epistemology.* Eugene, OR: Cascade, 2015.
Johnstone, H. W. "Towards an Ethics of Rhetoric." *Communication* 6 (1981) 306.
Kapic, Kelly M. *You're Only Human: How Your Limits Reflect God's Design and Why That's Good News.* Grand Rapids: Brazos, 2022.
Kauffman, Bradley, ed. *Voices Together.* Harrisonburg, VA: MennoMedia, 2020.
Kennedy, Thomas D. "Curiosity and the Integrated Self: A Postmodern Vice." *Logos* 4 (2001) 33–54.
Khalid, Amna. "The Futility of Trigger Warnings." *Persuasion*, February 17, 2023. Online. https://www.persuasion.community/p/the-futility-of-trigger-warnings.
King, Nathan L. *The Excellent Mind: Intellectual Virtues for Everyday Life.* New York: Oxford University Press, 2021.
———. "How Intellectual Virtues Can Help Us Build Better Discourse." *Christian Scholar's Review* 51.3 (2022) 315–30.
Kuhn, Thomas. *The Structure of Scientific Revolutions.* 2nd ed. Chicago: University of Chicago Press, 1970.
Langer, Rick. "Have We Become Moral Relativists about Gentleness?" *Christian Scholars Review*, May 26, 2022. Online. https://christianscholars.com/guest-post-have-we-become-moral-relativists-about-gentleness.
Langer, Rick, et al. "Introduction to the Theme Issue: Conviction, Civility and Christian Witness." *Christian Scholar's Review* 51.3 (2022) 267–70.
Lewis, C. S. *The Screwtape Letters.* London: Fontana, 1955.
———. *Surprised by Joy.* London: Fontana, 1955.
Lightman, Alan. *Searching for the Stars on an Island in Maine.* New York: Pantheon, 2018.

Locke, John. *An Inquiry Concerning Human Understanding*. Edited by Kenneth Winkler. Indianapolis: Hackett, 1996.
Lukianoff, Greg. *Unlearning Liberty: Campus Censorship and the End of American Debate*. New York: Encounter, 2014.
Lukianoff, Greg, and Jonathan Haidt. *The Coddling of the American Mind: How Good Intentions and Bad Ideas Are Setting Up a Generation for Failure*. New York: Penguin, 2018.
MacIntyre, Alisdair. *Whose Justice? Which Rationality?* London: Duckworth, 1988.
Mao, Bernard. *Ethics and the Moral Life*. London: Macmillan, 1958.
Mavrodes, George. *Belief in God: A Study in the Epistemology of Religion*. New York: Random House, 1970.
McCullough, David. *John Adams*. New York: Simon and Schuster, 2001.
Meek, Esther. *A Little Manual for Knowing*. Eugene, OR: Wipf & Stock, 2014.
———. *Longing to Know: The Philosophy of Knowledge for Ordinary People*. Grand Rapids: Brazos, 2003.
———. *Loving to Know: Covenant Epistemology*. Eugene, OR: Cascade, 2011.
Middleton, J. Richard. "Our Postmodern Moment, Part 3: Christian Discipleship in a Postmodern Moment." *Catalyst*, May 23, 2023. Online. https://jrichardmiddleton.files.wordpress.com/2024/02/middleton-our-postmodern-moment-part-3-christian-discipleship-in-a-polarized-world-catalyst-5-31-23.pdf.
Middleton, J. Richard, and Brian J. Walsh. *Truth Is Stranger Than It Used to Be: Biblical Faith in a Postmodern World*. Downers Grove, IL: InterVarsity, 1995.
Mill, John Stuart. *On Liberty*. Indianapolis: Hackett, 1978.
Mohler, Albert. "The Scandal of Biblical Illiteracy: It's Our Problem." *Albert Mohler*, January 20, 2016. Online. https://albertmohler.com/2016/01/20/the-scandal-of-biblical-illiteracy-its-our-problem-4.
Monteiro, Liz. "A Different Kind of Sunday Service." *Waterloo Region Record*, November 19, 2010. D7.
Mounk, Yascha. "Sam Harris on Whether Religion Really Does Make Everything Worse." Produced by John T. Williams and Brendan Ruberry. *Persuasion*, October 29, 2022. Podcast. https://www.persuasion.community/p/harris#details.
Muehlhoff, Tim, and Richard Langer. *Winsome Conviction: Disagreeing without Dividing the Church*. Downers Grove, IL: IVP Academic, 2020.
———. *Winsome Persuasion: Christian Influence in a Post-Christian World*. Downers Grove, IL: IVP Academic, 2017.
Nagel, Thomas. *The Last Word*. New York: Oxford University Press, 1997.
———. *The View from Nowhere*. New York: Oxford University Press, 1986.
Newbigin, Lesslie. *Proper Confidence: Faith, Doubt, and Certainty in Christian Discipleship*. Grand Rapids: Eerdmans, 1995.
Newman, Jay. *Fanatics and Hypocrites*. Buffalo, NY: Prometheus, 1986.
Nietzsche, Friedrich. *Philosophy and Truth*. Translated by D. Breazeale. London: Humanities, 1979.
———. *Twilight of the Idols and The Anti-Christ*. Translated by R. J. Holingdale. Harmondsworth, UK: Penguin, 1968.
Oberholtzer Lee, Heidi. "Critical Thinking or Just Critical? Reintroducing Humility to the Literature Classroom." *Christian Scholars Review* 39.4 (2010) 421–37.
Oxenham, Marvin. "A Renaissance of Character and Virtue in the Church and in Theological Education." *Evangelical Review of Theology* 44 (2020) 115–25.
Pascal, Blaise. *Pensées*. Translated by A. J. Krailsheimer. New York: Penguin, 1966.

Peters, R. S. *Authority, Responsibility and Education.* 3rd ed. London: Allen and Unwin, 1973.

Peterson, Eugene. *A Long Obedience in the Same Direction: Discipleship in an Instant Society.* Downers Grove, IL: InterVarsity, 1980.

Pew Research Center. "As Partisan Hostility Grows, Signs of Frustration with the Two-Party System." *Pew Research Center*, August 9, 2022. Online. https://www.pewresearch.org/politics/2022/08/09/as-partisan-hostility-grows-signs-of-frustration-with-the-two-party-system.

Plantinga, Alvin. *Warrant and Proper Function.* New York: Oxford University Press, 1993.

———. *Warranted Christian Belief.* Oxford: Oxford University Press, 2000.

Plato. *The Complete Works of Plato.* Edited by John M. Cooper. Indianapolis: Hackett, 1997.

Polanyi, Michael. *Personal Knowledge.* London: Routledge and Kegan Paul, 1958.

Quine, W. V. *From a Logical Point of View.* 2nd ed. Cambridge, MA: Harvard University Press, 1961.

Quine W. V., and J. S. Ullian. *The Web of Belief.* 2nd ed. New York: Random House, 1978.

Rabinow, Paul, ed. *The Foucault Reader.* New York: Pantheon, 1984.

Ratzsch, Del. *Philosophy of Science: The Natural Sciences in Christian Perspective.* Downers Grove, IL: InterVarsity, 1986.

Rawls, John. "The Idea of an Overlapping Consensus." *Oxford Journal of Legal Studies* 7 (1987) 1–25.

Roberts, Robert C., and W. Jay Wood. *Intellectual Virtues: An Essay in Regulative Epistemology.* Oxford: Clarendon, 2007.

Russell, Bertrand. *The Problems of Philosophy.* New York: Oxford University Press, 1969.

Schultz, William. "Don't You Know There's a War On?" *Sightings*, September 17, 2021. Online. https://divinity.uchicago.edu/sightings/articles/war-on.

Schuurman, Derek C. "You're Only Human: An Interview with Kelly Kapic." *Christian Scholar's Review*, March 6, 2023. Online. https://christianscholars.com/youre-only-human-an-interview-with-kelly-kapic.

Smedes, Lewis B. *Caring and Commitment: Learning to Live the Love We Promise.* San Francisco: Harper and Row, 1988.

Smith, James K. A. *Who's Afraid of Postmodernism? Taking Derrida, Lyotard, and Foucault to Church.* Grand Rapids: Baker Academic, 2006.

Smith, Richard L. "The Christian Academic Commission." *Such a Mind as This* (blog), May 22, 2023. Online. https://suchamindasthis.com/2023/05.

———. *Such a Mind as This: A Biblical-Theological Study of Thinking in the Old Testament.* Eugene, OR: Wipf & Stock, 2021.

Stackhouse, John G., Jr. *Humble Apologetics: Defending the Faith Today.* Oxford: Oxford University Press, 2002.

Stott, John R. W. *Your Mind Matters.* Downers Grove, IL: InterVarsity, 1972.

Stroehlein, Andrew. "The Other Navalnys." *Persuasion*, March 1, 2021. Online. https://www.persuasion.community/p/the-other-navalnys.

Thiessen, Elmer John. "The Bible and a Hermeneutic of Suspicion." *Elmerjohnthiessen's Blog* (blog), November 11, 2017. Online. https://elmerjohnthiessen.wordpress.com/2017/11.

———. *The Ethics of Evangelism: A Philosophical Defence of Proselytizing and Persuasion.* Milton Keynes: Paternoster, 2011.

———. *In Defence of Religious Schools and Colleges*. Kingston: McGill-Queen's University Press, 2001.

———. "In Pursuit of Intellectual Virtue." *Evangelical Review of Theology* 46 (2022) 12–23.

———. "A Philosopher Examines Peter Enns." *Elmerjohnthiessen's Blog* (blog), January 3, 2015. Online. https://elmerjohnthiessen.wordpress.com/2015/01.

———. "Question-Focused Christian Faith." *Elmerjohnthiessen's Blog* (blog), May 14, 2021. Online. https://elmerjohnthiessen.wordpress.com/2012/05.

———. "Review of *Who's Afraid of Postmodernism*, by James K. A. Smith." *Evangelical Quarterly* 83 (2011) 347–51.

———. *The Scandal of Evangelism: A Biblical Study of the Ethics of Evangelism*. Eugene, OR: Cascade, 2018.

———. "The Sin of Certainty." *Elmerjohnthiessen's Blog* (blog), May 4, 2018. Online. https://elmerjohnthiessen.wordpress.com/2018/05.

———. *Stumbling Heavenward: One Philosopher's Journey*. Chilliwack, BC: Mill Lake, 2021.

———. *Teaching for Commitment: Liberal Education, Indoctrination, and Christian Nurture*. Kingston: McGill-Queen's University Press, 1993.

Toulmin, Stephen. *Cosmopolis: The Hidden Agenda of Modernity*. New York: Free Press, 1990.

Vanhoozer, Kevin J. *Is There a Meaning in This Text? The Bible, the Reader, and the Morality of Literary Knowledge*. Grand Rapids: Zondervan, 1998.

Vazquez, Veola, et al. *Healing Conversations on Race: Four Key Practices from Scripture and Psychology*. Downers Grove, IL: InterVarsity, 2023.

Watson, Troy. "Question-Shaped Faith." *Canadian Mennonite*, February 6, 2012. 13.

Wells, Samuel. *Improvisation: The Drama of Christian Ethics*. Grand Rapids: Baker, 2008.

Weston, Paul. *Humble Confidence: Lesslie Newbigin and the Logic of Mission*. Eugene, OR: Cascade, 2023.

Winsor, Kim A., ed. *Cultivating Inquiry across the Curriculum*. Lexington, MA: Lexington Christian Academy, 2008.

Witte, John, and Richard C. Martin, eds. *Sharing the Book: Religious Perspectives on the Rights and Wrongs of Proselytism*. Maryknoll, NY: Orbis, 1999.

Wittgenstein, Ludwig. *On Certainty*. Edited by G. E. M. Anscombe and G. H. von Wright. Translated by G. E. M. Anscombe. New York: Harper and Row, 1972.

Wolters, Albert M. *Creation Regained: Biblical Basics for a Reformational Worldview*. 2nd ed. Grand Rapids: Eerdmans, 2005.

Wolterstorff, Nicholas. *Reason within the Bounds of Religion*. Grand Rapids: Eerdmans, 1976.

———. *Until Justice and Peace Embrace*. Grand Rapids: Eerdmans, 1983.

Wood, James R. "How I Evolved on Tim Keller." *First Things*, May 6, 2022. Online. https://www.firstthings.com/web-exclusives/2022/05/how-i-evolved-on-tim-keller.

Wright, N. T. *Following Jesus: Biblical Reflections on Discipleship*. 2nd ed. Grand Rapids: Eerdmans, 2014.

Zagzebski, Linda. *Virtues of the Mind: An Inquiry into the Nature of Virtue and the Ethical Foundations of Knowledge*. Cambridge, UK: Cambridge University Press, 1996.

Subject Index

(Note: Important virtues and vices have been starred.)

abortion debate, x, 2–3, 123, 131, 145, 164n12, 180n333
alternative facts, ix, x, 147
apologetics, 80, 174n207
Aristotle's Golden Mean, 5, 65, 164n15
arrogance, 58–60. See also *intellectual arrogance
autonomy, 50, 65, 68, 71, 77–78, 79, 171n138, 172n155, 173n192, 174nn197, 198, 180n326

beliefs, believing
  evidence for, 47, 52
  importance of, 48, 89, 101–2
  respect for others, 116. See also tolerance, forbearance
  tenacity in, 99
belief systems, 98, 100–102, 148, 177n261
biblical narrative, 13–15
  relation to intellectual virtues and vices, 19–27, 165nn42, 43

cancel culture, x, 132, 152
certainty, 93. See also confidence
  biblical references to, 96

Descartes' influence, 104
desire for, 72, 91
excessive, 105–6
fundamentalism and, 72
impossibility of, 40
proper, 103–5, 107
character
  biblical exhortations on, 15, 31, 124
  importance of, xii, 15, 143
  moral, 4, 8, 13
  relation to intellectual virtues, 6, 157, 164nn18, 19, 168n82, 183n386
Christian ethics. See ethics
*closed-mindedness, 108
  biblical references to, 7, 26, 35–36, 94
  conservative and liberal, xi, 4, 143
  definition, 88
  examples, 4, 85, 91–92
  objections to, 87
  origins in the fall, 22–23
  relation to dogmatism, 92
cognitive faculties, 5, 6, 20, 66, 75–77, 169n99

*committed openness, chapter 4. See also commitment, *open-mindedness
  biblical justification, 92–98
  definition, 90
  examples, 85, 107–8
  how to achieve, 102–3
  redemption of, 95–98
  related concepts, 89–90, 175n230
  in science, 176n259
commitment. See also *committed openness, confidence
  biblical references to, 92–98
  degrees of, 98–99, 102, 148
  need for, 86, 89, 91
  relation to believing, 85
  relation to faith, 93
confidence. See also certainty, *committed openness, commitment
  biblical references to, 91–97
  degrees of, 98–99, 132, 170n132
  humble, 93
  proper, 82, 93, 103–5, 107–8
  too little or too much, 90–92
conservative, 141
  need for, 99–100, 102
  theology, 2, 3–4, 79
  versus liberal, xi, 3, 4, 72, 85, 105, 125–26, 131, 145, 146
conspiracy theories, xi, 30, 46, 126–27
creation story, 20–22, 33, 43, 45, 69, 92–93, 167n67
*critical openness, 87, 89, 94, 97, 103, 106
critical thinking, 73, 87, 97, 104, 106
cultivating intellectual virtues, xii, 157–80
culture wars, 140–43, 146, 150, 156–70, 181n348
cure for unhealthy minds. See cultivating intellectual virtues
curiosity, 4, 21, 46
  idle, 53–54, 167n80, 168n81, 170n129, 171nn148, 149, 150

deconstructionism, 72, 103, 106–7
deep differences, 146–49

definitions
  intellectual vices and virtues, 4, 6
  virtues, 4–5
definitions of key virtues
  *committed openness, 90
  *fairmindedness, 125
  *intellectual courage, 131
  *intellectual forbearance, 115
  *intellectual humility, 65
  *love of knowledge and truth, 42
descriptions of key intellectual vices
  *dogmatism, 88, 105
  *hyper-criticism, 106
  *failures in fairmindedness, 127–29
  *failure to love knowledge and truth, 30, 51–54
  *fanaticism, 108
  *intellectual arrogance, 65–66
  *intellectual intolerance, 116, 121–23
Diagrams. See Illustrations
dignity of persons, 51, 110, 115–20
disagreement. See also deep differences
  defence of, 121, 123
  fact of, ix, 140–43
  how to overcome, 113–17, 144
  levels of, 146–49
  and the need for fairmindedness, 126
  and the need for forbearance, 110, 111, 114, 115–17
  and the need for an ideal of truth, 149–54
  and the need for love, 154–57
*dogmatism, 105, 108, 170n113. See also certainty, commitment, intellectual rigidity
  definition, 88
  relation to closed-mindedness, 92, 176n23
  relation to ideal of truth, 127, 154–55
doubt, 87, 98, 105–6, 177n273
  Descartes' methodological doubt, 104–5
  Jesus on, 107
  overemphasis on, 103–5
  proper, 107
dualism, 12

SUBJECT INDEX

education
    and autonomy, 77
    and critical thinking, 87, 106
    and neutrality, 86–87
    unable to overcome intellectual vices, xii, 143
Enlightenment
    and doubt, 166n45
    and intellectual courage, 180n321
    and knowledge and truth, 149, 154, 168n94
    opposed to humility, 68
    and reason, xii
epistemic autonomy, 50. See also autonomy
epistemology, 5, 8–9
    after the fall of Adam and Eve, 22–24, 33–34, 61–62
    biblical references to, 12–13, 16–18
    in Garden of Eden, 19–22, 33, 61, 69
    redemptive, 24–27
    Reformed, 10, 16
ethics
    biblical, 13–16, 118, 166n47
    rules in, 13
    universal or relative, 14, 85
    virtues, 7–9
    virtues of the mind, 142–45
evangelism, 19, 80, 127
evidence for beliefs
    and knowledge, 9, 36
    and love of knowledge, 30, 47, 52
    and open-mindedness, 84, 88, 90, 99, 103
    and vice of intellectual rigidity, 91

*fairmindedness, 125–29
    biblical justification of, 127
    in debating, 129
    definition, 125
    examples, 125, 127–28, 158
    failures in, 127–28
    how to achieve, 128–29
faith
    as beginning of knowledge, 10, 47, 92–93, 105, 176n239
    and certainty, 83
    and doubt, 104, 105
    falling away from, 94–96
    and reason, 10–12
*fanaticism, 91, 108. See also certainty, dogmatism, fundamentalism
fear of the LORD, 18, 43, 70–71
Figures. See Illustrations
fundamentalism, 79, 105, 153–54

gay marriage, xi, 140, 121, 146, 181n354. See also LGBTQ debate
Golden Rule, 19, 118, 127, 128
Great Commandment, 15, 18–19, 93, 118, 129

hermeneutics, 14–15
    humble, 72
    of suspicion, 73, 107, 173n182, 177n282
homosexuality. See LGBTQ debate, gay marriage
human nature, 5–6
    and belief and commitment, 98–100
    after the fall, 22–24
    in the Garden of Eden, 20–22
    and love of knowledge and truth, 32–36, 42, 48–49
    as persuading animal, 80
    fallibility, 20, 40, 69, 71, 74–75, 151
    finiteness, 20, 22, 33, 34, 40, 47, 54, 61, 67, 69, 71, 74–75, 92–93, 104, 118, 153, 168n69
    interdependence of, 50–51, 69, 77–78
humility
    -biblical references to, 58–60
    -false, 64–65
*hyper-criticism, 87, 104, 105–7. See also doubt, critical thinking

Illustrations
    Belief systems, 101
    Ladder of truth, 39
    Overlapping ellipses, 11
indoctrination, 78–79, 174n201
influencing others. See persuasion, evangelism
inquisitiveness, 4

intellectual abilities. See cognitive
    faculties
intellectual apathy, 4
*intellectual arrogance, x-xi
    biblical references to, 23, 58–64
    definition, 65
    emotional markers of, 76–77
    examples, 66, 67–68, 72–73, 74,
        76–77, 78–79, 80, 81, 142–43
    and intellectual courage, 134
intellectual bias, 4, 127–28
*intellectual carefulness, 52, 53, 168n82,
    170n130, 171n175
*intellectual carelessness, 4, 30
*intellectual courage, 129–37
    biblical justification, 22, 130, 135–37
    definition, 131
    examples, 129–30, 131, 132–33,
        135–37, 180nn333, 334
    importance of, 14
    question of excessive, 133–35
    relation to intellectual arrogance, 134
    relation to intellectual forbearance,
        137
    versus recklessness, 133–34
*intellectual cowardice, 133, 135
intellectual empathy, 126
intellectual faculties. See cognitive
    faculties
*intellectual flabbiness, 90–91, 108,
    175n231
    examples, 86, 90, 91
*intellectual forbearance, 113–25, 151.
    See also tolerance, safetyism
    biblical justification of, 116, 117–19
    definition, 115
    examples, 113, 126, 164n12
    importance, 111
    limits of, 119–25
    relation to tolerance, 114–15
intellectual hospitality, xi, 120–21
*intellectual humility, chapter 3, 111
    biblical references to, 16, 18, 20, 22,
        58–64
    definitions, 65, 172n168
    examples, 56–57, 66, 68–69, 107–8
    importance of, 57, 148, 172n152
    justification of, 68–70
intellectual justice, 113, 179n314

intellectual laziness, 4, 30
intellectual perseverance, 46, 180n331
intellectual pride, See *intellectual
    arrogance
intellectual recklessness, 133–34
intellectual rigidity, 90–92
intellectual scrupulousness, See
    intellectual carefulness
intellectual vices
    biblical references to, 22–24, 26
    definition, 4, 6
    how to overcome, 144, 157–60
    prevalence of, xi-xii
    study of, 9–10
intellectual virtues
    definition, 4, 6, 164n18, 168n82
    individual or collective, 111–12,
        178n285
    need for, 142–49
    objection to, 144–45
    oppositional, 112, 132
    relation to moral virtues, 5, 164n16
    study of, 9–10, 163n10, 165nn26–31
intolerance, 113–17, 151

LGBTQ debate, xi, 3, 123, 140. See also
    gay marriage
liberal/liberalism, 4, 125, 126, 131.
    arrogance of, xi, 105, 132, 164n12
    and autonomy. See autonomy
    versus conservatism, xi, 3, 4, 72, 85,
        105, 125–26, 131, 145, 146
    fundamentalism, 105, 164n12
    and rationalism, 143
    and tolerance, 114, 119
    and universities, 133
listening
    biblical references to, 18, 21–25, 34,
        53, 61–62, 96, 97
    failure in, 52, 128, 145
    importance of, 5, 19, 67, 99, 148
    and intellectual humility, 56, 65,
        67, 72
    and knowing, 17
    limits of, 120
    and love of knowledge and truth,
        31, 32, 46
    and open-mindedness, 88

love
- as answer to polarization, 154–57
- as binding intellectual virtues, 155
- of ideological enemies, 156
- *love of knowledge and truth, chapter 2, 16, 111
  - biblical references to, 18, 22
  - definition and description, 41, 42, 46–47
  - after fall of Adam, 22–24, 33–36
  - in Garden of Eden, 20–22, 33, 45
  - helping others in, 50–51
  - and human nature, 32–36, 99
  - importance of, 31, 168n80
  - justification of, 42
  - lack of, 51–52, 174n204
  - limits of, 47–50
  - and need for courage, 131–32
  - redemption of, 43–45

moral philosophy. See ethics
narrow-mindedness. See certainty, closed-mindedness, dogmatism, intellectual rigidity
*open-mindedness. See also *closed-mindedness, critical openness
- critique of, 87
- definition, 88, 175n223
- difficulty in assessing, 88
- examples, 85, 164n12
- importance of, 85
- misconceptions about, 86–87
overcoming differences, chapter 6. See also disagreement

persuasion. See also evangelism
- and arrogance, 80
- ethical, 19, 80
- and human nature, 80–81
- humble, 80, 182n358
- and intellectual hospitality, 121, 179n305
philosophy, 2, 7
- and the Bible, 12–13
- definition, 7
- Reformed. See Reformed epistemology
plausibility structures, 48–49
pluralism, 54, 119, 123

polarization, ix, x, 27, 140–43, 181n351. See also deep differences, disagreement, resolving disputes
- education as the answer, 143
- ideal of truth as the answer, 149–54
- information as the answer, 143–44, 181n355
- intellectual virtues as the answer, 142–54
- love as the answer, 154–57
postmodernism, 9, 72, 73, 86, 149–50
post-truth, x, 150
prayer about intellectual virtues, 160–61
pride. See arrogance
proper confidence. See confidence, committed openness

questionnaires, 27, 29–30, 55–56, 83–84, 109–10
- need for, 82, 157

rationalist delusion, 143, 181n356
Reformed philosophy and epistemology, 10, 16
relativism
- epistemological, x, 38, 40, 121, 150
- ethical, 7, 85, 144
- and open-mindedness, 108
- partial justification for, 153
- and tolerance, 114–15
resolving disputes, chapter 6

safetyism, 121–22, 179n306
self examination questionnaires. See questionnaires
Sermon on the Mount, 15
science, 12, 17, 37, 71, 176n259
sin
- Adam and Eve, 22–25
- cause of intellectual vices, xii, 6, 80, 94, 104, 143, 148, 151, 157
- and certainty, 105–6
- human nature and, 25, 40, 69, 99, 117, 154
- and hyper-criticism, 107
skepticism, 40, 73, 106, 153. See also critical thinking, *hyper-criticism
social constructivism, 38, 73–74, 150

straw man fallacy, 125, 128
submission to God's word and to truth, 72, 73–74

tolerance, 19, 114–15. *See also* forbearance
tradition vs. traditionalism, 79–80
Trump/trumpism, x, 126, 142–44, 147, 158, 181n348
truth, 38–41, 149–54
   biblical references to, 40–41
   consensus as a sign of, 153
   dangers of, 153–54
   definition, 41
   denial of, 38, 40, 74, 183n373
   and dogmatism, 127
   as freeing, 151
   as an ideal and with a capital "T", 8, 39–40, 150–51, 152, 170n112
   Ladder of truth diagram, 39
   search for, xi, 38–40, 150–51
   as socially constructed, 38, 74, 150

understanding, 37

university environment, x, 2–3, 38, 46, 56–57, 91–92, 122, 131, 132, 163n4

virtue ethics, 8, 15. *See also* intellectual virtues

weaponize, ix, 179n306
wisdom
   biblical references to, 43–45, 59, 63–64, 70, 159
   in creation, 20, 33
   definition, 37–38
   of God, 12, 66, 71
   love of, 18, 32–33, 43, 49–50, 61, 168n84
   need for, 49–50, 134, 140, 158
   of world, 63
worldview
   biblical references to, 13–16, 167n67
   and deep differences, 147
   in diagram of belief systems, 101
   evaluation of, 147–48
   examples, 11, 101, 135
   need for stability, 103

Scripture Index

(Note: This index is limited to instances where Scripture is quoted or discussed.)

Genesis

1–2	20–22, 33, 61
1:22	22
1:26	61
1:27–28	20
1:29–30	21
2:9	21
2:15	20, 61
2:17	34, 61
2:18–20	33
2:18	21
2:18–25	165n37
2:19–20	21
3	22–24, 61–62
3:1	22
3:5	22, 61
3:6	61
3:8	22
3:9–13	34
3:15	24
4–11	23
4:1–16	23
6:5	23
11:1–9	23, 118
21:1–3	24

Exodus

3:6	59
4	135
7:6	135
31:1	169n108
34:6	178n292

Leviticus

19:1	15
19:18	18, 178n297
19:34	178n302
25:35	178n302

Numbers

12:3	15, 58
14:18	178n292

Deuteronomy

5:16	78, 167n78
5:29	27
6:4–5	18, 93, 178n279
10:19	178n302
11:26–32	167n79

Deuteronomy (*cont.*)

11:27	176n245
11:28	174n204
27:9—28:68	167n79
28:14	174n204, 176n245
31:16–17	174n204, 176n245
31:21	94, 174n204
31:27	176n244
31:29	174n204, 176n245

Joshua

1:6–9	180n324
1:8	95
8:30–35	167n79

Judges

2:16–23	174n204, 176n245
21:25	182n360

1 Samuel

2:1–10	63
8	165n37

Job

19:25	95, 105
21:22	167n69
28:28	167n64, 173n178
36:26	167n69
38:2–3	20, 72
42:3	20

Psalm

1:1	59
1:2	44
11:3	152
11:10	173n178
14:1	34
17:10	60
18:2	96
25:9	62
31:5	39
32:8–9	34
33	44
33:9	20
36:9	45
39:3	ix
53:1	34
71:5	95–96
75:4–5	62
78:8	174n204, 176n244
81:11–12	35
86:15	178n292
92:5	167n69
92:6	34
94:8	34
94:11	34
95:10	174n204, 176n245
111:10	167n64
112:1	44
119	44
119:8–9	71
119:89–91	8, 182n360
131:1	62, 167n70
139:6	167n69
147:5	167n69

Proverbs

1:2–3	70
1:7	70, 167n64
1:22	34
2:1–6	43
2:6	38
3:5–6	71, 167n69
3:13–16	158
3:13	43
3:19–20	20, 38
3:19	71
3:34	60
4:7	44
8	20
8:10–11	158
9:10	167n64, 169n108, 173n178
10:14	38
14:29	178n298
15:14	44
15:18	178n298
16:18	59, 172n156
16:32	178n298
18:15	44
19:11	178n298

20:12	21	59:14–15	182n370
23:12	44	61:1–2	136
23:23	44	65:16	39
25:15	178n298,	65:17	170n126
26:12	55, 62, 172n153	66:2	62, 172n153

Ecclesiastes

12:9–10	54

Isaiah

1:19–20	167n79
2:2–4	45, 170n127
2:12	59
2:17	59
5:21	62, 172n153
6:1–7	24–25, 135
6:9–10	25–26, 35, 94, 135, 176nn241, 242, 169n97
6:11–13	135
10:19	178n298
11:6–9	26
11:9	45
11:12	178n298
13:3	178n298
13:11	59
15:1	178n298
15:4	178n298
17:28	178n298
22:23	41
26:4	176n248
28:23–29	12
29:10	176n243
30:29	176n248
32:1–5	96
33:6	167n64, 173n178
35:5	169n96, 176n241
40:14	167n69
40:28	167n69
42:20	169n96, 176n241
43:8	169n96, 176n241
44:18	35, 176n241
47:10	62
55:9	167n69
57:15	59, 172n153
57:18–19	26

Jeremiah

1:1–19	129–30
5:23	174n204, 176n244
7:28	182n370
8:6–7	182n360
10:14	169n105
11:10	174n204, 176n245
13:10	174n204, 176n245
14:10	176n245
15:10–21	130–31
16:19	176n248
17:17	176n248
18:15	174n204, 176n245
23	130
23:9–40	176n253
36	130
51:17	169n105

Lamentations

2:14	176n253

Ezekiel

13	176n253
28:1–2	63

Daniel

1:1–17	45
1:17	169n105
2	66
8:12	182n370
10:12	63

Hosea

4:5	176n245
4:6	169n105

Joel

3:16	176n248

Amos

2:6–8	165n37
4:1	132
8:9–14	40, 94–95, 174n204

Micah

6:8	59, 127

Nahum

1:17	176n248

Habakkuk

1:12	176n248

Matthew

5:1–10	15, 59
5:5	172n153
5:43–48	117, 129, 156
6:1–4	76
6:19–24	165n37
7:3	82
7:4–5	157
7:12	19, 118–19, 127
7:24–27	167n79
7:24	17
10:16	139
11:1–19	107
11:28	60
12:16	134
12:19	134, 134
13:9–16	94, 96, 169n97, 169n105, 176n242
13:14–15	169n97
14:1–12	136
15:1–20	96
16:17–20	179n312
18:1–4	59, 172n157
19:1–12	165n37
20:26–27	68
22:15–22	181n341
22:16	137
22:38	129
23:8–11	81
23:11	55
24:4–5	97
24:10–13	95, 96, 174n204
25:31–46	178n302
27:14	146

Mark

4:1–20	26, 166n58, 169n97, 176n242
7:20–23	60
12:13–17	181n341
12:29–31	18, 93, 178n297

Luke

1:4	96
1:51–52	63
2:41–52	18, 33, 44
3:19	135–36
4:16–30	136
10:21	63
11:37–54	136
11:52	35
12:54–56	45
14:11	172n153
16:14	136
16:15	76
18:14	172n153
20:1–8	136
20:9–19	136–37
20:20–26	137, 181n341
23:8–9	53
24:13–35	97

John

1:1–3	20
5:39	66–67
12:40	154
14:6	41
16:7	44
16:13	44
17:5	96
18:37	149
18:38–39	9, 40,
20:24–31	107
20:31	41
21:34	41

Acts

17:1–15	31
17:11	97
17:16–34	113, 116
17:21	53, 98
17:23	178n300
17:28	20
19:23–41	116–17
23:11	130
28:25–27	26, 169n97, 176n242

Romans

1:18–20	22, 35, 94, 154
1:21	22, 35, 154
1:28–32	23
2:4	117
3:24	24
3:25	117
7:14–25	25
8:5	25
9:22	117
10:2	148
11:7–10	176n243
11:33–36	71, 167n69
12:2	25, 176n246
12:3	75
12:17–21	117, 156
13:1–7	165n37

1 Corinthians

1:18—2:16	63
1:20	172n159
1:27–31	172n160
2:1	63
2:21	64
4:7	75, 172n160
8:1–13	179n312
11:2	176n249
13	155, 157
13:9	67, 153, 167n69
13:11	174n199
13:12	40, 48, 69, 153, 176n240
14:20	174n199
15:1–2	176n249
15:2	174n204
15:12–19	102
15:45	33
15:58	176n249

2 Corinthians

1:12	172n160
4:2	172n160
4:4	35, 94
4:7	173n185
5:12	172n160
10–13	172n160
11:29–30	173n185
11:4	179n312
11:6	169m105
12:8–10	173n185
12:20	60
13:5	27

Galatians

2:4–5	179n312
4:25–25	145
5:14	178n297
5:22	119
6:7–8	167n79

Ephesians

1:4	15
4:2	123–24
4:5	124
4:14	95, 174n204
4:15	119
4:22–24	25, 95
6:1–3	78
6:10–18	26, 151–52
6:12	152
6:14	174n204, 176n249

Philippians

1:9	170n125
2:3	64
2:5–11	59, 68–69
3:15	124, 183n384
4:5	178n299
4:8	48

Colossians

1:9	170n125
1:16–17	20
2:2–3	167n69, 170n125
2:5	176n249
2:18–19	77, 124
2:23	77
3:10	43, 95, 176n246
3:12–15	15–16, 124, 155
3:12	159
4:6	119

1 Thessalonians

5:21	44, 97

2 Thessalonians

2:10	29
2:15	96, 174n204, 176n249

1 Timothy

2:4	170n125
6:3	169n98
6:4–5	89–90, 172n159
6:20–21	95

2 Timothy

1:7	144
1:12	93, 96, 176n250
2:14	169n98
2:23	169n98, 172n159
2:24–25	129, 135, 170n125, 178n299
3:7	36, 86, 172n159
3:14	176n249, 176n250
4:3–4	35, 95, 97–98, 174n204

Titus

1:9	176n249

Hebrews

2:1	96
2:2	174n204
3:14	176n249
5:11–14	174n199
5:11	36
10:35	96
11:1	83, 105
12:14	139
13:2	178n302

James

1:6	90
1:19	67
1:21	72
1:22	166n58
3:1	80
3:5	80–81
3:13–18	145
3:13	166n58
3:17	109
4:6	60

1 Peter

1:16	15
2:17	119
3:15–16	119, 145, 178n299
5:5–6	59, 60, 172n53

2 Peter

1:5–7	1, 16, 46, 170n125
1:12	174n204, 176n249
2	179n312
3:5–7	20

1 John

2:16	60, 171n148
4:1–6	44, 174n204
4:1	97
5:6	44
5:21	148

2 John

10	121

Revelation

2:6	179n312	2:20	179n312
2:7	83, 96–97, 176n252	2:29	176n252
		3:3	176n249
		3:6	176n252
2:11	83, 176n252	3:13	176n252
2:16	179n312	3:22	176n252
2:17	83, 176n252